T5-BPY-782

Law in the Documents of the Judaean Desert

Edited by

Ranon Katzoff
& David Schaps

BRILL

LEIDEN • BOSTON

2005

Cover design: www.RAMVormgeving.nl

This book is printed on acid-free paper.

Library of Congress Cataloging-in-Publication Data

LC Control Number: 2004058554

BM
520.52
.L39
2005

ISSN 1384–2161
ISBN 90 04 11357 6

© Copyright 2005 by Koninklijke Brill NV, Leiden, The Netherlands.
Koninklijke Brill NV incorporates the imprints Brill Academic Publishers,
Martinus Nijhoff Publishers and VSP.

All rights reserved. No part of this publication may be reproduced, translated,
stored in a retrieval system, or transmitted in any form or by any means,
electronic, mechanical, photocopying, recording or otherwise, without prior
written permission from the publisher.

Authorization to photocopy items for internal or personal use is granted by Brill
provided that the appropriate fees are paid directly to The Copyright Clearance
Center, 222 Rosewood Drive, Suite 910, Danvers, MA 01923, USA.
Fees are subject to change.

PRINTED IN THE NETHERLANDS

Law in the Documents
of the Judaean Desert

Supplements

to the

Journal for the Study of Judaism

Editor

John J. Collins

The Divinity School, Yale University

Associate Editor

Florentino García Martínez

Qumran Institute, University of Groningen

Advisory Board

J. DUHAIME — A. HILHORST — P.W. VAN DER HORST

A. KLOSTERGAARD PETERSEN — M.A. KNIBB — J.T.A.G.M. VAN RUITEN

J. SIEVERS — G. STEMBERGER — E.J.C. TIGCHELAAR — J. TROMP

VOLUME 96

CONTENTS

LIST OF CONTRIBUTORS

Magen Broshi
  Israel Museum

Tiziana J. Chiusi
  Universität des Saarlandes

Hannah M. Cotton
  Hebrew University of Jerusalem

Werner Eck
  Universität zu Köln

Hanan Eshel
  Bar Ilan University

Ann Ellis Hanson
  Yale University

Timothy A.J. Jull
  University of Arizona

Ranon Katzoff
  Bar Ilan University

Joseph Mélèze Modrzejewski
  École Pratique des Hautes Études, Paris

Amihai Radzyner
  Bar Ilan University

Yosef Rivlin
  Bar Ilan University

Ze'ev Safrai
  Bar Ilan University

Michael L. Satlow
    Brown University

David Schaps
    Bar Ilan University

Lawrence H. Schiffman,
    New York University

Uri Yiftach-Firanko
    Hebrew University of Jerusalem

INTRODUCTION

Ranon Katzoff and David Schaps

During the last half-century the caves of the Judaean Desert have yielded a new and remarkable resource for the knowledge of Jewish history in antiquity—of the late first and early second centuries CE, to be more precise—namely, documentary papyri. Here for the first time one has written evidence on events, private events, of that era as presented by private individuals.[1] These must be sharply distinguished from the material from Qumran, even though they share provenance generally from the Judaean Desert and to a certain extent publication fora and responsible authorities. The two groups of material come from different groups of caves, in different ravines, with hardly any overlap. The Qumran material is entirely literary, largely sectarian, with not a single documentary (in the sense used by papyrologists) papyrus among them; the other material is almost entirely documentary, the only literary material being almost entirely fragments of the Hebrew Bible pretty much according to the masoretic text.[2] The Qumran material is generally considered to pre-date 70 CE; the documentary material is, with only a few exceptions, rather later, mostly from the first third of the second century CE.

The Qumran material, which has been seen by some as shedding light on the beginnings of Christianity, caught the imagination of the world public, producing many popular works, and even fiction, well before the entire corpus was published. The documentary material made less of a splash on the international scene (although in 1987 the Habima Israel National Theater did produce, with no

---

[1] A complete list is provided by Hannah Cotton in H.M. Cotton, W.E.H. Cockle, and F.G.B. Millar, "The Papyrology of the Roman Near East: A Survey," *Journal of Roman Studies* 85 (1995) 214–235, still most useful even though many of the listed documents have been published more recently with somewhat changed designations.

[2] It is very unlikely that the 17 documents published in P.Hever as "alleged" to be from Qumran are in fact from there. On the other hand, XHev/Se Eschatological Hymn, published in *DJD* XXXVIII, C.6, page 193, associated in the museum with the Nahal Se'elim documents, may well actually be from Qumran.

particular success, a drama by Miriam Kenan entitled "Babatha", attended by considerable attention on Israel public television); but for the history of the Jews it is if anything more compelling, giving us for the first time a non-rabbinic window on the actual lives and transactions of people whose relationship to religion and to law was not that of professionals. No less important was the role of the discoveries in giving us an important corpus of documentary papyri whose social and legal milieu was not Egyptian.

The documentary material of which we speak appeared first on the antiquities market in late 1951, and this led to controlled archaeological excavations in early 1952 in caves in Nahal Murabba'at to which Bedouins led the excavators. The material found there was published together in *Discoveries in the Judaean Desert. Volume II: Les Grottes de Murabba'at*, ed. P. Benoit, O.P., J.T. Milik, and R. de Vaux, O.P. (Oxford 1960), conventionally known as "P.Mur." In the course of the early 1950s Bedouins searched caves throughout the Judaean Desert in search of marketable written remains, and dozens of pieces appeared alleged to be from various ravines, both within the borders of Israel at that time and in the area then occupied by Jordan. For the most part they reached the Rockefeller Museum in Jerusalem, then known as the Palestine Archaeological Museum, where many were labeled as having been found in Wadi Seiyal (Nahal Se'elim). Little was done at that time to publish these documents.

Stimulated by reports of Bedouin finds on the Israeli side of the armistice line, Israeli archaeologists made sporadic attempts to search the caves, and finally in 1960 and 1961 made a concerted effort to scour the caves of Nahal Hever and Nahal Se'elim. The most important finds from the perspective of documentary papyrology were those discovered under the direction of Yigael Yadin in Cave 5/6 of Nahal Hever. The most dramatic of these were, in 1960, the letters—dispatches as Yadin called them—of Shim'on Bar Kokhba, the leader of the second Jewish revolt against Rome in the 130s CE. For legal history the most important find was, in 1961, the discovery of a pouch with some 35–40 legal documents, all connected to a certain Jewish woman named Babatha and to her immediate relations. The special value of these documents in contrast to the individual documents that had been found until then lies in the fact that the presence of other documents of the same persons provides a better base for scholarly speculation on the aims of the parties to the transactions and the purposes of the writers of the documents. While Yadin did publish detailed descriptions of many of these documents in several fora,[3] the full texts of most were not published for nearly three decades.[4] After Yadin's death in 1984 the Greek texts of the Babatha archive were published in *The Documents from the Bar Kokhba Period in the Cave of Letters. Greek Papyri*, ed. Naphtali Lewis. Aramaic and Nabatean Signatures and Subscriptions, ed. Yigael Yadin and Jonas C. Greenfield (Jerusalem 1989), conventionally known as "P.Yadin" or "P.Babatha." The non-Greek texts, those from the Babatha archives and others, were published in *The Documents from the Bar Kokhba Period in the Cave of Letters. Hebrew, Aramaic and Nabatean-Aramaic Papyri*, ed. Yigael Yadin, Jonas C. Greenfield, Ada Yardeni, and Baruch Levine (Jerusalem 2002). An incidental result of the study of the material known as P.Yadin is the demonstration that the papyri held in the Rockefeller Museum as coming from Wadi Seiyal must have come from the same cave in Nahal Hever as P.Yadin. These were published in *Aramaic, Hebrew and Greek Documentary Texts from Nahal Ḥever and Other Sites with an Appendix Containing Alleged Qumran Texts (The Seiyal Collection II)* ed. Hannah M. Cotton and Ada Yardeni (*Discoveries in the Judaean Desert XXVII*) (Oxford 1997), conventionally known as "P.Hever." Finally, a volume containing papyri of various types, found at various times and in various places, was published as *Miscellaneous Texts from the Judaean Desert*, ed. James Charlesworth et al. (*Discoveries in the Judaean Desert XXXVIII*) (Oxford 2000). This completes publication of the documentary material found to date. It should be said to the credit of the various editors of these volumes that the more important of the documents were published in scholarly periodicals well in advance of the appearance of the complete volumes, thus making the material available to scholars promptly.

---

[3] Notably in *IEJ* 12 (1963) 227–57, supplemented by H.J. Polotsky, ibid. 258–62, and especially the dramatic account in Y. Yadin, *Bar-Kokhba. The rediscovery of the legendary hero of the Second Jewish Revolt against Rome* (London, Jerusalem, New York 1971) 222–53.

[4] The Greek texts were entrusted to Prof. H.J. Polotsky, who after publishing three texts requested for reasons of ill-health to be relieved of this responsibility. Yadin himself undertook to prepare the non-Greek texts for publication, but soon was caught up in other major scholarly projects—the excavations at Masada and the publication of the newly acquired Temple Scroll, not to speak of the publication of the results of the earlier Hazor excavations—and in politics, organizing a new political party and becoming deputy prime-minister of Israel. He retired from politics and returned to scholarly pursuits in 1983, but died less than a year later.

Over 100 of these are legal documents, broadly defined—sales, leases, quittances, marriage documents, and the like; the rest are non-legal documents such as lists, accounts and letters. Somewhat over a third of the legal documents are written in Greek, the remainder in Hebrew, Aramaic, or Nabatean Aramaic.[5] These documents record private transactions, and the fulfillment (or demands for fulfillment) of the rights and obligations created by those transactions. The parties to the transactions and the scribes who recorded them were for the much greater part Jews living under Roman rule, a rule exercised for the most part in Greek by Greek-speaking officials. Are the rights and obligations recorded in these papyri, then, characteristic of Jewish society, as known from literary sources, mostly rabbinic? Are they characteristic of Roman society, as known from Roman legal and other literature? Are they characteristic of Hellenistic Greek society as known from the Greek papyri, mostly from Egypt? Were these rights and duties recognized as legal by Jewish law, by Roman law, or by Hellenistic law? Do the transactions presuppose rules of Jewish law, of Roman law, or of Hellenistic law? Do we learn from these documents anything new about Jewish law, about Roman law, or about Hellenistic law? Do we learn from these documents anything new about Jewish society, about Roman society, or about Hellenistic society? Questions of this sort are addressed by the studies in this volume.

Opening the series of studies, Joseph Mélèze Modrzejewski surveys the relationship between native Egyptian law and Greek law in Egypt as a possible model for the relationship of Jewish law and Hellenistic law that may be found in the Judaean papyri. On this basis, he argues, we should not expect to find in the documents under discussion any significant interpenetration of the two legal systems. Hannah M. Cotton and Werner Eck examine what is known on the matter of jurisdictional authority in the eastern provinces of the Roman empire so as to determine the role played by each of the Roman officials involved in our documents. For Hanan Eshel,

---

[5] Statistical figures are necessarily vague because of the uncertain nature of the criteria for counting. Sometimes several completely separate transactions are recorded on a single papyrus (e.g. P.Mur. 24); at others a single transaction is recorded on two separately numbered papyri (e.g. P.Yadin 21, 22). Some of the documents are so fragmentary that hardly anything can be learned from them other than the fact of their existence.

Magen Broshi and Timothy A.J. Jull the accurate dating of four legal papyri tips the scales in the scholarly controversy over the question of whether Bar Kokhba captured Jerusalem.

Michael Satlow examines the documents recording movement of property within a family so as to determine what the goals of the parties to the transactions were and the means by which they achieved these goals. Ann Ellis Hanson examines the life and legal activity of Babatha as a widow, comparing them with those of widows known from the papyri from Egypt, and finds much similarity but also some significant differences. Both Satlow and Hanson find that Babatha, although illiterate, was a canny businesswoman well able to use the available legal avenues to further her goals.

Uri Yiftach-Firanko explains the *ekdosis* clauses in the Judaean Desert documents in terms of the theory he has developed for their occasional presence in Greek documents from Egypt, with the result that the Judaean documents display a curious interplay of Greek and Jewish traditions.

Tiziana J. Chiusi studies the documents associated with the guardianship of Babatha's son, P.Yadin 12–15 and 27, and finds that they are best explained in terms of Roman law. Moreover, they contribute to the history of Roman institutions on guardianship. Ranon Katzoff defends the interpretation of P.Yadin 37 = P.Hever 65 in terms of Jewish law, either on the reading in P.Yadin 37 as reflecting the marriage of a minor orphan or on the reading of P.Hever 65 as a dowry receipt rather than a marriage contract.

Amihai Radzyner studies the contract recorded in P.Yadin 21 and 22 as a labor contract on the background both of Jewish law and Hellenistic practice. Yosef Rivlin examines the documents recording gifts, especially those in contemplation of death, in terms of Jewish law. Lawrence Schiffman examines the Aramaic documents of sale, and finds a high degree of correspondence with what is known from rabbinic literature on this subject.

Finally, in surveying the corpus as a whole, Ze'ev Safrai observes that the degree of correspondence with rabbinic law correlates with the place and language in which each document was composed. The Hebrew documents, and to a somewhat lesser degree the Aramaic documents, are saturated with halachic concepts and references; the Greek documents are drawn up in a legal universe very different from that of the rabbis, though there is little that is actually contrary to rabbinic instruction. In terms of geography, it is the documents from the area known to the rabbis as "the Rekem"—an area whose population is explicitly described in the Mishna and Talmud as halachically ignorant—that diverge the most widely from rabbinic teaching.

The studies presented here do not answer all the questions posed above, though some themes recur throughout. Over and over we find that correspondences exist between the documents and the legal systems in which they were written; that the correspondences are not exact; and that their presence or absence reveals much about the experiences and strategies of individuals born into one people, in contact with other peoples, trying to navigate a world ruled by yet others. If these studies stimulate further thought about these problems and those mentioned above, that will be the important contribution of this volume.

Nunc transeamus ad obligationes. These studies were presented orally in an Israel Science Fund Workshop on Law in the Documents from the Judaean Desert at Bar-Ilan University in 1998. The editors and authors are grateful to the Fund and to the University for their support. Special thanks are due to our editorial assistant (now Dr.) Uri Yiftach-Firanko who relieved the editors of much of the nitty-gritty of editing copy and checking references. Much of the editorial work by Ranon Katzoff was done during sabbatical leave spent as Visiting Fellow at Yale University, and he thanks its Department of Classics and Judaic Studies Program for their gracious welcome, and the staffs of its libraries, in particular the Judaica Curator, Dr. Nanette Stahl, for their help. Finally we thank Prof. John J. Collins, the editor of this series, for his encouragement and patience.

WHAT IS HELLENISTIC LAW? THE DOCUMENTS OF THE JUDAEAN DESERT IN THE LIGHT OF THE PAPYRI FROM EGYPT

Joseph Mélèze Modrzejewski

I. *Hellenistic law and Hellenistic culture*

1. *Legal history and "the seven wonders of the world."*—What kind of law can we observe in the documents of the Dead Sea—about fifty texts written in Greek, Hebrew and Aramaic, most of them from the 2nd century CE?[1] Is it a combination, the expression of "mixed cultures" within a space where the paths of several civilizations cross, or should we see in these documents the juxtaposition of varied elements, which represent distinct legal traditions and cultures: Jewish law, Greek law, Roman law? The question is fascinating, as much for the history of the Jewish people as for the history of law and civilizations. It is not an easy one. The multi-disciplinary inquiry it calls for must clearly define choices and methods.

The experience of legal papyrology, with its thousands of sources from Egypt, should help to start the project conceived by our Israeli colleagues. The history of law in Greek and Roman Egypt had to face problems similar to those of the law in the documents of the Judaean Desert: "mixed law" for the pioneers of our discipline, from Ludwig Mitteis[2] to Raphael Taubenschlag,[3] the law we know through the papyrological material from Egypt appears to us now as a complex phenomenon whose dominant feature is the pluralism of legal traditions which met in the Valley of the Nile without at any time combining. This evolution of legal doctrine corresponds to the change in our evaluation of Hellenistic civilization generally, of which law is only one component, along with its political systems, religions or art.

---

[1] My thanks are due to my colleagues Ranon Katzoff and Thomas Drew-Bear for improving the English version of my paper.

[2] L. Mitteis, *Reichsrecht und Volksrecht in den östlichen Provinzen des römischen Kaiserreiches* (Leipzig 1891).

[3] R. Taubenschlag, *The Law of Greco-Roman Egypt in Light of the Papyri 332 BC–640 AD* 2nd ed. (Warsaw 1955).

'Hellenistic law,' then—what does this mean? When this adjective applies to law, it needs to be explained, just as when it stands next to the words 'era' or 'civilization.' The idea of a "mixed civilization," advocated in the past by the historians of Antiquity, following Johann Gustav Droysen for whom the Hellenistic world was the result of a mixture of Greek Occident and Barbarian Orient, is usually abandoned. It resurfaces occasionally according to circumstances. So, in spring 1998, in Paris, on the occasion of an exhibition devoted to "the Glory of Alexandria" under the joint auspices of the French and the Egyptian governments, one could hear about a "Greco-Egyptian synthesis" which would have been carried out in the capital of the Ptolemies. The historians' scruples gave way to the interest of the excavations our archaeologists are bravely carrying out in the city and the port of Alexandria, where they think they might find the vestiges of the lighthouse of Pharos, one of the "seven wonders of the world."

Luckily, the lighthouse has nothing to do with the history of law; so we can eliminate with no regrets or hesitation the concept of a "mixed Greco-Egyptian law," that used to dominate research in legal papyrology. The meeting of local traditions with practices and ideas which the Greco-Macedonian immigrants imported to the provinces of the Achaemenid Empire conquered by Alexander the Great could surely not help but act upon the evolution of the law. The Greek traditions henceforth acted in a space larger than the narrow framework of the Greek state, *polis* or *ethnos*, and this necessarily entailed changes in the substance of law. For their part, the local legal cultures must have been influenced by the Greek element entrenched in an Egyptian or Oriental environment. An interplay of mutual influences started off and directed the lawgivers' action to solutions that could combine a Greek form with a content determined by the local heritage. But all this did not lead to a "mixture," and the idea of "Hellenistic law" can in no way refer to such a mixture.

Let us say it clearly: "Hellenistic law" is nothing else but Greek law practiced by the Greek-speaking immigrants within the kingdoms stemming from Alexander's conquests, as we know it thanks to the documents—papyri, parchments, ostraca, inscriptions—found mainly in Egypt, but also, though less often, in the Near East, at Dura-Europos or in the Judaean Desert, the object of the present volume.[4]

---

[4] H.J. Wolff, "Hellenistisches Recht," *ZSav* 90 (1973) 63–90 = "Hellenistic Private

Derived from the experience of ancient Greece, which was multi-sided by definition, it is characterized, as for its substance, by a high level of unity; as for its sources, it appears essentially as a law of custom, the source of which is not the legislation of a city or a sovereign, but notary practice. Because it is not the law of a limited group, as were the *nomoi* of the classical Greek cities or of the *ethne*, it is within the reach of all who can fit the definition of a "Hellene," through adherence to Greek culture and an origin foreign to the conquered country and reputed to be "civic"; in this respect, the case of the Jews of Egypt is particularly significant.[5] After the Hellenistic monarchies were reduced to the state of Roman provinces, Hellenistic law survived under the Principate in the practice of the provinces of the East.

2. *Greek contribution and local traditions.*—The Hellenistic era achieved the unity of the Greek law. The differences that were characteristic of the traditions of various cities or regions, the immigrants' fatherlands, diminished in practice. This process, which had already started in the 4th century BCE because of trade between cities under the dominating influence of Athens, became stronger in the melting pot which was Alexander's army. A Greek "common law" prevails in the Hellenistic world. The notion of legal *koine*, drawing a parallel between language and law, provides an explanation of this phenomenon.[6]

The new factor that ensured the success of this *koine* was not the kings' action, as one used to think, but the appearance of a new political structure: the Hellenistic monarchy, which is superimposed on the city. The city is no more the only framework of legal life for the Greeks. The Hellenistic state released the Greeks from obeying the laws of the city, which are factors of diversity, and created a terrain favorable to the unity of legal practice in private law. With the decline of civic autonomy, the fetters that confined the Greeks' legal life in distinct systems, for each independent *polis*, disappeared.

Law," in S. Safrai and M. Stern, eds., *Compendia rerum Iudaicarum ad Novum Testamentum I: The Jewish People in the First Century* (Assen 1974) 534–60. P.W. Pestman, "Hellenistic Law," in *Encyclopaedia Britannica, 15th ed.* (1974) IX, 746–8.

[5] J. Mélèze Modrzejewski, "Jewish Law and Hellenistic Legal Practice in the Light of Greek Papyri from Egypt," in N.S. Hecht et al., eds., *An Introduction to the History and Sources of Jewish Law* (Oxford 1996) 75–99.

[6] L. Gernet, "Introduction à l'étude du droit grec ancien," *Archives d'histoire du droit oriental* 2 (1938) 261–92.

Free of the particularism of the *polis*, Greek "common law" nevertheless kept a trace of its origin: in the judicial practice of Ptolemaic Egypt, it is called *nomoi politikoi*, "civic law." The city remains an ideological reference point that allows us to contrast, as regards politics or anything else, the Greek contribution with the local heritage.

The immigrants' "common law" was juxtaposed with the legal traditions of the conquered populations, which themselves were maintained and protected by the state. Ptolemaic Egypt gives a most instructive example of this coexistence.

Ancient Egyptian local law survived the Macedonian conquest and continued to be used by the natives. During the late Egyptian period, the rules of this law were recorded in writing in works kept by the temples; the tradition which attributes to Darius I the "codification" of Egypt's law prior to the Persian conquest suggests the existence of quite extensive collections. As for the Ptolemaic era, this impression has been confirmed by extracts of a "demotic priestly casebook" that were found in different religious centers; the most famous ones come from Tuna el-Gebel, the ancient Hermopolis West, which explains the widespread though misleading name "Hermopolis Legal Code."[7]

Actually, what we have here is a collection of practical instructions for judges and native lawyers, with models of deeds and sentences, or with solutions to hard cases. One could say it is a "handbook" ("prontuario legale" in Italian) due to the learned priests who produced and wrote down "holy books"—religious, scientific or legal collections for the Egyptian clergy and its "customers," in the "Houses of Life" of their temples. The priests who kept these books passed them on from one generation to the next, in variants that differed according to the religious centers.

The Egyptian priestly case-book has to be connected with another "holy book" existing in Ptolemaic Egypt: the Jewish Torah. Both of them were translated into Greek in the reign of Ptolemy II Philadelphus. The translation of the Jewish Law—the Alexandrian Septuagint— is well-known; its historicity has been confirmed by the fragments of the Pentateuch on rolls of papyrus anterior to the Christian era. A papyrus from Oxyrhynchus (P.Oxy. XLVI 3285) informed us over

---

[7] K. Donker van Heel, *The Legal Manual of Hermopolis [P.Mattha]. Text and Translation* (Leiden 1990).

twenty-five years ago that the demotic collection was also translated to Greek in the beginning of the 3rd century BCE, in the reign of Ptolemy II. In both cases, the Ptolemaic monarchy will have "sponsored" the undertaking.

Numerous documents preserved by demotic papyri add the testimony of everyday legal practice to these very formally normative texts. For the Ptolemaic period, they represent about half of the documentary papyrus material found in Egypt. They attest an undeniable continuation of the Egyptian legal traditions under the Ptolemies, that would be perpetuated under the Roman Empire and then appear again in the Coptic documents of the Byzantine and the Arabic eras. The Greeks call this *nomos* or *nomoi tes choras*, "the law of the country"; this expression should not be confused with "the laws of the Egyptians," *nomoi* (or *nomos*) *ton Aigyption*, mentioned by a few documents of the Roman period. We will come back to this point.

3. *Coexistence and interaction.*—Still without reaching an amalgam, the coexistence of different private laws could not help but lead to an interplay of mutual exchanges and borrowings between the rules and practices. Estimating their extent accurately is not easy. Let us make do with mentioning several significant facts.

Greek influence upon Egyptian law appears specifically concerning the form of legal deeds: this is the so-called "Doppelurkunde," written in duplicate and thought to have been borrowed from the Greeks by the Egyptian notaries. It is nevertheless not sure that the "Doppelurkunde" was invented by the Greeks: its prototype is the Mesopotamian "envelope tablet," which was replaced in the neo-Babylonian era by the multiple original, of which a copy was kept by each of the contracting parties. One is much less sure about other presumed borrowings from Greek law by Egyptian law.

Egyptian influences upon Greek law seem to be more numerous. But one has to be cautious. Thus, the changes characterizing Greek family law in Egypt by comparison with its classical roots should not necessarily be attributed to the action of local models; at the very most, the surrounding environment will have stimulated or accelerated an evolution already begun within Greek life. In some cases the new historical context contributed to the institutionalization of tendencies characteristic of a Greek practice which was until then secondary and marginal; this is notably the case, as we will see later, of women who give themselves in marriage or of endogamic unions.

Elsewhere—like the eldest son's privileged situation in matters of inheritance or the institution of *parapherna*—Egyptian influence seems to be more likely. But its effect is still limited.

One should distinguish the coincidences of the legal solutions from these mutual influences and borrowings. It would be banal to mention that distinct legal cultures, having reached the same stage of evolution, often elaborate similar solutions if the social and economical conditions are suitable: what seems to be an influence or a foreign element might just be a convergence. From the comparative point of view, detecting such parallelisms would be a fascinating undertaking. A careful study of the bilingual documents, including not only the truly bilingual ones and the translations, but also the documents written in one language according to the patterns characteristic of the other, would be particularly useful in this respect.

All in all, the exchanges and borrowings between the two bodies of law seem to be fewer than the supporters of the "mixed law" in the first half of the 20th century were willing to admit. Pluralism remains the dominant feature of legal life in the Hellenistic world. In Ptolemaic Egypt, it is maintained by a system of judicial organization that guarantees that Greek and the Egyptian traditions will be protected by official sanction.[8] The *nomoi politikoi* on the one hand, the *nomoi tes choras* on the other hand have been confirmed as *leges fori* of the courts specific to each of the two groups: the Greek dicasteries and the Egyptian *laocritai*. On this occasion, the Jewish Torah in Greek became a "civic law" (*nomos politikos*) of Egyptian Jews, being an integral part of the community of the "Hellenes."[9]

The Roman conquest of Egypt did not change this situation as far as the substance of the law is concerned. The local laws survived the conquest under the kindly eye of the Roman authority. The provincial judges were ready to respect the peregrine law, even if it meant filling the gaps, resolving the contradictions or restraining

---

[8] J. Mélèze Modrzejewski, "Law and Justice in Ptolemaic Egypt," in M.J. Geller, H. Maehler, and A.D.E. Lewis, eds., *Legal Documents of the Hellenistic World* (London 1995) 1–11.

[9] J. Mélèze Modrzejewski, "La Septante comme nomos. Comment la Tora est devenue une 'loi civique' pour les Juifs d'Égypte," *Annali di Scienze Religiose* 2 (Milan 1997) 143–58. English version: "The Septuagint as *Nomos*: How the Torah Became a 'Civic Law' for the Jews of Egypt," in J.W. Cairns and O.F. Robinson, eds., *Critical Studies in Ancient Law, Comparative Law and Legal History* (*Essays in Honour of Alan Watson*) (Oxford/Portland, Oregon 2001) 183–99.

extravagances by resorting to the scale of values which their own law, *ius urbis Romae*, gave them. They failed to see the difference between the Greek and the Egyptian origin of a local rule. Both were for them no more than a local tradition characteristic of the peregrines of the province of Egypt.[10]

The fact that the Greek version of the demotic collection made in the 3rd century BCE was copied in the Antonine era suggests the conclusion that this translation could enlighten the provincial judge on the situation of the law actually practiced by native Egyptians, as it might influence his decision in case of contention. But this does not mean that the measures included in this book, "the law of the country," can have imposed themselves as legal rules. Without a link that would connect them to a peregrine city, they could not aspire to the authority of a peregrine *ius civile* according to the Roman categories. For the Roman authority, they were only local customs.

This "law of the country" (*nomos tes choras*) should not be mistaken for the "law of the Egyptians" (*nomos ton Aigyption*) that a few documents of the 2nd century CE refer to. A careful analysis of these documents leads to the conclusion that the law known as "of the Egyptians" was "Egyptian" only by its name; actually, it was Greek law. The "Egyptians" in question were the peregrines of Egypt who were not citizens of a Greek *polis*. As for their *nomos*, in some cases, it could appear to be private collections made by local practitioners, using material taken from the royal legislation and the laws of the Greek *poleis* in Egypt.[11] For the Roman judge, it did not make any difference for the validity of this law: whether they are Greek or Egyptian, the rules recorded in these books were for him only customs specific to the peregrine populations—*mores provinciae, consuetudines loci*. After the generalization by Caracalla of Roman citizenship some of those customs, those in conflict with Roman law and order, would be left aside; others would survive as provincial customs, subordinate to the priority of the Roman "Reichsrecht."

---

[10] J. Mélèze Modrzejewski, "Diritto romano e diritti locali," in A. Schiavone, ed., *Storia di Roma* III 2 (Torino 1993) 985–1009.

[11] J. Mélèze Modrzejewski, "La loi des Égyptiens: le droit grec dans l'Égypte romaine," in B.G. Mandilaras, ed., *Proceedings of the XVIII International Congress of Papyrology (Athens, 25–31 May 1986)* (Athens 1988) 383–99 = in M. Piérart and O. Curty, eds., *Historia Testis: Mélanges d'épigraphie, d'histoire ancienne et de philologie offerts à Tadeusz Zawadzki* (Fribourg 1989) 97–115 = J. Mélèze Modrzejewski, *Droit impérial et traditions locales* (Aldershot 1990) IX.

From these general data, I would like to insist on a point that seems to be crucial for my purpose: the permanence of Hellenistic law within the monarchies of the successors of Alexander the Great and within the Oriental provinces that replaced them after the Roman conquest. I will limit myself to a few details about marriage, family structures and transmission of property by means of succession.

II. *Marriage and family: the permanence of Hellenistic law*

1. *Marriage.*—The new conditions in which the Greek immigrants' family life organized itself modified matrimonial law. In the Hellenistic world, heads of families no longer settle the question of concluding a marriage by themselves, as in classical Athens; it becomes a matter for the married couple itself. In the oldest Greek matrimonial agreement found in Elephantine (P.Eleph. 1, 310 BCE), an anacoluthon lets us hear the couple's voice in the first person plural, for the first time in the history of the Greek family. From now on it is a purely personal bond that appears in the marriage contracts preserved on papyrus. The diversity of the forms and of the terms that those contracts reveal goes hand in hand with the unity of social fact: conjugal cohabitation (*synoikein*) together with the idea of a durable common life.[12]

Nevertheless, the legal substance of marriage remains unchanged: it is based, as in the past, on the act of "giving" (*ekdosis*) the bride accomplished by her father, or, in his absence, by a close male relative, and failing that, by the woman herself. A patrimonial allowance— the handing over of the dowry—accompanies it; this is what gives the marriage its validity as a social institution. The classical *proix* gives place to the *pherne*; this term, which, in the ancient Greek sources, referred to the dowry in archaic or provincial practice, applies in Egypt to a matrimonial system now generalized because it is in accord with the needs of a new type of family organization. On the other hand, some formalities disappear, like *engyesis*, by which the father "placed" his daughter in the hands of the man who was

---

[12] U. Yiftach-Firanko, *Marriage and Marital Arrangements. A History of the Greek Marriage Document in Egypt. 4th cent. BCE–4th cent. CE* (Munich 2003).

about to become her husband. The written contract now assures the married woman of her being a lawful wife, *gyne gnesia*. The contract replaces the solemn statements that accompanied the bride's passage from her father's power to her husband's. The contractual clauses suffice to ensure all the effects that joinder of the marriage produces concerning the legal status of the wife and children.

A set of documents found in Abusir el-Meleq, dated from the Augustan era but certainly representing the Alexandrian matrimonial law prior to the Roman conquest, shows that in Alexandria, after drafting a written agreement (*synchoresis*), a second act was reached in order to strengthen the matrimonial union by a ceremony (or an agreement), passing before the *hierothytai*, the magistrates of the city. This dual formality of Alexandrian marriage gave rise to various attempts at explanation. The hypothesis of Egyptian influence was contemplated[13] but it sounds frail. One can certainly notice a parallelism between the Alexandrian dual deed of marriage and the Egyptian practice in the *chora* in which a "support agreement" could be followed by a "payment document." But comparing the Alexandrian *hierothytai* with the homonymous magistrates in the epigraphic and literary sources would rather suggest the idea of a Greek continuity. The intervention of the *hierothytai* was probably no more than a formality, necessary to the transmission of the family estate, under the control of the city.[14]

The barriers the Greek cities used to erect against mixed marriages collapsed in Egypt and in Greek-speaking circles in the East. It could well be that Alexandrian law required dual civic ancestry for acquiring the status of citizen, a principle whose panhellenic character is stressed by Aristotle (*Polit.* 1275b, 21–22). Monimos, son of Kleandros, Alexandrian by his father, lives in the *chora* with an Egyptian woman; Demetria, their daughter, in spite of her Greek name, is not an Alexandrian citizen.[15] On the other hand, a citizen of Ptolemais could certainly marry a foreign woman and, through this marriage, she could acquire the position of *aste* (citizen). So, the road was opened to vaster matrimonial exchanges than the ones the

---

[13] J. Winand, "Le rôle des hiérothytes en Égypte," *CdE* 60 (1985) 398–411.
[14] U. Yiftach, "The Role of the Syngraphe 'compiled through the Hierothytai.' A Reconsideration of W. Schubart's Theory in Light of a Recently Published Alexandrian Marriage Contract (P.Berol. 25423)," *ZPE* 115 (1997) 178–82.
[15] W. Clarysse, "Une famille alexandrine dans la chôra," *CdE* 63 (1988) 137–40.

epigamia clauses of the intercity treaties in the 4th century BCE used to allow.

In the *chora*, marriages between partners of different origins were possible and absolutely legitimate. In the middle of the 3rd century BCE, Demetrios, a Cyrenean who came to Egypt, following the example of Princess Berenice II, daughter of Magas, who had married Ptolemy III Euergetes, himself married an Egyptian woman; the law of his original fatherland, which allowed marriages outside the citizen body only with certain groups of the Libyan population, did not matter much to him (Inscr. Fay. I 2). The case is no different for Antaios, an Athenian settled in Egypt, who married Olympias, a Macedonian, in the beginning of the 2nd century BCE, unless one presumes that the Athenian law forbidding marriage with a foreigner was altered after the downfall of the democratic regime in 322 BCE (P.Giss. I 2, 173 BCE).

Demetrios the Cyrenean's union with Thasis the Egyptian represents an exceptional case. Marriages between "Hellenes" and natives are extremely rare in Hellenistic Egypt. They were not formally forbidden, but a sort of "cultural agamia" made them impracticable.[16] We are far from the mixing of populations that the supporters of a Greco-Egyptian civilization used to imagine. Exceptionally, the barrier is overcome in some circles and at certain times. That is how, in Pathyris, in Upper Egypt, in the 2nd century BCE, a certain mixture of Greek soldiers and the upper social class of the local population could take place. It was due to contingent reasons: a new form of military organization associating the Greek element with the Egyptian elites.

2. *Family structures.*—The Hellenistic era favored the endogamic tendencies of Greek matrimonial law. For the Greeks, legally, incest was only between relatives in direct line; unions between close collaterals, half-brother, half-sister, though morally disapproved of, were not illicit from the legal point of view. Cimon son of Miltiades, the

---

[16] J. Mélèze Modrzejewski, "Dryton le Crétois et sa famille ou les mariages mixtes dans l'Égypte hellénistique," in *Aux origines de l'hellénisme, la Crète et la Grèce. Hommage à Henri van Effenterre, présenté par le Centre Gustave Glotz* (Publications de la Sorbonne. Histoire Ancienne et Médiévale—15) (Paris 1984) 353–76 = J. Mélèze Modrzejewski, *Statut personnel et liens de famille* (Aldershot 1993) VIII.

Athenian, legally married Elpinice, his sister from the same father. Athenian law, since Solon, permitted marriage to a half-sister on one's father's side (*homopatrios*); one is less sure that Lacedaemonian law allowed marriage to a half-sister on one's mother's side (*homometrios* or *homogastrios*), the Spartan system being thus the opposite of the Athenian one. This information, resting on the sole testimony of Philo of Alexandria (*De spec. leg.* 3.22–24), might have simply been invented by the Jewish philosopher: his objective was not to give us information about the Greeks' matrimonial traditions but to contrast their endogamy with the biblical exogamy set down in chapter 18 of *Leviticus*.

In Hellenistic practice, a marriage between brother and sister having the same parents (*homognesioi*) became possible. Such an example was given in 278 BCE by King Ptolemy II Philadelphus who married Arsinoe II, his full sister. This marriage gave rise to various reactions. Theocritus, more a courtier than a poet on this occasion, compared it to the divine marriage of Zeus and Hera (*Idyll* XVII. 121–134): the Alexandrians may not have found this comparison very tasteful. Some people expressed criticism more or less sharply, the most violent being from Sotades of Maronea, the pornographer; this earned him a particularly severe punishment (Athenaeus, *Deipnosoph.* 14.620).[17]

Should one see in such a union the adherence to an Egyptian model? This is what Philo's text may suggest, as before him already Diodorus of Sicily, according to whom the Egyptians, "against the general custom of mankind," instituted a law authorizing a man to marry his sisters (*Bibl. hist.* 1.27.1). But in the present state of our sources, Egyptology does not let us maintain the idea that Ptolemy II and his sister had followed a Pharaonic example, unless one goes back a thousand years, to Amenophis III or Rameses II. The inevitable conclusion is that the children of the first Ptolemy pushed to its extreme limit a tendency conveyed by the Greek traditions favorable to endogamy.

Greek immigrants followed their example very quickly. As early as 267 BCE, at Tholthis, in the Oxyrhynchite nome, a certain

---

[17] J. Mélèze Modrzejewski, "'Paroles néfastes' et 'vers obscènes.' À propos de l'injure verbale en droit grec et hellénistique," in J. Hoareau-Dodinau and P. Texier, eds., *Anthropologies juridiques. Mélanges Pierre Braun* (Limoges 1998) 569–85 = *Dike* 1 (1998) 151–169.

Praxidamas had married a woman called Sosio who almost certainly was also his sister (P.Iena inv. No. 904 = SB XII 11053). One hundred and thirty years later, Dionysios, another Greek, gave his banker in Tebtunis an order to pay a tax for his sister Euterpe who was also his wife, as he specified (P.Tebt. III(1) 766, about 136 BCE). In the Roman period these practices were general; the numerous documents that attest them, and the tolerant attitude of the Roman authorities despite the regulations punishing endogamy according to the Roman law, lead us to think that they were already more frequent in Ptolemaic Egypt than is indicated by the two documents we have just mentioned. Such marriages are more common among the descendants of the "Hellenes" in the *metropoleis* than among village Egyptians; this is at variance with the opinion which derives marriage between brother and sister from an Egyptian tradition.

The Hellenistic era modified in various respects the status of Greek women. A woman was free to sell or buy, or to rent out her property; she could join her husband in giving their daughter in marriage, or she might do it herself when she was widowed or divorced. The power the head of the family had in classical Greece, as a *kyrios*, over the women under his control—wife, mistress, non-married daughters—was now limited to a sort of tutelage. In order to conclude a legal deed, the woman needed to be assisted by a *kyrios*; but the latter was no more a "lord and master": his intervention was just a formality, whose importance for the validity of the document is actually not obvious.

Some of those phenomena may appear as signs of "progress" in the evolution of women's status. But one should be careful of hasty generalizations. Thus, it is not certain that one can interpret as "progress" the alterations that the clauses of the matrimonial agreements preserved by the papyri reveal in matter of divorce. This includes, first, the sanction of behavior forbidden by the contract, particularly conjugal infidelity, which could result in the loss of the dowry for the wife and the husband's obligation to refund the dowry increased by 50% (*hemiolion*). But from the beginning of the 1st century BCE a new practice appeared, imposing on a husband who wanted to leave his wife the obligation of returning the simple amount of the dowry within a fixed time limit; the *hemiolion* had to be given only when the time limit was not respected. For her part, the woman obtained too the right to take the initiative for her divorce, giving her husband a time limit for the return of the dowry. Eventually, divorce as a sanction withdrew and gave place to divorce by mutual consent.

This situation, which seems to establish the equality of husband and wife in the matter of divorce, is not necessarily more favorable to the wife than the initial system in which the threat of the *hemiolion* towards the flighty husband effectively protected the wife who was blameless. On the other hand, one can very well consider as being "avant-garde" the women who themselves carry out the act of their *ekdosis*, that is to say who give themselves in marriage. In classical Greece, such a woman's "auto-ekdosis" was a sign of barbarism or of prostitution. On the contrary, in the Hellenistic world, the woman can indeed carry out her *ekdosis* with a legitimate union in mind. For Egypt, this fact is attested by two Ptolemaic documents (P.Giss. I 2, 173 BCE; P.Oxy. XLIX 3500, 3rd century CE). A document from Dura-Europos (P.Dura 30, 232 CE) and the novel *Chaireas and Callirhoe* by Chariton of Aphrodisias attest its expansion beyond the Egyptian context.[18]

3. *Succession.*—The data concerning marriage and the status of women can be usefully complemented by those concerning the transmission of family property *mortis causa*. The testamentary restrictions which, in ancient Greece, used to protect the *oikos*, family-household, in favor of the deceased's male descendants only, disappeared; daughters inherit in the same way as sons. At the same time also disappeared the epiclerate, an institution that made the deceased's unique daughter, legally incapable of being his heir, the one who would hand down the property by forcing her to marry a close relative on her father's side, the son descended from this union being destined to perpetuate the *oikos* of his grandfather on his mother's side.[19]

The compensation for the disappearance of institutions destined in the past to serve the classical *oikos* was the emergence of new practices of benefit to the individual family. Here is an example. Neither Greek nor Egyptian laws granted the surviving spouse

---

[18] E. Karabélias, "Le roman de Chariton d'Aphrodisias et le droit. Renversements de situations et exploitation des ambiguïtés juridiques," in G. Nenci and G. Thür, eds., *Symposion 1988* (Köln 1990) 369–96.

[19] E. Karabélias, "La situation successorale de la fille unique du défunt dans la koiné juridique hellénistique," in J. Modrzejewski and D. Liebs, eds., *Symposion 1977* (Köln 1982) 223–4.

intestate succession. In Hellenistic practice, this incapacity was alleviated by the husband's provisions by will in favor of his wife, notably the right of housing until her possible second marriage, and also, though more rarely, similar provisions on behalf of a woman in favor of her husband. Acts which combined a matrimonial agreement with the couple's provisions because of death (*syngraphodiathekai*) helped to attain the same objective.

The interaction of two legal cultures lets a few Egyptian influences appear on Greek practice. It seems indeed to be the case with the eldest son's privileged situation in matter of succession, which one can detect in the Greek papyri of Ptolemaic and Roman times,[20] and also with dowry rights, like the institution of *parapherna* derived from the demotic "Frauensachen."[21] On the other hand, P. Moscow dem. 123,[22] a will written in demotic in the 1st century BCE (April 18, 70 BCE), following a Greek pattern, cannot serve as proof in support of the hypothesis of Greek influence on the Egyptian law: this is a document of Greek law written in Egyptian language, and not testimony to the evolution of Egyptian law in contact with Greek law. We may be dealing with a similar situation in the Judaean Desert material.

The most striking new legal development in the matter of succession is the "invention" of the devolution to the state of inheritances without heirs, that is, to the royal treasury. The succession law of Dura-Europos, preserved in a copy on parchment from the Roman era, but whose substance dates to the beginning of this city which was built on the right bank of the Euphrates in about 300 BCE, decrees that, if there are no regular heirs—legitimate or adopted children, a non-remarried father or mother, collaterals up to the fourth degree (family ties with the grand-parents and with the cousins on the father's side)—the property of a settler who died intestate goes to the king (P.Dura 12, 14–16).[23] Paragraph 4 of the *Gnomon*

---

[20] E. Seidl, "La preminente posizione successoria del figlio maggiore nel diritto dei papiri," *Rendiconti dell'Istituto Lombardo, Classe di Lettere* 99 (1965) 185–92.

[21] G. Häge, *Ehegüterrechtliche Verhältnisse in den griechischen Papyri Ägyptens bis Diokletian* (Köln-Graz 1968).

[22] M. Malinine, "Partage testamentaire d'une propriété familiale," *Nachrichten d. Akad. d. Wiss. Göttingen, philol.-hist. Klasse* (n° 4 1965) 97–101; "Partage testamentaire d'une propriété familiale (Pap. Moscou No. 123)," *RÉg* 19 (1967) 67–85.

[23] J. Mélèze Modrzejewski, "La dévolution à l'État des successions en déshérence dans le droit hellénistique," *RIDA* 8 (1961) 79–113 = J. Mélèze Modrzejewski, *Statut personnel et liens de famille* (Aldershot 1993) IX.

of the Idios Logos, a collection of tax and legal provisions in force in Egypt under the Principate, suggests that the Roman system attributing *bona vacantia* to the imperial fiscus could have been inspired by such a rule of Hellenistic law.[24]

All in all, as we can see, the evolution of the Greek family law in the Hellenistic world acts according to its own dynamics, determined by political and social conditions, and not by the influence of the local environment. The same conclusions should be drawn in other fields, the law of property and the law of contracts. In no case should one speak about an "amalgam" or a "mixture."

* * *

In an article published in 1961, our German colleague Dieter Nörr asked the question whether the notion of legal *koine* should not be extended to the sense of an entity made up of Greek and Oriental elements: "eine hellenistische Rechtskoine, die aus griechischen und orientalischen Elementen gemischt wäre."[25] I am afraid that this would take us down a dangerous road. The conclusions drawn from the documentation of Egyptian origin certainly do not automatically apply to other regions of the Hellenistic Orient. But the idea of a mixed Greco-Palestinian or Greco-Babylonian law seems *a priori* to me as disputable as that of a mixed Greco-Egyptian law which, as we have just seen, never existed. A document or a file can reveal an interchange of borrowings or of influences, in Egypt or in the Judaean Desert, but one must be careful not to tackle the whole documentation with the preconceived idea that we have to deal with a "mixture." You can say it is Hellenistic law when the elements you have belong to a Greek tradition, provided that you separate them from what derives from Jewish tradition and what appears as obvious Roman practice. It is in this effort of analysis and identification that the experience of legal papyrology—and our thoughts about the content of Hellenistic law—may be of use to the study of the law revealed by the documents of the Judaean Desert.

---

[24] J. Mélèze Modrzejewski, "La dévolution à l'État des biens vacants d'après le Gnomon de l'Idiologue (BGU 1210 § 4)," in *Studi in onore di E. Volterra* VI (Milano 1971) 91–125 = J. Mélèze Modrzejewski, *Droit impérial et traditions locales (Aldershot* 1990) IV.

[25] D. Nörr, "Die Evangelien des Neuen Testaments und die sogenannte hellenistische Rechtskoine," *ZSav* 78 (1961) 92–141.

ROMAN OFFICIALS IN JUDAEA AND ARABIA AND CIVIL JURISDICTION

Hannah M. Cotton and Werner Eck

The family archives of two Jewish women, Babatha and Salome Komaise, are part of the Nahal Hever papyri.[1] Both archives originated in the Roman province of Arabia, created by Trajan in 106.[2] They consist primarily of legal documents written in Greek, Jewish Aramaic, and Nabatean Aramaic: deeds of gift, deeds of sale, contracts of loan, marriage contracts, receipts, concession of rights etc.[3] In addition they include two land declarations, P.Yadin 16 and P.Hever 62, submitted during the first Roman census carried out in the new province in 127.[4]

---

[1] This paper addresses only the part played by the imperial officials in the execution of justice in a Roman province, and leaves out the important role played by the self-governing units in a province, above all the cities. Furthermore, it does not cover criminal jurisdiction, which at least in theory devolved on the governor, but is so far not attested in the papyri. For vivid insights into the legal realities in a Roman province as revealed in Apuleius' *Metamorphoses* see F. Millar, "The World of the *Golden Ass*," *JRS* 71 (1981) 63–75 (= idem in H.M. Cotton and G.M. Rogers, eds., F. Millar, *Rome, the Greek World, and the East* II: *Government, Society and Culture in the Roman Empire* [Chapel Hill 2004] chapter 15). We thank Tiziana Chiusi and Dieter Hagedorn for discussing earlier versions of this paper with us.

For the Babatha archive see N. Lewis, ed., *The Documents from the Bar Kokhba Period in the Cave of Letters*. I. *Greek Papyri* (Judean Desert Studies 2) (Jerusalem 1989), and Y. Yadin, J.C. Greenfield, A. Yardeni and B. Levine, eds., *The Documents from the Bar Kokhba Period in the Cave of Letters* II. *Hebrew, Aramaic and Nabataean Aramaic Documents* (Judean Desert Studies 3) (Jerusalem 2002). The papyri in these two volumes are designated *P.Yadin*. For the archive of Salome Komaise see H.M. Cotton and A. Yardeni, eds., *Aramaic, Hebrew and Greek Documentary Texts from Nahal Hever and Other Sites. The Seiyâl Collection* II (Discoveries in the Judaean Desert XXVII) (Oxford 1997). The papyri in this volume are designated *P.Hever*. Cf. H.M. Cotton, "Documentary Texts from the Judaean Desert: A Matter of Nomenclature," *SCI* 20 (2001) 113–19.

[2] All dates are CE.

[3] H.M. Cotton, "The Languages of the Legal and Administrative Documents from the Judaean Desert," *ZPE* 125 (1999) 219–231.

[4] Cf. H.M. Cotton, "Ἡ νέα ἐπαρχεία Ἀραβία: The New Province of Arabia in the Papyri from the Judaean Desert," *ZPE* 116 (1997) 204–208; P.Hever 61 is a fragment of such a declaration.

It is precisely because of their legal-administrative nature that the documents provide important new information on the judicial system in a Roman province; from them we learn about the issuing of *vadimonia* to summon a person to the governor's court,[5] the assize system (*conventus*), the application of Roman law, and other matters.

The Roman judicial system, however, seems to be present in the documents in the person of the provincial governor *alone*. In other words, the governor emerges from the documents as the sole representative of Roman provincial power in the province and the sole dispenser of justice there.[6] This is true of Ti. Iulius Iulianus (P.Yadin 13, 14, 15), T. Aninius Sextius Florentinus (P.Yadin 16, P.Hever 62) and T. Haterius Nepos (P.Yadin 23, 25, 26).[7] Nevertheless, this impression is false: the governor was not the only one involved in the dispensation of justice in a Roman province—even if he embodied in his person the highest state authority. The presence of other officials invested with judicial competence in a Roman province can safely be assumed even when unattested, as happens to be the case in the archives from Arabia. In fact the Empire went further than the Republic in extending the judicial competence of an office-bearer charged with administrative duties; under the Empire he became *iudex competens* for all matters falling within his sphere.

In order to rescue the governor from this unhistorical "splendid isolation" and put the legal matters which we encounter in the papyri in the right context, we offer below an outline of all the officials present in a Roman province who are likely to have been involved with the dispensation of justice.[8]

---

[5] On the *vadimonium* to the governor's court see G.P. Burton, "The Lex Irnitana, Ch. 84. The Promise of Vadimonium and the Jurisdiction of Proconsuls," *CQ* n.s. 46 (1996) 217–21.

[6] Cf. H.M. Cotton, "The Rabbis and the Documents," in M. Goodman, ed., *Jews in a Graeco-Roman World* (Oxford 1998) 167–79 at 171 ff. on the total absence of other courts.

[7] T. Haterius Nepos' term as governor of Arabia coincided with the outbreak of the Bar Kokhba revolt in Judaea in 132 AD. He may have been the cause for the flight of the Jews from Arabia to Judaea, and thus indirectly for the presence of legal documents from Arabia in the cave of Nahal Hever; see W. Eck, "The Bar Kochba Revolt: The Roman Point of View," *JRS* 89 (1999) 76–89, and H.M. Cotton, "The Bar Kokhba Revolt and the Documents from the Judaean Desert: Nabataean Participation in the Revolt (P.Yadin 52)," in P. Schäfer, ed., *The Bar Kokhba War Reconsidered* (Tübingen 2003) 133–152.

[8] No exhaustive survey of the officials occupied with administering justice in a Roman province exists. Of special significance to the discussion here is G.P. Burton,

1. *Roman office-holders and the dispensation of justice*

Arabia and Judaea at the time belonged to what is known as the imperial provinces, the *provinciae Caesaris*.[9] The governor of an imperial province was designated *legatus Augusti pro praetore*. The title reveals that the governor was a senator with the rank of praetor; furthermore he was the emperor's representative and in possession of an *imperium*. Whether this *imperium* was independent or delegated by the emperor remains disputed,[10] but is of no consequence for his competence as a judge: for all practical purposes the legate had full *iurisdictio*, as can be inferred from Gaius 1.6.[11]

Despite their identical title, the governors of Judaea and Arabia held different ranks in the senatorial hierarchy. The governor of Arabia was an *ex praetore*, and assumed office some time after having served as praetor and before becoming consul; the legate of Judaea on the other hand was already a consular when entering office,[12]

"Proconsuls, Assizes, and the Administration of Justice under the Empire," *JRS* 65 (1975) 92–106. For Judaea/Syria Palaestina one may consult (warily) A.M. Rabello, "Civil Justice in Palestine from 63 BC to 70 AD," in R. Katzoff, ed., *Classical Studies in Honor of David Sohlberg* (Ramat Gan 1996) 293–306 and idem, "Jewish and Roman Jurisdiction," in N.S. Hecht et al., eds., *An Introduction to the History and Sources of Jewish Law* (Oxford 1996) 141–167 (not always accurate); F.M. Ausbüttel, *Die Verwaltung des römischen Kaiserreiches* (Darmstadt 1998) 54–61 (superficial). For the role of "arbitration" see H.M. Cotton, "Jewish Jurisdiction under Roman Rule: Prolegomena," in M. Labahn and J. Zangenberg, eds., *Zwischen den Reichen: Neues Testament und Römische Herrschaft. Vorträge auf der Ersten Konferenz der European Association for Biblical Studies*, (TANZ 36) (Tübingen 2002) 5–20. For municipal jurisdiction in civil and criminal matters (not discussed here) see: D. Nörr, *Imperium und Polis in der Hohen Prinzipatszeit* (Munich 1966) 30–34 and H. Galsterer, "Statthalter und Stadt im Gerichtswesen der westlichen Provinzen," in W. Eck, ed., *Lokale Autonomie und römische Ordnungsmacht in den kaiserzeitlichen Provinzen vom 1. bis 3. Jahrhundert* (Munich 1999) 243–56.

[9] For greater detail see the various essays in W. Eck, *Die Verwaltung des Römischen Reiches in der Hohen Kaiserzeit. Ausgewählte und erweiterte Beiträge* I–II (Basel 1995; 1998).

[10] The *s. c. de Cn. Pisone patre*, lines 34–36, implies that, unlike proconsuls, the legates had a merely delegated *imperium*; see W. Eck, A. Caballos, and F. Fernández, *Das senatus consultum de Cn. Pisone patre* (Munich 1996) 160–162.

[11] *Ius autem edicendi habent magistratus populi Romani; sed amplissimum est in edictis duorum praetorum . . . quorum in provinciis iurisdictionem praesides earum habent.* "The right of issuing edicts is possessed by magistrates of the Roman people. Very extensive law is contained in the edicts of the two praetors, . . . whose jurisdiction is possessed in the provinces by the provincial governors."

[12] Note though that his administrative rank remained that of a praetor as the title *pro praetore* makes clear; the emperor was the only *pro consule* in the imperial provinces.

since the province had received consular status at the latest in
Hadrian's first years.[13] Consequently the governor of Judaea was on
average several years older than his colleague in Arabia. But neither senatorial rank nor age made any difference as far as the governor's official competence was concerned, including, of course, its
judicial aspect. The only difference lay in the number of subordi-
nates whom the governor could use for various tasks, above all in
the judicial sphere.

There was never to be more than one legion stationed in Arabia.
It was the *legio III Cyrenaica* in the first years after annexation and
again from the 20s or 30s of the second century onwards.[14] The legion's
headquarters were in Bostra in the north of the province. The governor of Arabia was also the commander of the single legion,[15] and
was thus the only high-ranking senatorial official in Arabia.

The garrison of Judaea, in contrast, numbered two legions from
the early years of Hadrian: the *legio X Fretensis* had its headquarters
in Jerusalem; the second had its military quarters probably right from
the outset at Caparcotna/Legio in the north of the province. The
identity of this second legion in the 20s and 30s is a matter of dispute,[16] but it is of no significance here. With the stationing of the
second legion, the governor of Judaea no longer, as previously, dou-
bled as commander of the *legio X Fretensis*. Each legion was com-
manded by a senatorial legionary legate (*legatus legionis*) with praetorian
rank. Having served as a praetor in Rome, the commander of the
legion was not without some experience in the administration of justice, with the result that the governor could transfer judiciary duties
to him—a somewhat problematic situation if we believe that the governor himself had only a delegated *imperium*.[17] Be this as it may, it

---

[13] Cf. H.M. Cotton and W. Eck, "Governors and their Personnel on Latin
Inscriptions from Caesarea Maritima," in *Proceedings of the Israel Academy of Sciences
and Humanities* VII 7 (2001) 215–30.

[14] For a while it was replaced by the *legio VI Ferrata*; see contributions by H.M.
Cotton, S. Daris and P.-L. Gatier in Y. Le Bohec, ed., in *Les légions de Rome sous
le Haut-Empire. Actes du Congrès de Lyon (17–19 septembre 1998)*, (Lyon 2000).

[15] Generally on this G.W. Bowersock, *Roman Arabia* (Cambridge, Mass. 1983)
76 ff., 160 ff.

[16] Later on it was certainly the *legio VI Ferrata*; see B. Isaac and I. Roll, "Judaea
in the Early Years of Hadrian's Reign," *Latomus* 38 (1979) 54–66 = B. Isaac, *The
Near East under Roman Rule. Selected Papers* (Leiden 1998) 182–197, and the works
cited supra note 14.

[17] See supra note 10.

constitutes no obstacle in practice: legionary legates, especially in times of peace, are found deeply involved in the civil and judicial administration of the province, as is convincingly attested for the legate of the *legio VIII Augusta* Iuventius Caesianus in Upper Germany probably in 186.[18] Iuventius Caesianus ruled in a controversial inheritance case, either at the legion's camp of Argentorate or in the city of Arae Flaviae.[19] Thus in Judaea, in addition to the governor in Caesarea, there were two additional senatorial officials, one stationed in Jerusalem/Aelia Capitolina and the other in Caparcotna/Legio, who could adjudicate legal disputes between provincials. Presumably an appeal against their decisions could go to the governor. In the more important cases the governor could summon the two commanders to his *consilium* to help him reach a verdict.[20]

In addition to the legionary legates, the governor could delegate legal cases to the senior officers of the legion. Each legion had six military tribunes, one of senatorial rank and five of equestrian rank. While the senatorial tribunes generally were no more than 20 to 25 years of age, the equestrian tribunes were generally older, as were the equestrian commanders of the auxiliary troops, the cohorts and the *alae*, who held the title of *praefectus* or *tribunus*. Many of these equestrian officers had been active in public life in their home towns prior to their military service, as *IIviri iure dicundo* in Roman colonies and *municipia*, or in the parallel magistracies in the Greek *poleis*.[21] The administrative and judicial experience which these tribunes and prefects had acquired at home could be exploited by the governor in the province.

Thus, for example, P.Yadin 16 and P.Hever 61,[22] copies of two land declarations from the *census* of 127, reveal to us a Priscus, prefect

---

[18] J.C. Wilmanns, "Die Doppelurkunde von Rottweil und ihr Beitrag zum Städtewesen in Obergermanien," *Epigraphische Studien* 12 (1981) 1–182, especially 54–72.

[19] He probably acted on his own authority i.e. by virtue of the general jurisdiction delegated to him by the governor rather than as *iudex datus*; see infra text to notes 24–25.

[20] As can be learned from the *consilium* of the proconsul of Sardinia L. Helvius Agrippa where the proconsular legate and the provincial *quaestor* were present, *CIL* X 7852 = *ILS* 5947.

[21] On this see various contributions by H. Devijver, *The Equestrian Officers of the Roman Imperial Army* (Amsterdam 1989) 137 ff., 246 ff., 273 ff.; Volume 2 (Stuttgart 1992) 341 ff.; E. Birley, *The Roman Army Papers* (Amsterdam 1988) 147 ff.

[22] H.M. Cotton, "Another Fragment of the Declaration of Landed Property from the Province of Arabia," *ZPE* 99 (1993) 115–122.

of a cavalry unit (*praefectus alae*), attaching his subscription (*subscriptio*) to the original declarations; he must have been the recipient of the census-returns. Although his subscription has reached us in Greek, it was originally written in Latin since it is explicitly stated there to be a translation.[23]

The governor was able to call on these tribunes and prefects for the dispensation of justice as well;[24] he could transfer cases to them by appointing them *iudices dati* in civil cases which did not call for proceedings before a magistrate. Using these officers in such functions was all the more necessary in the province of Arabia, where at the time reflected in the papyri few held Roman citizenship, even among the leading families of the cities. It is just possible, as we shall see below, that one of the documents of the Babatha archive attests a *praefectus* as *iudex datus* (see part 3 below). Another solution to the paucity of people with Roman citizenship in the province would be the appointment of non-Romans as judges (especially as *recuperatores*), something that was surely done in the procedure reflected in P.Yadin 28–30.[25]

Finally, military tribunes, like the legionary legates of the consular governor, were called to the governor's *consilium*, which acted also as a court of law. A papyrus from 64 in Egypt reveals five military tribunes on the *consilium* of the *praefectus Aegypti* Caecina Tuscus, in addition to the *iuridicus*.[26]

---

[23] On the languages of administration and jurisdiction in this part of the Empire see A. Stein, *Untersuchungen zur Geschichte und Verwaltung Ägyptens unter römischer Herrschaft* (1915, reprinted 1974); see most recently A. Wacke, "Gallisch, Punisch, Syrisch oder Griechisch statt Latein?," *ZSav* 110 (1993) 14–59, who restricts himself to legal (i.e. "normative") sources. It remains to be seen whether or not his conclusions are borne out by the documentary evidence; on this see W. Eck, "Lateinisch, Griechisch, Germanisch . . .? Wie sprach Rom mit seinen Untertanen," in L. de Blois and E.A. Hemelrijk, eds., *The Empire at the Local Level: Effects of Roman Rule on Life in Italy and the Provinces. Proceedings of the 4th workshop of Impact of Empire, Leiden 25–28 June 2003*, (Leiden, forthcoming).

[24] Normally a governor had legal advisers at his side. For Syria Palaestina we have the testimony of Grégoire le Thaumaturge, *Remerciement à Origène*, Sourc. Chrét. 148 (Paris 1969) 5.6, pp. 118–120: Gregorius Thaumaturgus' brother in-law, who like him came from Neocaesarea in Cappadocia, held office as *nomikos* (perhaps *boethos*) on the staff of the governor in 233–8.

[25] See the convincing arguments of Dieter Nörr in: "The Xenokritai in Babatha's Archive," *Israel Law Review* 29 (1995) 83–94; idem, "Zur condemnatio cum taxatione im römischen Zivilprozess," *ZSav* 112 (1995) 51–90; idem, "Prozessuales aus dem Babatha-Archiv," *Mélanges André Magdelain* (Paris 1998) 317–41; idem, "Zu den Xenokriten (Rekuperatoren) in der römischen Provinzialgerichtsbarkeit," in W. Eck, ed., *Lokale Autonomie* (supra note 8) 257–301.

[26] P.Fouad I 21; on Baebius Iuncinus as *tribunus militum* of the *legio XXII Deiotariana*

All these Roman officials—legionary legates, tribunes, and prefects of the legions and auxiliary units—could exercise jurisdiction only *per delegationem*, i.e. the source was the governor's judicial competence inherent in his *imperium*. The legionary legates were likely to have been delegated general jurisdiction, whereas the lesser officers were entrusted with jurisdiction for specific and isolated cases (see part 3 below).

There were, however, in a province office holders whose authority was independent of the governor, and whose jurisdiction was not delegated by him. These were the imperial procurators of equestrian rank. We use the plural deliberately since, albeit often overlooked, in the course of the second and third centuries, in addition to the financial procurator proper so-to-speak one or two supplementary procurators were appointed to collect taxes. They make their appearance in the different provinces at different times.

The most important equestrian official in a province governed by a senator was the financial procurator, who was in charge of all taxes levied on a regular basis, above all the poll tax and the land tax. This official was appointed immediately after the Nabataean kingdom was annexed and reduced into the province of Arabia.[27] In Judaea, which had formerly been governed by prefects (later perhaps procurators), the financial procurator proper made his appearance once a senatorial governor was appointed for it—perhaps as early as 67, and certainly from 70 onwards (see text to note 55 below). From the outset this procurator had his headquarters in Caesarea; recent excavations have revealed structures and produced inscriptions which pin down the precise spot of this official's *praetorium*.[28] The rank of the procurator was determined by his salary-grade. Initially he was a centenary, i.e. he received an annual salary

in this year see *CIL* X 6976 = *ILS* 1434 and W. Eck, "Die Laufbahn eines Ritters aus Apri in Thrakien," *Chiron* 5 (1975) 365–92 at 381 f.

[27] For the procurators of Arabia see H.-G. Pflaum, *Les carrières procuratoriennes équestres sous le Haut-Empire romain* (Paris 1960) III 1083; *Supplément* (Paris 1982) 133; on *CIL* III 14157, 1 see *AE* 1993, 1649; *IGLS* XXI 29; F. Zayadine, ed., *Jerash Archaeol. Project 1981–1983*, Vol. I (Amman 1986) 384.

[28] See on this J. Patrich, "A Government Compound in Roman-Byzantine Caesarea," *Proceedings of the Twelfth World Congress of Jewish Studies, Jerusalem, July 29–August 5, 1997. Division B. History of the Jewish People* (Jerusalem 2000) 35*–44*; W. Eck, "New Inscriptions from Caesarea in Judaea/Syria Palaestina" in J. Patrich, ed., *Caesarea Maritima. Final Report* (forthcoming) with a list of newly discovered procurators.

of 100,000 sesterces. With the arrival of a second legion and a consular governor, that is when Judaea acquired consular rank (see above), the procurator's rank was raised as well: he was now a ducenary, i.e. receiving an annual salary of 200,000 sesterces.[29] His duties and responsibilities remained the same as those of the centenary procurator in Arabia, who had his headquarters in Gerasa and not where the governor of the province resided, first probably in Petra and later on in Bostra.[30]

At first the fiscal procurator was in charge of all financial matters in the province (and the legal issues arising from them), even those taxes and customs which were not regularly levied, e.g. "the five percent inheritance tax" *(vicesima hereditatium)* or "the five percent emancipation tax" *(vicesima libertatis)*, as well as of all legal issues arising from them. Only for a large imperial domain would a special procurator be assigned, as was C. Herennius Capito for Iamnia (in Judaea) at the time of Tiberius and Caligula.[31] Whether or not this particular function continued later is unknown.

The assumption that a special *procurator vicesimae hereditatium* (i.e. in charge of "the five percent inheritance tax") existed for Syria Palaestina (formerly Judaea) *alone* as early as 145, based on a false restoration of an inscription from Caesarea in Mauretania Caesariensis, should now be rejected.[32] It was unlikely to begin with, given the scanty evidence, that we should assign a special procurator for the collection of the *XX hereditatium*—to which only Roman citizens were liable—to a province like Syria Palaestina, where few Roman citizens resided at the time. Furthermore, the small size of the province should have discouraged belief in the presence of this official here

---

[29] See Pflaum, *Suppl.* (supra note 27) 33–7. No evidence, however, supports Pflaum's dating of the upgrade to shortly after 123; Sempronius Senecio's career points to an earlier date, perhaps 117.

[30] At first the governor resided in Petra: cf. R. Haensch, *Capita provinciarum. Statthaltersitze und Provinzialverwaltung in der römischen Kaiserzeit* (Mainz 1997) 238–9; 556–63; see more in part 2 below.

[31] *AE* 1941, 105.

[32] *proc(urator) XX heredi[tatium]/provinciae [Syriae Palaest]inae*, so read by L. Leschi, *CRAI* 1945, 144–62, especially 152 = *AE* 1946, 113, and accepted by Pflaum, *Carrières* (note 27 above) I, 375–9 as also by I. Piso and G. Alföldy in the works cited in note 35. The inscription should be restored differently: *proc. XX heredi[t., proc.]/provinciae [Syriae Palaest]inae*, i.e. a procurator of the the *XX hereditatium* in Rome who was previously the financial procurator of Syria Palaestina; see in detail W. Eck, "Zu Inschriften von Prokuratoren," *ZPE* 124 (1999) 228–41 at 238 f.

when everywhere else in the Empire at the time several provinces shared a *procurator vicesimae hereditatium*, e.g. the *procurator XX hereditatium per Baeticam et Lusitaniam*, or the *procurator XX hereditatium per Asiam, Lyciam, Pamphyliam, Phrygiam, Galatiam, insulas Cycladas*.[33]

By the third century in many provinces certain taxes, and especially the *XX hereditatium*, were taken out of the provincial procurator's responsibility and transferred to a separate official. This may well be attested for Arabia and Syria Palaestina if we accept the restoration of [*proc(urator) vice*]*s(imae) h*[*e*]*red*[*itatium provincia*]*rum Syr(iarum)* [*Phoen(ices) et/ Palaestin*]*ae at Ar*[*abiae*][34] in an inscription from Sarmizegetusa in Dacia.[35]

As pointed out before, like other Roman officials, the financial procurator had jurisdiction in cases arising from his administrative, or rather financial, functions. The financial procurators were assisted by imperial freedmen and slaves. Of particular significance in the dispensation of justice was the imperial freedman (*libertus Augusti*), who like the equestrian procurator bore the title of *procurator*. He was the deputy of the financial procurator, and as such was allowed from Claudius' time onward to exercise jurisdiction, limited of course to issues arising from tax collection.[36]

True, this administrative position is not everywhere attested, and has therefore been called into doubt by some.[37] By a happy chance his presence in Syria Palaestina, alongside that of the equestrian procurator, is borne out by a new interpretation of papyrus *SB* XII 11043, published for the first time in 1974, and the discovery of a new inscription in recent excavations in Caesarea Maritima mentioned above.

---

[33] See the lists in Pflaum, *Carrières* (note 27 above) 1049, 1074; see also 1054, 1056, 1077. A similar combination of provinces is to be found in an inscription from Prusias ad Hypium: *IGR* III 1420 = *I. Prusias* 57, where, however, the official may be a *procurator ludorum* rather than a *procurator vicesimae hereditatium*.

[34] Or: *Syr*[*iae/ Palaestin*]*ae et Ar*[*abiae*].

[35] See I. Piso, "Die Laufbahn eines Ritters aus Pamphylien," *Chiron* 8 (1978) 515–527; G. Alföldy, "Zum cursus honorum des Aurelius Tuesianus," *ZPE* 34 (1979) 247–72.

[36] Tac. *Ann.* 12.60; cf. F. Millar, "Some Evidence on the Meaning of Tacitus' *Annals XII.*60," *Historia* 13 (1964) 180–7; P.A. Brunt, "Procuratorial Jurisdiction," in idem, *Roman Imperial Themes* (Oxford 1990) 163–87.

[37] See F. Millar's review of H.-G. Pflaum, *Carrières* (supra note 27) in *JRS* 53 (1963) 194–200 (= idem in H.M. Cotton and G.M. Rogers, eds. [supra note 1] chapter 8).

The papyrus was written in Caesarea Maritima in 152 and later made its way to the Fayyum in Egypt.[38] Its relevant part reads as follows in John Rea's translation:[39]

> ... (day, month) in the consulship of Glabrio and Homullus, in Caesarea in the temple. When Valerius Serenus, veteran, from the village of Meason(?) in the Peraea, petitioned to be received into the number of those who heard a proclamation(?) which took place before Quintianus, Aelius Amphigethes, procurator, freedman of the Augustus (Αἴλιος Ἀμφιγέθης ἐπίτροπος Σεβαστοῦ ἀπελεύθερος), said: "Are you in possession?" Said Serenus: "I am." Amphigethes said: "No-one will eject you. You will remain in possession and I shall ... in the record-office and if the muster-roll of the veterans is found, I shall certify for you in your name what it is necessary for me to testify."

Leaving aside some difficult readings in the text, its message is clear: the imperial *libertus et procurator* Aelius Amphigetes confirms here the rights of possession of the veteran Valerius Serenus, thereby implementing a general ordinance issued by a Quintianus, referred to in the preamble to the proceedings which are now taking place before Aelius Amphigetes. The casual reference by the imperial freedman to Quintianus, merely by cognomen and without naming his official title, sits hard with the identification of the latter as the senatorial governor of Syria Palaestina at the time, suggested by John Rea (although one cannot exclude *per se* the possibility of collaboration between an imperial freedman and a senatorial governor).[40] Quintianus and Aelius Amphigetes appear to be on close, almost intimate, terms with each other, a situation now fully accounted for by an inscription, palaeographically dated to the second half of the second century, which was found in what used to be the *praetorium* of the financial procurator in Caesarea:[41]

---

[38] First published in H. Maehler, "Ein römischer Veteran und seine Matrikel," in E. Kießling and H.-A. Rupprecht, eds., *Akten des XIII. Internationalen Papyrologenkongresses, Marburg/Lahn, 2.-6. August 1971* (Munich 1974) 241–250; cf. H.M. Cotton, W. Cockle and F. Millar, "The Papyrology of the Roman Near East: A Survey," *JRS* 85 (1995) 214–35, no. 335.

[39] J. Rea, "Two legates and a procurator of Syria Palaestina," *ZPE* 26 (1977) 217–22.

[40] Cf. e.g Hesperus, *libertus et procurator*, who worked together with the proconsul of Asia, Avidius Quietus; *CIL* III 355 = U. Laffi, "I terreni del tempio di Zeus ad Aizanoi," *Athenaeum* 49 (1971) 3–53, text on pp. 9–11.

[41] W. Eck (supra note 28) no. 2.

[. . ?*Calp*]*urnio Quin-*
[?*tian*]*o proc(uratori) Aug(usti)*
[*prov]inc(iae) S[y]r(iae) Pal(aestinae)*
[—/—].

Once the extremely attractive and plausible identification of the [Calp]urnius Quin[tian]us of this inscription with Quintianus of the papyrus is accepted,[42] everything falls into place: Aelius Amphigetes is involved in settling a legal issue (perhaps within the precincts of the procuratorial *praetorium* itself),[43] in the wake of some general ruling pronounced by his superior. The freedman is all but a deputy of his equestrian superior in the administrative sphere of which the dispensation of justice is an important component.

Our initial impression on reading the Babatha archive, of the "splendid isolation" of the Roman governor in the province should be corrected in the light of the evidence submitted above: more Roman officials were actively involved in the dispensation of justice and the execution of administrative measures in a Roman province than the documents allow for. Nevertheless, the fact that the governors of Arabia are directly or indirectly present in the majority of the Greek legal documents of the Babatha archive[44] is in itself highly significant; it underscores the governor's paramount authority, his dominant and central position in the judicial system of a province—which should by no means suggest that he was acting alone. It tells us more of how the provincial subjects perceived Rome's government in the province than of the division of work within that government itself.[45]

---

[42] W. Eck, "Ein Prokuratorenpaar von Syria Palaestina in P.Berol. 21652," *ZPE* 123 (1998) 249–55.

[43] The ναός (temple) of the papyrus could well be part of the *praetorium*, see Eck (supra note 42) 253.

[44] Legal issues in P.Yadin 12 (appointment of guardian by the council of Petra), 13 (petition to the governor) 14 and 15 (summons and deposition), 16 (land declaration), 17 (deposit between husband and wife), 18 (marriage contract), 19 (deed of gift), 20 (concession of rights), 21 and 22 (purchase of date crop), 23 (summons) 24 and 25 (deposition and summons), 26 (summons), 27 (receipt), 28–30 (three identical copies of a legal formula issued by the governor), 31–36 (fragmentary). There are 6 Greek legal documents in the archive of Salome Komaise, most of them of private character (supra note 1): P.Hever 60 (receipt), P.Hever 61 (subscription to land declaration), P.Hever 62 (land declaration), P.Hever 63 (concession of rights), P.Hever 64 (deed of gift), P.Hever 65 (marriage contract).

[45] See H.M. Cotton, "The Guardianship of Jesus Son of Babatha: Roman and Local Law in the Province of Arabia," *JRS* 83 (1993) 94–108.

2. *The operation of the Roman judicial system and the Babatha archive*

Apuleius tells us in the *Golden Ass* of a physician's wife in Corinth who, realizing that she had been poisoned, ran to the house where the proconsul of Achaia was residing (*ad ipsam praesidis domum*). With her screams she caused both his door as well as his ears to unlock (*et domus et aures praesidis patefierent*). However, no sooner had she been admitted to tell her dire tale than the poison took its effect and she expired at the governor's feet (*ante ipsos praesidis pedes exanimis corruit*).[46] The anecdote may be pure fiction, but the circumstances and the expectations implied are real enough: the Roman provincial governor, although acknowledged by all to be the most powerful man in the province, was not an aloof and distant head of a bureaucratic apparatus. His accessibility in his role as a judge was taken for granted by Rome's subjects, who expected it from the emperor himself: "then do not be a king", said a woman to the emperor Hadrian, in the famous anecdote told by Cassius Dio, when he told her that he had no time for her.[47]

It is precisely in order to increase the governor's accessibility, and make an audience with him a matter of routine, that the *conventus* (assizes) system was created in some provinces, already in republican times;[48] it seems likely that it spread into all the provinces in the imperial period, even if it is not attested for all of them.[49] The *conventus* (*dioikesis* in the eastern part of the empire) was a judicial region whose central city (the *conventus* centre) was visited by the governor annually at a fixed time of the year. Each province was divided into a number of *conventus* whose inhabitants convened at the *conventus* centre when the governor sat in judgment there. Doing the annual round of the province, the governor "attended" his subjects rather than the other way around. But it is not unlikely that the subjects could also present themselves before the governor outside

---

[46] Apuleius *Metamorphoses* 10.27; see F. Millar (supra note 1).
[47] Cassius Dio 69.6.3; the anecdote strikes the key-note to F. Millar, *The Emperor in the Roman World* (London and Ithaca 1977, 2nd ed. 1992) 3.
[48] A.J. Marshal, "Governors on the Move," *Phoenix* 20 (1966) 231 ff.
[49] For recent literature see R. Haensch, "Zur Konventsordnung in Ägypten und den übrigen Provinzen des römischen Reiches," in B. Kramer et al., eds., *Akten des 21. Internat. Papyrologenkongresses, Berlin, 13.–19.8.1995* (Stuttgart, Leipzig 1997) 320–1.

the *conventus*, and above all in his permanent seat. Some of the documents in the Babatha archive, as will be seen, suggest as much.

In Asia the number of *conventus* centres was fixed at twelve. Changes occurred on some occasions:[50] thus Tralleis lost its status as a *conventus* centre under Tiberius after a devastating earthquake, and Thyateira received this privilege from Caracalla in the second decade of the third century.[51] While an attempt to obtain the rank of a *conventus* by some cities in the southern part of Crete-Cyrene was resisted by both Hadrian and Antoninus Pius on the ground that the proconsul could not visit more cities than he already did, it was considered entirely improper to deprive cities already enjoying the coveted status of a *conventus* centre of their hereditary rights.[52] Hence existing arrangements tended to remain unchanged. The system appears to have been more rigid in Asia and Crete-Cyrene where the governors were required to visit the individual traditional *conventus* centres every year; in Egypt by contrast matters seem to have been organized in a more flexible fashion.[53] The *praefectus Aegypti* appears to have been able every year to draw up a different list of *conventus* to be attended by him, so long as the provincials were acquainted with the newly planned circuit well in advance, and the time of year spent "on the move" remained restricted to the first four months of the year. That this was so is attested in numerous papyri from Egypt, which are precisely dated. The prefect was accompanied on these journeys by other high office-holders, such as the *iuridicus* or the head of the *idios logos*, who were equestrian like him and subordinate to him.[54] We can exclude the possibility that the financial procurators in other provinces accompanied the governor on these journeys in order to settle tax disputes: they belonged to the equestrian hierarchy and consequently were never subordinate to the senatorial governor. It would seem that legal cases connected with financial matters had to go to the financial procurator's headquarters, as happened in Caesarea Maritima in 152.

---

[50] Cf. on all this Burton (supra note 8) 92–4.

[51] *IGR* IV 1287 = *TAM* V 2, 943.

[52] J.H. Oliver, *Greek Constitutions of Early Roman Emperors from Inscriptions and Papyri* (Philadelphia 1989) 274–84, nos. 120–4.

[53] So Haensch (supra note 49) 322 ff. But this observation is determined, at least in part, by the vast difference in both quality and quantity between the Egyptian documentation and that coming from the rest of the empire.

[54] The latter was in charge of one of the two imperial property administrations; cf. Haensch (supra note 49) 322–42.

To this day we have no explicit evidence for the existence of the *conventus* system in Judaea/Syria Palaestina. True, Josephus tells us about the travels of the prefects of Judaea, which was governed at least until 41, if not as late as 66/7, as an administratively autonomous part of the province of Syria.[55] We also hear that on Passover the prefects normally resided in Jerusalem, but this was so as to maintain order in the crowded city; indeed legal proceedings conducted on those occasions in the form known as *cognitio extra ordinem* were the direct result of religious riots which broke out then.

Be this as it may, several reasons must have come together to make the introduction of the *conventus* system into Judaea (if it was not already established there) necessary, once it became an independent province with a senatorial governor at its head. The size alone of the now enlarged territory made it necessary to apply here the Roman principle of catering to the legal needs of the subjects by meeting them halfway. Otherwise the inhabitants would have had to spend several days on the road from the more remote corners of the province to the governor's seat in Caesarea: 100 km from Ascalon, some 125 km from Caesarea Philippi, at least 150 km from Hebron, no less than 160 km from Ein Gedi, and over 200 km from the southern tip of the Dead Sea.[56] No doubt the drastic curtailment of Jewish judicial independence—expressed *inter alia* in the dissolution of the Sanhedrin—in the wake of the suppression of the revolt of 66–70 made it all the more necessary to have recourse to a Roman court of law.[57] Thus it is reasonable to assume that in addition to Caesarea, the *caput provinciae*, also Ascalon in the south, Aelia Capitolina, the province's second *colonia*, and Scythopolis functioned as *conventus* centres, i.e. the governor held court in them regularly.

---

[55] Judaea was annexed to Syria in 6; see *AJ* 17.355; 18.2. It may have become an independent province already under Claudius in 41 when its provincial status was restored, but perhaps as late as 66/67 or even 69; cf. H.M. Cotton, "Some Aspects of the Roman Administration of Judaea/Syria-Palaestina," in W. Eck, ed., *Lokale Autonomie* (supra note 8) 75–91.

[56] By way of comparison it should be noted that the distance from Petra to Bostra was around 300 km; to cover this distance, eight travelling days were required according to Iulius Apollinarius of P.Mich. VIII 466, who was employed in 107 as *librarius*, probably with the *legio III Cyrenaica*.

[57] For judicial autonomy see E. Schürer, G. Vermes, and F. Millar, *The History of the Jewish People in the Age of Jesus Christ, 175 BC–AD 135*, vols. 1–3 (Edinburgh 1973–87), vol. 2, 197–8; 218 ff.; for its curtailment cf. Cotton (supra note 3); Cotton (supra note 8).

The absence of explicit evidence for the *conventus* system in Judaea/ Syria Palaestina is of no significance. There was no proof whatever for the existence of a *conventus* in Lycia-Pamphylia in southern Asia Minor until 1984. In that year a single inscription from the third century revealed that the *conventus* system was introduced into this province as soon as it was created, i.e. in 43.[58]

However, the best proof for the existence of the *conventus* system in Judaea is its introduction to Arabia, probably soon after the annexation of the Nabataean Kingdom in 106,[59] although it is attested there for the first time only in 125.

In P.Yadin 14, written on 11 or 12 October 125,[60] Babatha summons one of the guardians of her orphan son before witnesses (ἐπὶ τῶν ἐπιβεβλημένων μαρτύρων παρήνγει[λεν Βαβαθα Cιμωνος], lines 20–21): "Therefore, I summon (παραγγέλλω) you to attend (παρεδρεῦcαι)[61] at the court (βῆμα)[62] of the governor Iulius Iulianus in Petra the metropolis of Arabia until we are heard in the tribunal (τριβουνάλιον)[63] in Petra on the second day of the month Dios (?) or at his next sitting (παρουcία)[64] in Petra" (lines 29–33 of the outer text).[65] These summonses were served in the village of Mahoza (ἐν Μαωζᾳ περὶ Ζ[οαραν], line 20). A reference to the summons served in P.Yadin 14 can be found in P.Yadin 15 of the same date and written by the same scribe (lines 3 ff. = lines 17 ff.), also in Mahoza.

Five years later, on 17 November 130, Besas son of Jesus from Ein Gedi, the guardian of the orphan children of Babatha's brother

---

[58] *SEG* 34, 1306 = *AE* 1989, 724.

[59] In fact the onus of proof nowadays is on those who deny some form of the *conventus* system in a given province. Cf. Bowersock (supra note 15) 79 f. and 86 for Arabia.

[60] Probably also in the badly damaged P.Yadin 13 of the same year.

[61] Cf. προcεδρεύcαι in P.Amh. 81.9 = M.Chr. 54.

[62] Βῆμα is restored from the inner text.

[63] Τριβουνάλιον is restored from the inner text—where it is also partially a restoration.

[64] For παρουcία of a governor see P.Oxy. 1764; for the παρουcία of Hadrian in Egypt see SB 9617; cf. B.A. Groningen, "Preparatives to Hadrian's Visit to Egypt", in: *Studi in Honore di Calderini e R. Paribeni* 2 (1957) 253–6. See also P.Ness.19, a settlement of a law suit mentioning παρουcίᾳ ἐμῇ of a *scriniarius* in the camp of Nessana.

[65] διὸ παραγγέλλω cοι παρεδρεῦcαι [ἐπὶ βῆμα]τος Ἰουλίου Ἰουλιανοῦ ἡγεμόνος ἐν Πέτρᾳ [μητροπόλει τῆ]c Ἀραβίας [μέχρι οὗ διακουcθῶμεν ἐ]ν τῷ ἐν Πέ[τρᾳ τριβουναλίῳ τῆ]c δευτέρας ἡ μέρᾳ τ[οῦ Δίου μηνὸc ἢ εἰς τὴν αὐτοῦ ἔγγιcτα . . .]ι ἐν Πέ[τρᾳ π]αρου[cίαν].

in law, Jesus son of Eleazar Khthousion, serves a summons in Mahoza (ἐν Μαωζᾳ τῇ πε[ρ]ὶ Πέτραν, P.Yadin 23, line 23) on Babatha "to meet him before Haterius Nepos, *legatus pro praetore*, in Petra or elsewhere in his province ([ἢ] ἄλλ[ου ἐν τῇ α]ὐτοῦ ἐπ[αρχίᾳ]) . . . and, equally important, to attend every hour and day until judgement" (P.Yadin 23, lines 1–8 = lines 10–19).[66]

Over half a year later, on 9 July 131, Iulia Crispina, the *episcopos* of the same orphans,[67] acting for both herself and the sick Besas, their guardian, summons (παραγγέλλω) Babatha "pursuant to the subscription (ὑπογραφή) of his Excellency the governor to accompany me in person to Petra . . . and, equally important, to attend in Hadrianic Petra until we are heard" (P.Yadin 25, lines 6–12 = lines 37–43).[68] To which Babatha replies as follows: "Seeing that before this you summoned me to Hadrianic Petra before his Excellency the governor . . . until we were heard on your false charge against me of resorting to violence, and I submitted a notice (πιττάκιον)[69] against your side to his Excellency the governor and he instructed me by his subscription (ὑπέγραψεν μοι) to perform the legal formalities with you in Petra, now therefore I summon (παραγγέλλω) you first before his Excellency the governor in Rabbath-Moab . . ." (P.Yadin 25, lines 15–24 = lines 47–59).[70] To which Iulia Crispina responds: "I have carried out the legal formalities for the judgement of his Excellency the governor in Petra, and if you have any complaint against me you have the option of attending the guardian(?) of the said orphans before the said Nepos [i.e. the governor, Haterius Nepos]" (P.Yadin

---

[66] ἐπὶ [τ]ῶν ἐπιβεβλημένων [μαρτύρω]ν παρήνγιλεν Βη[cᾶc Ἰ]η[c]ου[ο]υ [ἐ]πίτρ[οποc τῶν ὀρ]φανῶν Ἰ[ηc]ουου Ἐλεαζαρου Χθουcίωνοc Ἡνγαδην[ὸ]c [Β]αβαθαν Cιμωνοc Μαωζηνῆ⟨ν⟩ ἐπέρχεcθαι αὐτῷ ἐπὶ Ἀτερίῳ Νέπωτι πρεcβευτ[ῇ] καὶ ἀντιcτρατήγου [ε]ἰc Πέτραν [ἢ] ἄλλ[ου ἐν τῇ α]ὐτοῦ ἐπ[αρχίᾳ] . . . οὐδὲν δὲ ἧccον καὶ παρεδρεύιν πρὸc πᾶcαν ὥραν καὶ ἡμέραν μέχρ[ι δια]γνώcεωc (quoted from the outer text).

[67] For the role of the *episcopos* see Cotton (supra note 45) 97.

[68] νυν[εὶ] παραγγέλλω [coι] κατὰ [τ]ὴν [ὑ]πογραφὴν τοῦ κρατίcτ[ο]υ [ἡγεμόνο]c cυνεξελθῖν αὐτῆ⟨ν⟩ εἰc Πέ[τ]ρ[α]ν . . . [οὐδὲν δὲ ἧccον καὶ παρεδρ]εύι[ν ἐν Ἀδρια]νῇ Π[έτ]ρᾳ μέχρι οὗ δ[ιακου]cθῶμεν (quoted from the outer text).

[69] Cf. P.Yadin 16 lines 1 and 3; cf. S. Krauss, *Griechische und lateinische Lehnwörter im Talmud, Midrasch und Targum*, II (1899), 441 f.

[70] ἐπὶ πρὸ τούτου πα[ρ]ήνγιλεc με [εἰ]c Ἀδριανὴν Πέτραν πρὸc τὸν κράτ[ι]c[τ]ον [ἡ]γ[ε]μόνα . . . μέχρι διακουcθῶμεν βίαν μοι χρωμένη cυκοφαντοῦcά μοι καὶ ἔδωκα καθ᾽ ὑμῶν πιττάκιν τῷ κρατίcτῳ ἡγεμόνι καὶ ὑπέγραψέν μοι εἰc Πέτραν cὺν ὑμῖν τ[ὰ ν]όμιμα χρᾶ[c]θ[αι], κα[ὶ τ]ὰ [ν]ῦ[ν πα]ρα[γγέλλω coι π]ρ[ώ]τ[αc π]ρὸc τὸν κράτιcτ[ον ἡγεμόνα εἰc Ῥα]ββαθμωαβα (the text cited here is mainly—but not always—from the outer text).

25, lines 24–29 = lines 60–63).[71] It is to be assumed that on each of the three occasions the summonses were served in Mahoza, as stated at the end of the document, where two copies were made of the entire document ([ἐ]πράχθη [ἐν] Μαωζα περὶ Ζ[οο]ρων ὑπατίας Λαίνα Πο[ν]τιανοῦ καὶ Μά[ρ]κου ʼΑντ[ω]νίου ʽΡ[ο]υφίνου πρὸ ἑπτὰ εἰδῶν Ἰουλ[ί]ων. ἐγρ[ά]φη ἀντίτυπα δύω, P.Yadin 25, lines 64–66).

On the same day, the same scribe executed yet another set of reciprocal summonses in Mahoza (ἐν Μαωζα περ[ιμ]έτ[ρ]ῳ Ζ[οορων], P.Yadin 26, line 18), this time between Babatha and her late husband's ex-wife (or other wife),[72] Miriam, daughter of Beianos. Babatha summons Miriam "to accompany her in person before Haterius Nepos, *legatus Augusti pro praetore*, wherever he happens to be on his judicial circuit of the province, . . . and, equally important, to attend before the said Nepos until judgement (διάγνωϲιϲ)" (P.Yadin 26, lines 3–11).[73]

All these summonses and counter-summonses[74] were issued in Mahoza which was not a *conventus* centre itself. However, we can infer from them that Petra (P.Yadin 14, 23, 25) and Rabbath Moab (P.Yadin 25) served as assize centres; even more importantly, that other places could serve for the same purpose (P.Yadin 23: "in Petra or elsewhere in his province ([ἢ] ἄλλ[ου ἐν τῇ α]ὐτοῦ ἐπ[αρχία])"; P.Yadin 26: "wherever he happens to be on his judicial circuit of the province (ὅπου ἄν ᾖ ὑπʼ αὐτοῦ ὑπαρχ[ί]α')".

Rabbath Moab was no doubt a *conventus* centre, but Petra may have been more than that: it may have continued to function as the capital of the province (*caput provinciae*) for a while after annexation. In fact the dates of the summonses surveyed above greatly favour

---

[71] τὰ νόμιμα τοῦ κρα[τ]ίϲτου ἡγεμόνοϲ εἰϲ Πέτραν τῇ δικαιοδοϲίᾳ ἀπήρτιϲα, καὶ εἴ τι λόγον ἔχιϲ πρὸϲ ἐμὲ παρεδρεύιν ἐπὶ τὸν αὐτὸν Νέπωτα[ν] ἐπιτροπ . . . ἔχιϲ τῶν αὐτῶν ὀρφανῶ[ν] (quoted from the outer text).

[72] Lewis (supra note 1) 113 opted for polygamy; see however R. Katzoff, "Polygamy in P.Yadin?" *ZPE* 109 (1995) 128–32 and A. Schremer, "How Much Polygamy in Jewish Roman Palestine?" *Proceedings of the American Academy for Jewish Research* 63 (1997–2001) 181–223.

[73] ϲυνεξέρχεϲθαι αὐτὴν ἐπὶ ʼΑτέριον Νέπωταν πρε(ϲ)βευτοῦ Ϲεβαϲτοῦ ἀντιϲτρατήγου ὅπου ἄν ᾖ ὑπʼ αὐτοῦ ὑπαρχ[ί]α . . . οὐδὲν δὲ ἧϲϲον καὶ παρεδρεύιν ἐπὶ τὸν αὐτὸν Νέπωτα μέχρι διαγνώϲεωϲ. Our translation differs from Lewis', but we agree on the sense. P. Yadin 34 may represent another petition to the governor concerning the same controversy, but it is too fragmentary to be of much use here.

[74] P.Yadin 35, perhaps from 132, also contains a summons but is likewise too damaged to be of any use here.

the supposition that at the time they were issued Petra had not yet lost its status to Bostra.[75] The length of time implied by the summons to Petra—October in P.Yadin 14, November in P.Yadin 23 and July in P.Yadin 25—is far too extensive for Petra to have been a *conventus* centre; it is most unlikely that a governor would hold court in the same *conventus* centre in July as well as in October and November. All in all Petra emerges from the archive as the place where the governor would normally be present when not on his annual circuit of the *conventus* centres in the rest of his province.[76] This, we believe, is especially clear in P.Yadin 23 of 17 November 130 where Besas son of Jesus summons Babatha "to meet him before Haterius Nepos . . . *in Petra or elsewhere in the province* in the matter of a date orchard" etc. (lines 1–5 = lines 10–16). Clearly, if for some reason a litigant could not attend the assize centre (*conventus*) nearest to his place of residence, it was always possible to go to Petra where the governor resided on a more permanent basis.

This underlying assumption, which pervades the documents, namely that Petra is a ready fall-back, "an assize centre by default" so to say, is by no means contradicted by the fact that on one and the same day, 9 July 131, while Iulia Crispina summoned Babatha to Petra, the latter summoned her opponent to Rabbath Moab (P.Yadin 25); nor by the fact that on this very same day Babatha also invites Miriam to meet her "wherever [the governor] happens to be on his judicial circuit of the province" (P.Yadin 26). It would be a mistake to use ploys and tricks practiced by litigants against each other as a means to date the governor's movements precisely. The *conventus* system was not merely available to Rome's provincial subjects; it could be used by them to gain advantage over their legal opponents. This is precisely what we witness in P.Yadin 25 and 26. There are explanations at hand for the opponents' actions: whereas Iulia Crispina seeks to obtain a rapid settlement by going to Petra where the governor is often to be found, Babatha plays for time by suggesting Rabbath Moab, the *conventus* centre which normally catered for the needs of the residents of Mahoza,[77] but where the governor

---

[75] See above text to note 30; see also Cotton (supra note 7) 152.
[76] Similarly Haensch (supra note 30) 241.
[77] As being the nearest city. Note also that land declarations by the residents of Mahoza were submitted in Rabbath Moab: cf. B. Isaac, "Tax Collection in Roman

is present only once a year. Nor should we see any sign of undue urgency in Babatha's invitation to Miriam to meet her before the governor "wherever he happens to be on his judicial circuit of the province".

The procedure worked at least as far as the sequence "petition—subscription—summons" went,[78] but it could at times be slow, inefficient and cumbersome.[79] As an extreme example we may cite *P.Euphrates* 1 of 246, in which the villagers of Beth Phouraia on the Euphrates complain that they had waited for over eight months in Antioch, the capital of Syria Coele, for a decision by the governor.[80] However, as we pointed out in the first part of this paper, the governor was not the only person to exercise jurisdiction in a Roman province— furthermore, jurisdiction could be delegated even within his own sphere. It is just possible that such a case can be detected in the Babatha archive.

3. *P.Yadin 14 and a case of* iudex datus *in the Babatha archive*

As we have seen, in P.Yadin 14 written on 11 or 12 October 125[81] Babatha summons one of the guardians of her orphan son, Johanes son of Joseph Eglas (or son of Eglas)[82] before witnesses [ἐπὶ τῶν ἐπιβεβλημένων] μαρτύρων παρήνγει[λεν Βαβαθα Cιμωνοc], lines 20–21): "Therefore, I summon (παρανγέλλω) you to attend (παρεδρεῦcαι) at the court (βῆμα) of the governor Iulius Iulianus in Petra the metropolis of Arabia until we are heard in the tribunal (τριβουνάλιον) in

---

Arabia: New Evidence from the Babatha Archive," *Mediterranean Historical Review* 9 (1994) 256–66 (= Isaac, *The Near East under Roman Rule* [supra note 16] 322–333).

[78] See in detail Cotton (supra note 45) 102–7.

[79] See Burton (supra note 8) 102.

[80] D. Feissel and J. Gascou, "Documents d'archives romains inédits du Moyen Euphrate (IIIᵉ s. après J.-C.), 1," *JSav* (1995) 65–119 at 84; cf. Cotton, Cockle and Millar (supra note 38), no. 9. A remedy to similar situations in Italy is offered in the *s. c. de sumptibus ludorum gladiatorum minuendis* from Marcus Aurelius' late period, *CIL* II 6278.40–44 = *ILS* 5163 = *FIRA* I² no. 49. There it is said that a citizen, or alternatively a community, in urgent need of a legal decision in the subject matter of that enactment can turn to any Roman authority within reach. Albeit not yet attested, it may have applied to the provinces as well.

[81] Probably also in the badly damaged P.Yadin 13 of the same year.

[82] Ἰωάνη Ἰωσηπου τοῦ Ἐγλα; cf. P.Yadin 18 lines 4–5 (inner text): Ἰουδα[τι υἱῷ] Ἀνανιου Cωμαλα and: Ἰουδατι ἐπικαλουμένῳ Κίμβερι υἱῷ Ἀνανιου τοῦ Cωμαλα (lines 34–5, outer text).

Petra on the second day of the month Dios (?) or at his next sitting (παρουϲία) in Petra" (lines 29–33 of the outer text).[83]

The contrast with the other summonses in the Babatha archive which "do not specify a date but simply demand attendance in court until the case is heard and decided" led the editor to offer an explanation for the precise dating: "Obviously it must have been known that the governor of the province would be holding his annual assizes (*conventus*) in Petra then, and presumably the present summons was drawn up after notification of a date on the court calendar for the instant suit."[84]

Even if a list of cases to be heard at the assizes was published in advance, the ruling known from Egypt that defendants had to attend for the whole *conventus* period, and the absence of evidence that cases were taken before the governor in a fixed order,[85] suggest a different solution for the fixed date in P.Yadin 14. Such a procedure is familiar from the hearings before a *iudex datus*, where a date had to be fixed in advance for both litigants and the *iudex* to be present.[86] And indeed a *iudex datus* may well be mentioned in the inner text of P.Yadin 14, lines 10–14, which differs from the parallel passage in the outer text discussed exclusively so far:[87]

[παρ]εδρεῦϲαι ἐπὶ βήμα[τ]ο[ϲ Ἰ]ου[λίο]υ Ἰουλι[ανοῦ ca. ? μητροπό]λει τῆϲ
Ἀραβίαϲ μέχρ[ι οὗ δ]ιακουϲ[θ]ῶ[μεν ca. ? τριβουν]αλίῳ ἐπὶ Ἰουλίαν[ο]ῦ
ἐπά[ρχου ca. ? Δίου μηνὸϲ] ἢ εἰϲ τὴν αὐτοῦ ἔγγιϲτα παρ[ουϲίαν ca. ?]

Lewis' translation is a combination of the inner and outer text, but he notes the variation in a footnote. We reproduce here Lewis' text modified by his note:

> to attend at the court of the governor Julius Julianus in Petra the metropolis of Arabia until we are heard in the tribunal in Petra before Iulianus, governor, on the second day of the month Dios(?) or at his next sitting in Petra.

---

[83] διὸ παρανγέλλω ϲοι παρεδρεῦϲαι [ἐπὶ βήμα]τοϲ Ἰουλίου Ἰουλιανοῦ ἡγεμόνοϲ ἐν Πέτρᾳ [μητροπόλει τῆ]ϲ Ἀραβίαϲ [μέχρι οὗ διακουϲθῶμεν ἐ]ν τῷ ἐν Πέ[τρᾳ τριβουναλίῳ τῆ]ϲ δευτέραϲ ἡμέραϲ τ[οῦ Δίου μηνὸϲ ἢ εἰϲ τὴν αὐτοῦ ἔγγιϲτα . . .]ι ἐν Πέ[τρᾳ π]αρου[ϲίαν].

[84] Lewis (supra note 1) 57 at lines 13 and 32 of the papyrus.

[85] Cf. Burton (supra note 8) 100.

[86] For specific cases of *iudices dati* in Egypt see Haensch (supra note 49) 338, note 83 and 358–360.

[87] Lewis (supra note 1) 56.

It would seem that the scribe *not only* introduces in line 13 of the inner text an otiose repetition of the governor's name, Iulius Iulianus, already spelled out in line 11, *but also* changes the correct title of ἡγεμών (the generic title of a governor) of the outer text (line 30) to the incorrect one of ἔπαρχος, *praefectus*. The latter term may suit the governor of Egypt, the *praefectus Aegypti*, who was of equestrian rank, but cannot under any circumstances be applied to the governor of Arabia, who right from the beginning was of senatorial rank. Not once is the title ἔπαρχος, *praefectus* applied to the governor in the Babatha archive, where the governors make their appearance on six occasions altogether, always bearing a correct title of ἡγεμών or πρεcβευτὴc καὶ ἀντιcτράτηγοc.[88] This alone should suggest that the discrepancy between inner and outer text is not a scribal error,[89] but that two different persons are referred to in lines 11 and 13 of the inner text: the senatorial governor Iulius Iulianus in line 11 and an equestrian *praefectus* also called Iulianus in line 13. The latter was a *iudex* to whom the governor delegated jurisdiction in accordance with a well-known procedure practised in Rome as well as in the provinces in order to lighten the load of the judge. A prefect of an auxiliary unit stationed in the province would be an obvious candidate for a *iudex datus*. Iulianus can be very nearly compared to the prefect Priscus put in charge of accepting land declarations in Rabbat Moab during the census of 127 by the governor, Aninius Sextius Florentinus.[90]

The only obstacle to accepting this conjecture seems to be the coincidence of the same cognomen borne by both governor and prefect. But then one has to bear in mind that Iulianus is one of the most common Roman *cognomina*—also among the highest orders: the *Prosopographia Imperii Romani* (*PIR*) lists 113 individuals with this name in the senatorial and equestrian orders.[91] Hubert Devijver lists 19 equestrian prefects with this *cognomen*.[92] Iulianus is almost as frequent as Priscus, which is listed 142 times in the most recent volume of the *PIR* published in 1998. It is therefore not particularly surprising

---

[88] P.Yadin 13, 14, 15, 16, 23, 25.
[89] As Haensch (supra note 30) 559 no. 42 believes.
[90] P.Yadin 16 and P.Hever 61 and 62.
[91] *PIR*² IV pp. 120–125.
[92] *Prosopographia Militiarum Equestrium quae fuerunt ab Augusto ad Gallienum. Partes I–V* (Leuven 1976–93), pars tertia, p. 1071; pars quarta, p. 1841; pars quinta, p. 2334.

if an auxiliary prefect with the same cognomen was employed under a governor Iulianus.[93]

We suggest that P.Yadin 14 of 125 contains a summons to appear before an auxiliary prefect Iulianus, to whom Iulius Iulianus, the *legatus Augusti pro praetore* of Arabia, delegated the power to adjudicate in the legal dispute between Babatha and one of the guardians appointed for her orphaned son by the council of Petra. In other words, we have here yet another instance of the early application of a common Roman legal practice to the new province of Arabia.

However, no less worthy of comment is the fact that the case was not taken to the council of Petra who appointed the guardian, but to the court of the Roman governor. Later Roman law (e.g. *C.* 5. 50.1 of 215) put charges against a guardian explicitly within the competence of the governor of the province, and not of the appointing city-council.[94] The rule may have been in existence some hundred years prior to its attestation in the Roman legal sources. Alternatively, the later Roman law reflects *ad hoc* provisions by Roman officials in the provinces or local customs adopted by them.[95]

---

[93] Finally, the legate of Arabia had under his command a whole series of auxiliary units, probably at least 12; see M.P. Speidel, "The Roman Army in Arabia," *ANRW* II 8 (Berlin 1977) 687–730, especially 699–712 (in a new military diploma soon to be published by Peter Weiß even more are attested; we are grateful to him for the information). Hence it is perfectly possible that one of them had the cognomen Iulianus.

[94] *Pupillus, si ei alimenta a tutore suo non praestantur, praesidem provinciae adeat*; cf. Cotton (supra note 45) 102 ff.

[95] See the pioneer study of H.J. Wolff, "Römisches Provinzialrecht in der Provinz Arabia," *ANRW* II.13, 1980, 763–806; T. Chiusi, "Zur Vormundschaft der Mutter," *ZSav* 111 (1994) 155–196 at 178 ff., and T. Chiusi's contribution in this volume, "Babatha vs. the Guardians of her Son: A Struggle for Guardianship—Legal and Practical Aspects of P.Yadin 12–15, 27."

FOUR MURABBAʿAT PAPYRI AND THE ALLEGED
CAPTURE OF JERUSALEM BY BAR KOKHBA

Hanan Eshel, Magen Broshi and Timothy A.J. Jull

A problem much debated by students of the Second Jewish Revolt
is whether Bar Kokhba captured and occupied Jerusalem. Some
scholars believe there is evidence showing that the insurgents were
able to conquer the city and even reestablish the Temple cult,[1] while
others hold that there is no evidence for such an occupation.[2] Our
paper will deal with four papyri from Wadi Murabbaʿat which have
been claimed as evidence for the first view.

According to Milik, the editor of the Hebrew and Aramaic texts
discovered in the Murabbaʿat caves, one of the Aramaic double deeds
of sale, P.Mur. 25, carries the date "[In the . . . of Marheshvan] year
three to the Freedom of Jerusalem".[3] The restoration "Marheshvan"
is based on the parallel text in the preserved fragment of the "open"

---

[1] P. Schäfer, *Der Bar Kokhba Aufstand. Studien zum zweiten jüdischen Krieg gegen Rom*
(Tübingen 1981) 119.
[2] See notes 12 and 13 below.
[3] J.T. Milik, "Textes hébreux et araméens," in P. Benoit et al., eds., *Les Grottes
de Murabbaʿat (Discoveries in the Judaean Desert II)* (Oxford 1961) 67–205. Greenfield
claimed that P.Mur. 25 belongs to the Nahal Seelim lot. See J.C. Greenfield, "The
Texts from Naḥal Seʾelim (Wadi Seiyal)," in J. Trebolle Barrera and L. Vegas
Montaner, eds., *The Madrid Qumran Congress 2* (Leiden, New York, Köln 1961) 661–5
at 664. This means that the papyrus was not found in Wadi Murabbaʿat but in
Nahal Hever (sic!). The similarity of this document to three others found in Murabbaʿat
(P.Mur. 29, 30, 22) makes it difficult to accept his claim. Now, after the publica-
tion of the Seʾelim lot, it is apparent that Greenfield meant P.Mur. 26 and not
P.Mur. 25. See H.M. Cotton and A. Yardeni, *Aramaic, Hebrew and Greek Documentary
Texts from Naḥal Ḥever and Other Sites (Discoveries in the Judaean Desert XXVII)* (Oxford
1997) 123–9. Ada Yardeni added a fifth fragment to the four assembled and published by Milik as P.Mur. 26. See Milik, *ibid.*, 137–8. For the fifth fragment cf.
Cotton and Yardeni, *ibid.* Yardeni is of the opinion that the five fragments belong
to the deed kept in the Catholic Institute in Paris, attesting to the sale of a field.
See J.T. Milik, "Deux Documents inédits du Désert de Juda," *Biblica* 38 (1957)
245–68. It so happens that the same document carries three designations: The deed
for the sale of a field—P.Jud.Des.2; The four fragments—P.Mur. 26; Yardeni's—
P.Hever 50. Yardeni maintains, justly, that this papyrus was found in Wadi Murabbaʿat
and not in Nahal Hever. Cf. Cotton and Yardeni, *ibid.*, p. 6. Therefore, there is
no doubt that P.Mur. 25 and P.Mur. 26 originated indeed from Cave 2 of Wadi
Murabbaʿat.

part of the deed. Milik ascribed the papyrus to the end of 133 CE, i.e. to the beginning of the third year of the Bar Kokhba revolt.[4] In another document, written in Hebrew, P.Mur. 29, Milik read: "On the fourteenth of Elul, year two to the redemption of Zion, in [. . .] אלים [. . .]" (fig. 1). He dated it to 133 CE, some two months earlier than the aforementioned Aramaic deed.[5] Both documents are poorly preserved and there is no telling what the nature of the business they were meant to record was, but it is quite probable that they deal with real estate. A Hebrew deed recording the sale of a field, P.Mur. 30, was written "On the twenty first of Tishri, year four to the redemption of Israel in אלים [. . .]", i.e. at the end of the Feast of Tabernacles. The vendor, Dosthos, sold a field to a man whose name was not preserved. Milik dated this deed to the end of 134 CE, i.e. to the fourth year of the Bar Kokhba revolt.[6] In an addendum Milik corrects himself and reads in P.Mur. 29: "On the fourteenth of Elul, year two to the redemption of Israel, in Jerusalem" and he believes that Jerusalem is also the location where the transaction of P.Mur. 30 was executed. In P.Mur. 29 the vendor is Kleopos son of Eutrapelos from Jerusalem.[7] In a fourth, Hebrew, document, P.Mur. 22, the opening clause is: "On the fourteenth of Marheshvan, year four of the redemption of Israel."[8] Thus the deed recording the sale of real estate was written about a month after the Feast of Tabernacles of year four of the redemption of Israel. If we assume that these deeds date to the Bar Kokhba revolt, it means that the revolt ended after Marheshvan 135 CE and that Jerusalem was kept by the insurgents until the winter of the fourth year.

Determining when the revolt ended is not simple, but most scholars agree that it lasted no more than three and a half years.[9] The Mishna asserts that Beitar, the last stronghold of the revolt, fell on the ninth of Ab (M.Taanit 4.6), i.e. two months before the Feast of

---

    [4] J.T. Milik, "Textes hébreux etc." (supra note 3) 134–137.
    [5] *Ibid.*, 140–4.
    [6] *Ibid.*, 144–8.
    [7] *Ibid.*, 205.
    [8] Milik read "year one" and dated the deed to year 131 CE, *ibid.*, 118–21. However, Yardeni, who re-examined the document, is certain that it belongs to the fourth year. See A. Yardeni, *The Aramaic and Hebrew Documents in Cursive Script from Wadi Murabba'at, Nahal Hever and Related Material. A Paleographic and Epigraphic Examination* (Ph.D. dissertation, Hebrew University) (Jerusalem 1991) 12–4 (Hebrew).
    [9] Schäffer (supra note 1) 10–28.

Tabernacles.[10] If this tradition is reliable, Milik's dates are problematic, for it is inconceivable that in the year four, after the fall of Beitar and the death of the leader of the revolt, fields would still be sold and Jerusalem held by the rebels.

Papyri 29 and 30 are exceptional in having the names of members of a judicial court who signed and ratified the deals to be specified below. Such an arrangement is not found in any of the economic documents dated unequivocally to the Bar Kokhba revolt.[11] Therefore these papyri should be dated to a different period.

In the archaeological excavations carried out in Jerusalem prior to 1982 a total of 13,629 coins were found, but only 3 of them were overstruck by the Bar Kokhba administration. Two of these were unearthed south of the Temple Mount and the third in the Citadel.[12] The negligible number of Bar Kokhba coins led many scholars to conclude that Jerusalem did not fall into the hands of the insurgents.[13] Some, out of historical considerations, even rejected Milik's reading Jerusalem.[14]

In 1991 A. Yardeni offered new readings to the Murabba'at documents and she also read the name of Jerusalem in P.Mur. 25, 29 and 30.[15] H. Misgav, who dealt with P.Mur. 29 and 30, reached the same readings.[16] This is an interesting situation: The three epigraphists (Milik, Yardeni and Misgav) read "Jerusalem" and simply assumed that the insurgents captured the city; the archaeologists and

---

[10] It is highly plausible that the precise date, the ninth of Ab, ascribed to the fall of Beitar is apocryphal, made to conform to the date of the fall of the First and Second Temples.

[11] H. Misgav, "Jewish Courts of Law as Reflected in Documents from the Dead Sea," *Cathedra* 82 (1996) 17–24 (Hebrew).

[12] D.T. Ariel, "A Survey of the Coin Finds in Jerusalem (Until the End of the Byzantine Period)," *Studium Biblicum Franciscanum. Liber Annuus* 32 (1982) 273–326 at 293.

[13] S. Applebaum, *Prolegomena to the Study of the Second Jewish Revolt (A.D. 132–135)* = BAR Supplementary Series 7 (London 1976) 27, 83, note 241; L. Mildenberg, "Bar Kokhba Coins and Documents," *Harvard Studies in Classical Philology* 84 (1980) 312–35 at 320; Schäffer (supra note 1) 87–8.

[14] M.D. Herr, "The Causes of the Bar Kokhba War," *Zion* 43 (1980) 1–11 at 9–10, note 44 (Hebrew); A. Oppenheimer and B. Isaac, "Research History of the Bar Kokhba War," in A. Kloner and Y. Tepper, eds., *The Hiding Complexes in the Judean Shephela* (Tel Aviv 1987) 405–28 at 423 note 95 (Hebrew); M. Mor, *The Bar-Kochba Revolt, Its Extent and Effect* (Jerusalem 1991) 157 (Hebrew).

[15] Cf. Yardeni (supra note 8) 16, 22, 26.

[16] Cf. Misgav (supra note 11).

most of the historians were of the opinion that the city was not conquered and therefore doubted the reading. Some of the latter did
so out of historical considerations, some because of the almost total
lack of Bar Kokhba coins in the archaeological finds in Jerusalem.
S. Applebaum, who was one of the first scholars who concluded that
paucity of the numismatic evidence shows that the city was not occupied by the rebels,[17] changed his mind and later held that the city
was still held by them in Year Four (135 CE).[18]

As the name of Simeon son of Kosiba was not mentioned in the
dating formula of P.Mur. 22, 25, 29 and 30 there exists the possibility that those documents date from the First Revolt, i.e. from the
years 68–69 CE. It ought to be noted that among the Murabbaʿat
documents there are some which belong unequivocally to the Second
Commonwealth and the First Revolt. The earliest of these is an
ostracon, P.Mur. 72, recording two decisions of a court of justice,[19]
dated on paleographical grounds to 125–100 BCE.[20] Another document is a bill dating to Nero's second year, i.e. 55/56 CE, written
in Sobah, in which Zachariah son of Yehohanan from Kesalon
declares that he owes Absalom son of Hanun 20 denarii.[21] Both
localities are near Jerusalem to the west, and they belong to refugees
seeking shelter in the Murabbaʿat caves at the end of the First Revolt.

Another document from that time is a divorce bill from Masada,
P.Mur. 19, dated to Year Six. Yehosef son of Neqsan, residing in
Masada, divorces Miriam daughter of Yehonathan, also of Masada.
Milik was of the opinion that the date is according to the era of the
Provincia Arabia established in 106 CE, i.e. 111 CE.[22] Yadin did not
agree with Milik, on the grounds that the lack of the formula
על מנין הפרכיה דא ('according to era of this province') points to a
different date. Rather, he believed that the date is according to the
First Revolt era and that the year is 71 CE. A year after the fall of

---

[17] S. Applebaum (supra note 13), *ibid.*
[18] Idem, "The Bar Kokhba War and its Consequences," in U. Rapaport, ed.,
Judea and Rome—the Jewish Revolts (Jerusalem 1983) 229–60 at 245–6, 254 (Hebrew).
[19] Cf. Misgav (supra note 11).
[20] F.M. Cross, "The Development of the Jewish Scripts," in E.G. Wright, ed.,
The Bible and the Ancient Near East, Essays in Honor of William Foxwell Albright (Garden
City 1961) 133–202 at 148, fig. 3:2.
[21] J. Naveh, *On Sherd and Papyrus. Aramaic and Hebrew Inscriptions from the Second
Temple, Mishnaic and Talmudic Periods* (Jerusalem 1992) 84–8 (Hebrew).
[22] Milik (supra note 3) 104–9.

Jerusalem Miriam left Masada and took with her the bill of divorce. Yadin suggested, it seems correctly, that at Masada that year they could not use the standard formula "Year Six to the Freedom of Israel" or "to the Freedom of Jerusalem" since nearly all the country was in Roman hands and Jerusalem was in ashes. Therefore the bill carries simply the legend "Year Six."[23]

Even if Yadin was wrong about P.Mur. 19 (though we believe his suggestion is highly plausible), the document from Nero's second year shows that refugees from the vicinity of Jerusalem sought shelter in Wadi Murabba'at at the end of the Second Commonwealth. Hence we propose that the other four papyri, P.Mur. 22, 25, 29 and 30, all mentioning Jerusalem, are also to be dated to the First Revolt.

In order to test our hypothesis we submitted the documents to radiocarbon tests. One of the papyri, P.Mur. 30, had already been tested in Zurich at the Institut für Mittelenergiephysik, ETH- Hoenggerberg in 1990, and the date range obtained was 69–136 CE,[24] with the result that the document could belong either to the First or to the Second Revolt. The whereabouts of P.Mur. 25 is unknown.[25] We submitted, then, the remaining two documents for tests at NSF Arizona Accelerator Mass Spectrometer Facility, The University of Arizona, Tucson, a laboratory which had already examined twenty manuscripts from the Judaean Desert.[26] The results are as follows:

Sample Number	Test Number	Document	Radiocarbon date
1. A882	AA-26201	P.Mur. 22	1990 ± 45
2. A836	AA-26202	P.Mur. 29	1980 ± 45

Both documents can be dated, after calibration, with 95% probability, to a period stretching between 91 BCE and 78 CE. These data

---

[23] Y.Yadin, "The Excavations of Masada 1963/4, Preliminary Report," *IEJ* 15 (1965) 1–120 at 119, note 112. The latest coin found in Masada is from 111 CE, so the Roman garrison occupied the site at least up to that date. Cf. Y. Meshorer, "The Coins of Masada," *Masada* 1 (Jerusalem 1989) 127, no. 3840. As Yadin has noted, there was no sign of Jewish settlement between the First and the Second Revolt. It is inconceivable that the Romans would have allowed any Jew a foothold in Masada. Therefore it is well nigh certain that the divorce bill is from 71 CE.

[24] G. Bonani et al., "Radiocarbon Dating of the Dead Sea Scrolls," *Atiqot* 20 (1991) 27–32 at 29–30.

[25] S.A. Reed, *The Dead Sea Scrolls Catalogue* (Atlanta 1994) 230.

[26] A.J.T. Jull et al., "Radiocarbon Dating of Scrolls and Linen Fragments from the Judean Desert," *Atiqot* 28 (1996) 85–91.

would ascribe both to the First Revolt, not the Second, the Bar Kokhba Revolt.

Two Aelia Capitolina coins found in the same context with four Bar Kokhba coins in the el-Ji cave in Nahal Michmash (Wadi Suweinit)[27] indicate that Aelia, built over the ruins of Jerusalem, minted coins before 135 CE. A Gaza coin from 133/4 found in the same cave with the Aelia coins is further support for Herr's suggestion that Aelia started minting during the Second Revolt, probably in 133 CE.[28] It seems, therefore, that the Aelia was founded in 130 CE during the visit of the emperor Hadrian. The building activity lasted for some years, and sometime during the Bar Kokhba revolt the city started minting coins in which Hadrian is depicted as founding it by symbolic ploughing. (Figure 2). It is quite conceivable that the slogan "For the Freedom of Jerusalem" appearing on the late Bar Kokhba coins is a reaction of the insurgents to this development. This slogan has been explained as a battle cry intended to encourage the rebels when the prospects of the war started to look grim.[29] It seems, though, that it was a battle cry meant literally, a call to fight against the conversion of Jerusalem into a pagan city.

To sum up: the four documents, P.Mur. 22, 25, 29 and 30, were written during the First Revolt and they do not indicate that Jerusalem was captured by the Bar Kokhba combatants.

---

[27] H. Eshel, "Aelia Capitolina, Jerusalem No More," *Biblical Archaeology Review* 23 no. 6 (1997) 46–8, 73; H. Eshel, B. Zissu and A. Frumkin, "Two Refuge Caves in Wadi Suweinit," in H. Eshel and D. Amit, eds., *Refuge Caves of the Bar Kokhba Revolt* (Tel Aviv 1998) 93–103 (Hebrew); H. Eshel and B. Zissu, "Coins from the el-Jai Cave in Nahal Mikhmash (Wadi Suweinit)," *Israel Numismatic Journal* 14 (2002) 168–175.

[28] Herr (supra note 14) 65–6 and notes 42, 44.

[29] A. Kindler, "The Bar Kokhba War Coinage," in A. Oppenheimer, ed., *The Bar-Kokhba Revolt* (Jerusalem 1980) 159–77 (Hebrew).

MARRIAGE PAYMENTS AND SUCCESSION STRATEGIES IN THE DOCUMENTS FROM THE JUDAEAN DESERT

Michael L. Satlow

When the elder Jesus died in 110 CE, he did not leave his son out in the cold. Jesus, or his brother and business partner Joseph, left his share of the family business to his minor son in the form of a bill of deposit. Whether the elder Jesus himself or his brother set up this strategy of succession, its potential advantages are clear. Jesus' money could be kept within the family and at work in the family business. Uncle Joseph may well also have served as a guardian to his nephew, thus again keeping outsiders away from the family property. The elder Jesus was apparently wiser than his son. After profiting from his father's foresight, the younger Jesus married, had a son, and himself died without making provisions for his own son, thus setting up a series of legal confrontations between his widow, Babatha, and the council-appointed guardians of their only son.[1]

P.Yadin 5, the instrument of deposit that established Jesus' trust fund, nicely illustrates how one Jew from antiquity manipulated a flexible legal instrument, in this case the deposit, to achieve his goals of succession. P.Yadin 5 is not unique; if the documents from the Judaean Desert teach us anything, it is that their authors were not simpletons or rubes. When it came to using legal instruments to achieve their sometimes complex goals, they were shrewd players.

H.L.A. Hart has observed that civil legal instruments ". . . provide individuals with *facilities* for realizing their wishes, by conferring legal powers upon them to create, by certain specified procedures and subject to certain conditions, structures of rights and duties within the coercive framework of the law."[2] Richard Saller has applied this instrumental approach to the Roman law of succession, showing how Roman legal institutions provided a "tool-kit" of strategies that Romans, facing a wide variety of personal circumstances, could manipulate in order to bequeath their property in an orderly fashion

---

[1] P.Yadin 13, 14, 15.

[2] H.L.A. Hart, *The Concept of Law* (Oxford 1961) 27 (original emphasis).

that conformed both to social norms and to their own idiosyncratic wishes.[3] Seen in this way, the certificate of deposit of P.Yadin 5 is an answer to a "unique" problem of succession, in which a man whose capital is tied up in the family business leaves a single child, a minor son.[4]

Devolving property to a lone son was a relatively simple procedure when compared to the problems that daughters in a patriarchal society presented for the orderly devolution of property. The primary problem in any patriarchal or patrilocal society is that daughters marry, and whatever property they take with them (e.g., as dowry or inheritance) would pass out of their families and into their husbands'. Indeed, the primary complaint of women against their husbands in the papyri from Greco-Roman Egypt is the treatment of the property that they brought with them into the marriage.[5] Among the documents from the Judaean Desert, Hannah Cotton has recently noted, "[t]here seems to be a close relationship between marriage, dowry, and the bestowal of gifts on daughters."[6] The purpose of this paper is to explore the nature of and reasons for this "close relationship."[7]

---

[3] R.P. Saller, *Patriarchy, Property and Death in the Roman Family* (Cambridge 1994) 155–244.

[4] According to the family tree given in Lewis *P.Yadin* page 25, the son, Jesus, had at least one other brother, Joseph, and perhaps a second one as well. Lewis's evidence for the existence of the brother Joseph appears to be P.Yadin 13, a fragmentary petition from the latter half of 124, which mentions "his brother Joseph, from his own [funds?]" (line 8). Lewis writes: "Given the date of this document, this Joseph must be not the Joseph of **5**, but that man's son, the brother of Babatha's first husband, Jesus" (*P.Yadin* page 53). This statement contains both an unwarranted assumption and a non-sequitur. The lines are too fragmentary to assume that this Joseph is not precisely the Joseph of P.Yadin 5, the brother of Jesus, the father of Babatha's first husband. The complaint of lines 17–19 might then be that this Joseph, with whom Jesus still had a deposit when he died, did not provide any of this money to Jesus' orphaned son. More problematic is the non-sequitur. Even if Lewis is correct that this Joseph must be the son of the Joseph of P.Yadin 5, that would make him Babatha's husband's first cousin, not his brother.

Jesus' hypothetical brother, "Jacob son of Jesus," mentioned at P.Yadin 17.5 (128 CE) (not P.Yadin 19, as indicated by Lewis, *P.Yadin* page 25 note *) as Babatha's guardian for her loan to her second husband, Judah Khthousion, is far more speculative. I see no reason to think, *pace* Lewis, that he "is not likely to have been a stranger" (74, note *ad* lines 5 and 23).

[5] I. Arnaoutoglou, "Marital Disputes in Greco-Roman Egypt," *JJP* 25 (1995) 11–28.

[6] *P.Hever* page 203.

[7] Cotton has vaguely linked this relationship to the law of succession, which she

My approach to these documents is instrumental. I am assuming that those who used these legal instruments viewed them as flexible tools to be used in order to accomplish specific goals for the devolution of property. This brief paper contains three parts. In the first, I present a "strong" reading of the documents in order to underscore patterns and timing of property movement. The second part focuses on the function of marriage payments, and the last part deals with why the marriages in these documents are often accompanied by the bestowal of a gift on the wife by her family.

The Movement of Property

In 99 CE, Babatha's father, Shimeon ben Menahem, bought four date groves for 132 silver *selas*, the equivalent of 528 *denarii*.[8] He gave Babatha these date groves at her first marriage, in 120 CE, to Jesus (the orphan of P.Yadin 5).[9] Babatha registered this property in 127 CE, declaring it to be a little over 24.5 *bet seahs*, on which she must pay in taxes in kind something over 135 *seahs* of dates and 100 *seahs* of "splits" (a better kind of date), and a monetary tax of 12 "blacks" and 105 *lepta*.[10] While there is much debate over the quantity of these terms, it is clear that her holdings were large and productive.[11] Her dowry for her first marriage, although unknown, was

---

originally claimed did not entitle a daughter to inherit from her father under certain conditions. H.M. Cotton and J.C. Greenfield, "Babatha's Property and the Law of Succession in the Babatha Archive," *ZPE* 104 (1994) 211–24 at 220. She has more recently retreated from this view. Cf. H.M. Cotton, "The Law of Succession in the Documents from the Judaean Desert Again," *SCI* 17 (1998) 115–23.

[8] P.Yadin 3, described by Y. Yadin, "Expedition D—the Cave of Letters," *IEJ* 12 (1962) 227–57 at 239–241. On the equivalency clause, see Y. Yadin, J.C. Greenfield, and A. Yardeni, "Babatha's *Ketubba*," *IEJ* 44 (1994) 75–101 at 89–92; M.A. Friedman, "Babatha's *Ketubba*: Some Preliminary Observations," *IEJ* 46 (1996) 55–76 at 56–60.

[9] There is no direct evidence for this transfer, its timing, or the date of Babatha's marriage. Nevertheless, the same courtyards that Shimeon bought in 99 CE appear in Babatha's land declaration of 127 CE (P.Yadin 16), and Shimeon's gift to his wife in 120 CE (P.Yadin 7, first published by Y. Yadin, J.C. Greenfield, and A. Yardeni, "A Deed of Gift in Aramaic Found in Nahal Hever: Papyrus Yadin 7," *ErIsr* 25 [1996] 383–403 [Hebrew] with summary in English at 103*) was most likely occasioned by his daughter's marriage (attested to in 24–25). Cf. Cotton and Greenfield (supra note 7).

[10] P.Yadin 16. See also *P.Hever* pages 181–5.

[11] Lewis (*P.Yadin* page 69, note *ad* 18–20) suggests that each *seah* is about thirteen liters, and each *bet seah* about a fifth of an acre. Cotton suggests that a "black" is

probably in the range of 200–400 *denarii*, the size of nearly all of
the other marriage payments found in these documents as well as
Babatha's own second marriage.[12]

Shortly after giving his daughter these date groves, Shimeon wrote
over his other properties to his wife, Miriam.[13] Although an "eter-
nal gift," this was really a conditional gift in contemplation of death.
Miriam would only receive this property if she was still his wife at
the time of his death, and she had no right of alienating the property until her husband died. This "gift in contemplation of death"
prevented Miriam from selling the property until her husband died.[14]

Babatha's and Jesus' marriage was short-lived but fertile. They
had a son, Jesus, before (Babatha's husband) Jesus died, in 124 CE.[15]
By the end of 127 CE, Babatha had married for the second time,
to Judah Khthousion.[16] In their Aramaic marriage contract, Judah
Khthousion obligated himself, among other things, to (1) "bring you
(into my house) by means of your *ketubba*"; (2) cause their male children to inherit her *ketubba* money if he predeceased her; and (3) support their female children until they marry.[17] Soon after marrying,
Judah Khthousion borrowed from Babatha, by means of an instrument of deposit, another 300 silver *denarii*.[18] Six weeks later Judah
used 200 *denarii* of this money to dower his daughter by his first

---

worth half a *denarius* (*P.Hever* page 171, note *ad* lines 8–9). These figures would give
Babatha land holdings of around 6 acres, and a tax burden of some 3,055 liters
of dates and 6–7 *denarii*. This does not include the fixed percentage of half of her
crop that she must pay in taxes on her smallest plot.

[12] An exception is P.Hever 69, where the dowry is 500 *denarii*. I will return below
to the interpretation of Babatha's *ketubbah* as a dowry. Jesus' own mother's "marriage money" was 710 "blacks" (355 *denarii*?), and when Babatha remarried, by 128
CE, her "marriage money" was 400 *denarii*. See P.Yadin 5.15, 10.6, 8–9.

[13] P.Yadin 7.

[14] The conditions are at P.Yadin 7.16–18, 28–29. Cf. Reuven Yaron, "Acts of
Last Will in Jewish Law," in *Acts of Last Will* (*Recueils de la Société Jean Bodin pour
l'histoire comparative des institutions* 59, Brussels 1992) 29–45; H.M. Cotton, "Deeds of
Gift and the Law of Succession in the Papyri from the Judean Desert," *ErIsr* 25
(1996) 410–5 (in Hebrew).

[15] P.Yadin 12, dated between 27 February and 28 June, 124 CE.

[16] Lewis suggests (*P.Yadin* page 58) on the basis of Judah's appearance as the
guardian of Babatha in P.Yadin 15 (11 or 12 October, 125 CE), that they were
already married by this time. This supposition is unnecessary, and in fact the lack
of his explicit designation as a husband in this document would mitigate against it.
They are certainly married by the time of P.Yadin 16, more than two years later.

[17] P.Yadin 10.5, 12–13, and 14, respectively. Lines 12–13 are almost entirely
reconstructed.

[18] P.Yadin 17.

wife, Shelamzion, to which her husband made a "dowry addition" of another 300 *denarii*.[19] Eleven days later Judah Khthousion gave Shelamzion a gift of half of a courtyard in Ein-Gedi, with the other half to follow after his death.[20] At some point, and in some manner, Shelamzion acquired another courtyard in Ein-Gedi from her grandfather, Judah's father.[21] Babatha's second marriage lasted no longer than her first. Judah Khthousion died by 130 CE, apparently insolvent, and Babatha seized three of his date groves "in lieu of my dowry and debt."[22] These properties were, apparently, still not worth the 700 *denarii* that she was owed, for she then got into a legal battle with her co-wife for Judah's remaining possessions.[23]

The second best documented family archive from the Judaean Desert is that of Salome Komaïse, daughter of Levi. Her mother, Salome Grapte, the daughter of Menaham, no doubt knew Babatha: "their families' properties were abutted by the same neighbors, and the same witnesses signed their documents."[24] She may have been several years older than Babatha, for she appears to have married her first husband, Levi, before 113 CE.[25] They had at least two children, a son and a daughter. Sometime before 127 CE the daughter,

---

[19] P.Yadin 18. Cf. N. Lewis, R. Katzoff, and J.C. Greenfield, "*Papyrus Yadin* 18," *IEJ* 37 (1987) 229–50.

[20] P.Yadin 19. This is the same courtyard that Judah mortgaged for his father in 124 CE (P.Yadin 11). See H. Cotton, "Courtyard(s) in Ein-Gedi: P.Yadin 11, 19, and 20 of the Babatha Archive," *ZPE* 112 (1996) 197–201.

[21] P.Yadin 20. As Cotton notes (supra note 20), this courtyard is not mentioned in P.Yadin 11 and 19. Cotton suggests that Shelamzion acquired this courtyard directly from her grandfather, perhaps even after her father's death. I think that this is unlikely. In P.Yadin 11, written in 124 CE, Judah mortgages a courtyard which, he acknowledges, belongs to his father. In P.Yadin 19, Judah is in full possession of this courtyard, and is able to give it to his daughter. The implication is that his father had died in the interim, leaving him the courtyard, and perhaps also the one in P.Yadin 20. If so, then the claimants of P.Yadin 20 (representing the children of Judah's deceased brother) would be acknowledging that the (intestate?) transmission of this property from Eleazar to his son Judah (and not his son Jesus) was valid. Judah's ability to transfer this property to his daughter would not be questioned. In any case, the document that transfers possession to Shelamzion did not survive.

[22] P.Yadin 22.9–10 (trans. by Lewis in *P.Yadin* page 99): κατέχω αὐτὰ ἀντὶ τῆς προ{ο}ʹκός μου καὶ ὀφιλῆς.

[23] P.Yadin 26. Miriam appears to have been Judah's first wife, and Babatha's co-wife. See N. Lewis, "Judah's Bigamy," *ZPE* 116 (1997) 152. Cf. R. Katzoff, "Polygamy in P.Yadin?" *ZPE* 109 (1995) 128–32.

[24] H.M. Cotton, "The Archive of Salome Komaise Daughter of Levi: Another Archive from the 'Cave of Letters'," *ZPE* 105 (1995) 171–208 at 172.

[25] According to P.Hever 63 Levi had died by 127 CE (?) and his daughter, Salome,

Salome Komaïse, married Sammouos son of Simon; they were divorced by 129 CE.[26] No financial details of this marriage survive, but I suggest that upon marrying, Salome Komaïse did not receive a gift of property which she felt due to her. While there is absolutely no explicit evidence in the archive for this suggestion, it would serve to explain the rather odd renunciation of claims against her mother that she filed in 127 CE (*P.Hever* 63). In this document, Salome Komaïse, represented by her husband, renounced all claims against her mother "regarding the properties left by Levi, her late husband, and (those left by)... her late son, the brother of the declarant."[27] This renunciation was intended, the document continues, to end the "controversy" (*amphisbeteseos*).

I suggest the following course of events. In 127 CE (or shortly before), Levi, Salome's father, died. His son (and Salome's brother), Levi, was the sole inheritor of his property. Very shortly thereafter, Levi himself died.[28] At this point, the property apparently passed

---

was represented by her husband. Assuming that she was at least 13 years old at this time, and that she was their first child, Levi and Salome Grapte could not have married later than 113 CE. It is likely that they married even earlier. My observation about Salome Grapte's age relative to Babatha's assumes, of course, that they both entered their first marriage at around the same age, and that Babatha was married at or around 120 CE.

[26] This interpretation is highly speculative. In P.Hever 63 (dated between 25 April and 31 December, 127 CE), in which Salome Komaïse renounces claims against her mother (see below), Salome Komaïse is represented by her husband, whose name is fragmentary. Cotton plausibly suggests, however, that Sammouos son of Simon, mentioned on a receipt from 125 CE (P.Hever 60) should be restored (*P.Hever* page 161). Their marriage had ended by 131 CE, the date of the contract of her second marriage (P.Hever 65 = P.Yadin 37). Sammouos appears for the last time in a deed of gift from Salome Grapte (herself remarried) to her daughter, Salome Komaïse, in 129 CE, where he is mentioned as owning an abutting plot of property (P.Hever 64). In this document he is not termed her husband. Cotton maintains that because Salome's archive contained Sammouos's papers divorce was unlikely (*P.Hever* page 162). Yet it could be that after the divorce—the divorce document, if there was one, has been lost—Salome simply neglected to clean out her "file." The receipt for which Sammouos served as a go-between (P.Hever 60) was relatively unimportant to him. P.Hever 62, a land declaration from 127, is an important, but not critical, document, as the original was filed in the government offices. Alternatively, these documents might really be from Sammouos' archive, and he himself was hiding with his ex-wife in the same cave.

[27] P.Hever 63. 6–7. About the "controversy," Cotton states that "it is likely to have concerned the property left after the death of both father and son" (*P.Hever* page 195).

[28] P.Hever 63. Cotton plausibly suggests that this son is the subject of P.Hever 61, the conclusion of a land declaration dated to April 25, 127 (*P.Hever* pages 174–5). His death then occasioned the renunciation of claims later that year.

back to Levi's mother, Salome Grapte. Feeling slighted, her daughter, Salome Komaïse, threatened to sue for the marital "gift" that she thought she rightfully deserved. Such a threat may or may not have amounted to a valid legal claim, but it would have provoked her mother to work out some kind of compromise with her, as a result of which Salome Komaïse had to renounce all of her claims.

This reconstruction would then also explain why Salome Komaïse received a gift from her mother in 129 CE. She and Sammouos were divorced, and when she entered her second, at first "unwritten" marriage with Yeshua son of Menahem, her mother gave her a date grove and half of a courtyard.[29] The tax on this grove was ten *seahs* of "splits" and six *seahs* of regular dates—less than a tenth of Babatha's tax assessment. This gift was most likely linked to Salome's renunciation of claims against her mother: her mother may have promised her a gift, and the occasion of her second marriage was an opportune time to fulfill this promise. Two years later, Salome Komaïse and Yeshua drew up a marriage contract that acknowledged receipt of a dowry consisting of her trousseau, appraised at 96 *denarii*, ". . . with his [= Yeshua son of Menahem's] undertaking to feed [and clothe both her] and her children to come in accordance with Greek custom and Greek manner," converting this marriage into a written one.[30] There is no way to know why they converted their marriage at precisely this point; perhaps Salome was pregnant.[31]

Marital Payments

The Judaean Desert papyri testify to at least two kinds of marital payments: dowry and, in a single case, an indirect dowry or dowry addition. The dowry, a sum of money (or a trousseau or other movables) which the bride brings into the marriage, is by far the most

---

[29] P.Hever 64.

[30] P.Hever 65. 9–10: σὺν αἱρέσει τροφῆς [καὶ ἀμφιασμοῦ αὐτῆς] τε καὶ τῶν μελλόντῳ[ν τέκ]νῳν νόμ[ῳ] | ἑ[λλη]γικῶ καὶ ἑλλ[η]γικῷ τρόπῳ. There is some controversy over whether this document is converting an unwritten marriage into a written one, or that it indicates that Salome, as an orphan and a minor, was living together with her husband from the time of her betrothal. I here follow *P.Hever* pages 226–9. Cf. Lewis, Katzoff, Greenfield (supra note 19) 240–1. [See the contribution by Katzoff in this volume.]

[31] Birth of a first child would both "cement" a relationship as well as call for legal documents that clarify the succession of property.

common marital payment found in these documents, as in other Greek and Roman marriage documents from antiquity.[32] It has also been widely assumed that these documents contain evidence of a *ketubba* payment. The *ketubba* payment, known to us from rabbinic sources, is a husband's pledge of a certain sum of money, payable to the wife upon the dissolution (by death or divorce) of the marriage.

I have argued elsewhere that the *ketubba* payment arose in the rabbinic period, and if it ever did gain popularity in antiquity, it did so at a time well after these desert documents were authored.[33] My interpretation of these documents has been in a similar vein. The Judaean Desert documents do not offer a single clear example of a *ketubba* payment, as known from rabbinic sources. The Greek marriage documents all explicitly mention dowries. The three Aramaic marriage contracts are more debatable. One mentions money, but the surviving fragment does not indicate how much or whence it came.[34] The other two mention the *ketubba* money, and of these only one, Babatha's marriage contract, contains a sum.[35] Was this the *ketubba* money known from rabbinic sources, an endowment pledge on the part of the husband? None of the Aramaic documents contains a clause recording receipt of a dowry, although in two, and possibly in all three, such a clause may have been lost. Such a receipt may have been part of a very fragmentary marriage contract from Nahal Hever.[36]

The strongest evidence that the *ketubba* payment (in the rabbinic sense) was known among the authors of these documents is Babatha's marriage contract, to her second husband Judah Khthousion (P.Yadin 10). This Aramaic document mentions that Judah owes Babatha the 400 *zuz* (= *denarii*) of her *ketubba* money. It does not record that Babatha brought this money into the marriage, nor does it include a receipt for the dowry. On the other hand, it seems odd that

---

[32] P.Mur. 115 (124 CE): 200 *denarii*; P.Mur. 116 (early second century): 2,000 *denarii* (?); P.Yadin 18 (128 CE): 200 *denarii* plus a 300 *denarii* dowry addition; P.Hever 69: 500 *denarii*; P.Yadin 37 = P.Hever 65 (131 CE): 96 *denarii*. On dowry additions, see R. Katzoff, "*Donatio ante nuptias* and Jewish dowry additions," *YCS* 28 (1987) 231–44.

[33] M.L. Satlow, "Reconsidering the Rabbinic *Ketubah* Payment," in S.J.D. Cohen, ed., *The Jewish Family in Antiquity* (Atlanta 1993) 133–51.

[34] P.Mur. 20 (117 CE?).

[35] P.Yadin 10; P.Mur. 21.

[36] P.Hever 11.3: [ל[מפרעה ואנה מקב]ל].

Judah—who seems perpetually strapped for cash—would marry not only without acquiring a dowry, but also obligating himself to pay a significant sum of money. Moreover, the clause "bring you (into my house) by means of your *ketubba*" makes little sense if Judah is supplying the *ketubba*. I am hence inclined to see P.Yadin 10 as well as an instance of dowry.

In theory, a dowry can have four overlapping economic (as distinct from symbolic or ceremonial) functions. In practice, different societies emphasize different functions depending on their own needs. The four (perceived) functions are: (1) economic compensation to the husband for support of his wife; (2) "getting by" money for a new widow or divorcée; (3) hindrance to hasty divorce; and (4) early inheritance. The society that produced the Judaean Desert documents clearly saw the primary purpose of the dowry as (1), with (2) and perhaps (3) serving secondary functions.

Some of the marriage contracts explicitly indicate that the use of the dowry is intended to compensate the husband for his feeding and clothing her and their children. Hence, in the marriage contract of Shelamzion, her husband Judah Cimber received her dowry and pledged an addition, "pursuant to his undertaking of feeding and clothing" her.[37] The canceled marriage contract from Nahal Hever might explicitly say that dowry (or its usufruct) should be used to nourish and clothe the wife.[38] When Judah Khthousion says that he will bring Babatha into his house "by means of your *ketubba*" it similarly appears to mean that use of her dowry compensates him for these obligations.

For how long could a freshly divorced or widowed woman get by with her dowry of 200–500 *denarii*? It is generally thought that in Palestine in the first century CE a person needed about one *zuz* (= *denarius*) each day to live at sustenance level.[39] An "average" dowry, at this rate, would last about a year, at which time a woman would have to rely on her own resources, get remarried, or return to her

---

[37] P.Yadin 18.15–16: ἀκολούθως αἱρέσει | τροφῆς καὶ ἀμφιασμοῦ. The same idea is found at P.Hever 65.9. The phrase is substantively the same as "*ad sustinenda onera matrimonii*," found in Roman legal texts.

[38] P.Hever 69.10: ἐφ᾽ ᾧ ἔσται ἡ Σελαμπιους τρεφομένει καὶ ἀμφ[ιαζο]μ[ενῆ. Could the ἐφ᾽ ᾧ refer to the dowry money?

[39] See the price lists in D. Sperber, *Roman Palestine 200–400: Money and Prices* (Ramat Gan 1991) 101–44.

family home. But we are seriously hampered here by our lack of data regarding contemporary prices and their fluctuation. During the Bar Kokhba revolt, for example, there seems to have been an enormous increase in the value of money. Babatha's share of her date crops (covering about 25 *bet seahs*) in 130 CE would have amounted to 84 *denarii* and 65 "blacks" (before taxes?).[40] Three or four years later, in the Nahal Hever documents, the most expensive plot of land sold is for 36 *zuzin* (= *denarii*).[41] A plot of land of three *bet seahs* sold for 28 *zuzin*.[42] On an IOU written during the rebellion, four witnesses attested to the loan of a tetradrachm, which just a few years earlier would have been regarded as a paltry sum.[43] There can be little doubt that the increased buying power of the average dowry would have been countered by the increasing inability in such economic circumstances to return the full dowry. A full appraisal of Palestinian prices in the first and second centuries CE, though, will have to await for a fuller documentary record.

If the wives and their parents in these documents expected that their large dowries would discourage divorce, they were mistaken. One of the marriages with a large dowry, 500 *denarii*, appears to have ended in divorce. Salome Komaïse, I have argued, was divorced, and P.Mur.115 testifies to a remarriage with a dowry of 200 *denarii*. One supposes that her original dowry was no less. Several other testimonies of divorce survive in the papyri, and although they do not reveal the amounts, they do indicate that the husbands returned their wives' dowries.[44] It is possible that the relatively numerous testimonies in these documents to divorce are a function of ancient source preservation—that is, divorce was accompanied by documents that both parties would want to save—but it is also likely that divorce among these Jews was neither difficult nor uncommon. If one is looking for parallels, one need go no further than contemporary Rome, in which

---

[40] P.Yadin 21 and 22; cf. *P.Hever* page 185. The monetary sum indicates the fine that the sharecropper would owe should he not deliver the contracted amount of dates. I assume that this would be at or above the expected market price.

[41] P.Hever 8.

[42] P.Hever 9.

[43] M. Broshi and E. Qimron, "A Hebrew I.O.U. Note from the Second Year of the Bar Kokhba Revolt," *JJS* 45 (1994) 286–94. My thanks to Hanan Eshel for this reference.

[44] See, e.g., P.Mur. 19 (111 CE?); P.Hever 13 (134 or 135 CE).

large dowries were said to discourage divorce, but in actuality probably had little impact on the divorce rate.[45]

The fourth conceivable function of a dowry, ante-mortem inheritance, is the least important role of dowries in these documents. The
land that families gave to their daughters upon their marriage appears
to have been worth more than their dowries. Babatha's case is the
best documented: her marital "gift" of date groves cost her father
over 500 *denarii* about twenty five years before her second marriage.
These marital gifts, not dowry, represents a daughter's true patri-
mony. While the documents surveyed above are the only ones that
testify directly to the practice of giving land to a woman after she
marries, several other papyri provide indirect testimony that such a
practice was common. In a deed of sale of a house from 134 or
135 CE, for example, a seller's wife declares that she neither has nor
will have any claim to that house.[46] Years ago, Rabinowitz suggested
connecting this line with the rabbinic law in *m. Ketub.* 4:7, by which
a woman can place a lien on her husband's property for payment
of her *ketubba*.[47] While this is not impossible, the relative scarcity of
such a renunciation in surviving deeds of sale of property makes it
unlikely. Rather, I suggest that the reason the woman renounces her
rights is that the property was originally hers—she transferred or
sold it to her husband who then sold it to a third party. This buyer
then sought a guarantee that the wife would not at some later date
contest her transfer of her property to her husband. Perhaps a clearer
example can be seen in a deed of sale from 134 CE. Here, a man
sold a plot of 5 *bet seahs* for 88 *denarii*. At the end of the document,
the man's wife renounced her claim on this land, but with a catch:
"And I, Shalom, wife of this Dostes, daughter of Honi son of
Yehonatan, on the condition that I am paid 30 [*zuzin*] each year
after [your death, and live] in your house, my lord, I have no claim
in this sale."[48] That is, Shalom made a deal with her husband whereby

[45] Cf. S. Treggiari, "Divorce Roman Style: How Easy and how Frequent was
it?" in B. Rawson, ed., *Marriage, Divorce, and Children in Ancient Rome* (Canberry and
Oxford 1991) 30–46, which deals mainly with the period of the Republic. Several
rabbinic stories of "the rabbi with a bad wife who has a large *ketubba*" follow this
literary trope.

[46] P.Hever 8a.12–13.

[47] J.J. Rabinowitz, "Some Notes on an Aramaic Contract from the Dead Sea
Region," *BASOR* 136 (Dec 1954) 15–6.

[48] P.Mur. 30.25–28.

he could sell this property if he were to promise her (additional?) support after his death. A woman could only make a deal like this from a position of strength, and the strongest position that she could have had was if she herself owned the property that he sold.[49]

First and foremost, then, husbands saw the dowry as compensation for the upkeep of a wife. Secondarily, assuming that her husband was solvent, it provided enough liquid capital to a widow or divorcée to prevent her from starving before she found another husband or returned to her parental estate.[50] But a dowry most likely made nary an impact on the divorce rate, and was not seen as a daughter's share of her inheritance.

Deed of Gift

Babatha, Shelamzion, and Salome Komaïse all received at least part of their inheritance by means of a deed of gift given around the time of—I presume shortly after—their marriages. The granting of these gifts to daughters upon their marriage is, as we shall see, a particularly shrewd move. By using and appropriately timing these deeds of gifts parents were able to realize several goals simultaneously.[51]

The reason that parents would want to transfer their property to their daughters by deeds of gift rather than as dowries is obvious: it kept the property out of the hands of their sons-in-law. The legal instruments themselves demonstrate the concern that parents had for the property of their daughters. Nearly all the surviving marriage

---

[49] Cf. P.Mur. 29 (133 CE), which contains just the signature of a woman, who in the lost part of the document probably renounced claims to the property.

[50] It is interesting to note that this gift, which should technically conclude the financial relationship between a daughter and her natal family, did not necessarily mean that she was expected never to return to her family. P.Yadin 7 makes this clear: Babatha's father's gift to his wife stipulates that should Babatha be widowed she is allowed to reside on this land.

[51] One goal that these gifts probably did not serve to realize was a circumvention of inheritance laws. Cotton and Greenfield (supra note 7) have suggested that the purpose of these gifts was to devolve property to daughters in a legal system in which a man's brother's sons took precedence over his daughters in matters of inheritance. Cotton has recently emphasized that the evidence for this argument is less than compelling (supra note 7). It is indeed possible that the inheritance laws put women at a great disadvantage, but for my argument this is largely irrelevant. Deeds of gift to women might have secondarily served to circumvent these laws, but their primary function had nothing to do with them.

documents contain a "pledging clause," in which a husband pledges all that he has or will acquire as surety for the return of his wife's dowry.[52] Not content with a single protection of the woman's property, they also contain a second guarantee in the form of the inheritance clause, which assures a woman that her marriage money would be inherited by her male children, and would not count against any other shares that they had in their father's estate.[53]

These two clauses protect against the two scenarios that might have kept a young bride's parents awake at nights. A father's nightmare (and perhaps his daughter's as well) was to see his estate pass to his son-in-law's children *by a woman other than his daughter*. Equally horrifying to him would be the thought that his son-in-law would squander the large dowry that he gave to his daughter. Should the son-in-law go broke after having (illegally) squandered the dowry, sue as they might, there would simply be nothing left to collect. This, of course, is what happened to Babatha. After her second husband, Judah Khthousion, died, she seized his date crops, "which [she] distrained, as [she] said, in lieu of marriage money and debt."[54] Babatha's seizure and the formulation of this clause, which appears in her agreement with Simon son of Jesus to sharecrop the dates, raise two questions. First, was her seizure legal? Although Judah pledged all of his assets as security for the seven hundred *denarii* that he owed her, Babatha may have acted on her own, without legally executing her rights. "As you say," Simon son of Jesus states, absolving himself of responsibility should someone challenge Babatha's legal possession of these date groves. That she may not have legally taken possession of these groves might also be indicated by her continued possession of the uncanceled marriage contract (P.Yadin 10) and deed of deposit (P.Yadin 17), which, had they been discharged, we would expect to have been destroyed or marked.[55] It is possible

---

[52] P.Yadin 18.17–19; P.Hever 65 = P.Yadin 37.10–12; P.Hever 69.10–11; P.Yadin 10 (only traces; see Yadin, Greenfield and Yardeni [supra note 9] 92); P.Mur. 20.12–13; P.Mur. 21.17 (traces); P.Mur. 115.12–14. Its absence from P.Mur. 116 is most likely due to the poor state of the document.

[53] P.Hever 69.12 (traces); P.Yadin 10 (traces); P.Mur. 20.7–8 (reconstructed); P.Mur. 21.12–14; P.Mur. 115.17; P.Mur. 116.7–8. It is absent from P.Hever 65 and P.Yadin 18. Cf. M.A. Friedman, *Jewish Marriage in Palestine: A Cairo Geniza Study* I (Tel Aviv and New York 1980) 379–85.

[54] P.Yadin 21.11–12 (= P.Yadin 22.10, with minor variations).

[55] This argument is obviously not conclusive, as Babatha may have given receipts

either that Babatha decided that she had to act quickly after Judah's death so that she would not lose the crop, or that she was afraid of a legal challenge either from Judah's nephews or from Miriam, and thought she could avoid the hassle by taking possession illegally. She was mistaken.[56]

The second question, whether or not Judah's property was worth the 700 *denarii* that she was owed, is more difficult to answer. It does appear, though, given continuing litigation between those who claimed to be Judah's heirs, that Judah did not have enough at the time of his death to discharge his financial obligations. At the end of the day, somebody would not be paid.

Judah Khthousion was not a father-in-law's dream: he squandered his daughter's (that is, his own) money. Judah was not the only man in history to die insolvent, and it was no doubt the fear of irresponsible use of the dowry that led parents to grant property to their daughters in a way that would prevent their sons-in-law from alienating it. Property given to a woman by deed of gift rather than as dowry fulfilled this function well, for unlike dowry, it could not be alienated or mortgaged by the husband.

But deeding property to one's daughter or wife, from the perspective of her father or husband, had a potential downside: it gave her freedom. This is the fact that governed the timing of these gifts. Fathers, who may have been insecure about their ability to govern the marital choices of their daughters under normal conditions, could use the deed of gift as additional leverage. Once a woman married an appropriate man, the father would write over his property. If he wanted to maintain some control over her, he might make part of the gift contingent on his death; if she misbehaved he might cancel (or at least think that he could cancel) this part of the bequest.[57]

---

when these obligations were discharged and kept the original, unmarked, instruments of debt. According to Katzoff (supra note 19), "The practice recorded in Greek papyri was that receipts for payment of private debts were issued only in special circumstances, such as the death of the principal creditor or debtor, loss of the debt document, or partial or early payment. Otherwise the normal practice was to return and tear the document recording the obligation" (243).

[56] Judah's nephews, of course, did sue (P.Yadin 23, 24, and 25), but it is unclear which date groves they were claiming that Babatha illegally appropriated. See Lewis, *P.Yadin* page 107, note *ad* 4–6. P.Yadin 26 indicates that Babatha and Miriam did engage in litigation over their deceased husband's property.

[57] In Talmudic law, a "gift in contemplation of death" was, under normal circumstances, irrevocable. It is not clear whether this was so in the laws that govern

This is the form of Judah Khthousion's gift to Shelamzion.[58] Should, however, the father not approve of the match, he could refuse to give her any property: I have argued that this is exactly what happened in Salome Komaïse's first marriage. So too, a man could exercise control over his wife by "a gift in contemplation of death" conditional on her remaining married to him, as in the case of Babatha's parents. Such a gift could never have been immediate and irrevocable, for the men of antiquity, rightly or wrongly, would have loathed the loss of control that would follow from an immediate gift to one's wife.

The Judaean Desert papyri provide a more or less coherent picture of one kind of succession strategy. While these documents present variations on a theme, they all begin from a common problem: how to devolve property to one's only child, who is female. The ancient solutions to other problems are more obscure. P.Yadin 5, I have suggested, provides one answer to a very specific problem that involved an only son. Indirectly, the small plots of land or shares in a house or courtyard that one regularly finds in the papyri indicate that family estates were divided among multiple siblings rather than conserved in the hands of one or two. A more interesting, but completely unattested, problem is the case of sons and daughters competing for limited resources.

Throughout this paper I have tried to avoid explaining the papyri in light of rabbinic or "Hellenistic" law or practice. I have done this not because I believe, *a priori*, that such comparisons are methodologically unsound; indeed, in this particular case the rabbinic material nicely illustrates and confirms some of the suggestions offered here. Rather, my goal has not been to see how "Jewish" or "Hellenized" Babatha and her friends were, but to try to understand a family at work, negotiating the mundane and treacherous terrain of money and familial relationships. Unsurprisingly, these problems, and not the more abstract and theoretical decisions about self-identity, were what drove these people daily. Jews and non-Jews, then and now, all faced and face similar problems. Only our answers have changed.

---

the papyri. See Yaron (supra note 14). [See the contribution of Rivlin in this volume.]

[58] P.Yadin 19.

JUDAEAN DESERT MARRIAGE DOCUMENTS AND *EKDOSIS* IN THE GREEK LAW OF THE ROMAN PERIOD

Uri Yiftach-Firanko

The starting point of this discussion is P.Yadin 18, a marriage document from 128 CE from Maʿoza in the province Arabia, published for the first time in 1987.[1] The unmistakable common formulaic features that this document shares with the Greek marriage documents from Egypt, on the one hand, and its evident peculiarities, on the other, have given rise to a heated discussion of its legal identity. According to one school it represents marriage customs of assimilated Jews who adopted and acted according to Greek legal institutions. According to another school, this document shows that the Jewish population of the Dead Sea region held on to its own legal traditions, and used Greek formulas, when it did so, only for the attestation of its non-Greek practices.[2] Yet despite the diversity of the interpretations of this document, some of the clauses incorporated in it are generally agreed to be of Greek origin. Such is the clause attesting the act of *ekdosis*, which will be designated henceforth as the *ekdosis*-clause.[3]

The latest study dealing with the *ekdosis*-clause, as with the legal mechanism of Greek marriage in the Hellenistic world in general,

[1] N. Lewis, R. Katzoff, J.C. Greenfield, "P.Yadin 18," *IEJ* 37 (1987) 229–50. I would like to express my gratitude to all those who contributed to the present article by reading its earlier versions and discussing their contents with me. I thank in particular Hannah Cotton of the Hebrew University of Jerusalem, Ranon Katzoff of Bar-Ilan University and Joseph Mélèze-Modrzejewski of the Sorbonne and the École Pratique des Hautes Études, Paris.

[2] The first view is represented by A. Wasserstein, "A Marriage Contract from the Province of Arabia Nova: Notes on Papyrus Yadin 18," *JQR* 80 (1989) 93–130 at 109–13, 117–8; J. Geiger, "A Note on P.Yadin 18," *ZPE* 73 (1992) 67–8; H.M. Cotton, "A Canceled Marriage Contract from the Judaean Desert," *JRS* 84 (1994) 64–86 at 77, 82. For the second view see R. Katzoff, in Lewis, Katzoff and Greenfield, (supra note 1) 240–1, 247; idem, "Papyrus Yadin 18 Again: A Rejoinder," *JQR* 82 (1991) 171–6 at 173; idem, "Hellenistic Marriage Contracts," in M.J. Geller and H. Maehler (eds.), *Legal Documents of the Hellenistic World* (London 1995) 37–45 at 41.

[3] Katzoff (supra note 1) 238; (supra note 2, 1991) 173; (supra note 2, 1995) 40; Wasserstein (supra note 2) 109.

was "La structure juridique du mariage grec", by Mélèze in 1981.[4]
Since then, however, the number of documents containing the *ekdosis-*
clause has increased dramatically. Compared to nine marriage documents containing this clause that had been published up to that
year,[5] we now have fourteen. Of the five new documents, two come
from the Judaean Desert (P.Yadin 18 and P.Hever 69),[6] and three
from Roman Oxyrhynchos (P.Oxy. XLIX 3491, 3500, and PSI
Congr.XX 10 lines 14–29). Worth mentioning is also P.Amst. I 40,
published in 1980 and not treated by Mélèze. This influx of new
material allows us, therefore, to re-assess the issue of the Greek *ekdosis*
in Egypt before turning to its Judaean counterpart.

The main features of the Ekdosis *according to the Egyptian material*

In the Greek marriage laws and customs as known from Classical
Greece, the act of *ekdosis* consisted of the shifting of the legal authority over a daughter from her previous male *kyrios*—that is her father,
or, in his absence, another agnate male next-of-kin—to her new one,
her husband. This shifting was signified by a "handing over" of the
daughter "for the sake of being a wedded wife and begetting legitimate children."[7]

---

[4] J. Mélèze-Modrzejewski, "La structure juridique du mariage grec," *Scritti in onore
di Orsolina Montevecchi* (Bologna 1981) 231–68, reprinted in idem, *Statut personnel et
liens de famille dans les droits de l'Antiquité* (Aldershot 1993). For a detailed account of
the history of research on the issue see now Yiftach-Firanko, *Marriage and Marital
Arrangements: A History of the Greek Marriage Document in Egypt, 4th century BCE– 4th century CE* (Münchener Beiträge zur Papyrusforschung und Antiken Rechtsgeschichte.
Heft 93) (Munich 2003) 1–3, 45–6, 54–63, 81–3, 105–8, 197.

[5] P.Dura I 30 (232 CE-Dura Europos); P.Eleph. 1 = MChr 283 (310 BCE-
Elephantine); P.Giss. 2 = C. Ptol.Sklav. 55 (173 BCE-Fayum); P.Mur. 115 = SB X
10305 (124 CE-Bethbassi [Judaea]); P.Oxy. III 496 = MChr 287 (127 CE-Oxyrhynchos);
P.Oxy. III 497 (II CE-Oxyrhynchos); P.Oxy. VI 905 (170 CE-Oxyrhynchos); P.Oxy.
X 1273 = Sel.Pap. I 5 (260 CE-Oxyrhynchos); P.Vind.Bosw. 5 (304 CE-Hermopolis).
An *ekdosis*-clause also appears in the *descriptum* P.Oxy. II 372 descriptum.2 (74–75
CE-Oxyrhynchos) (Yiftach-Firanko [supra note 4] pp. 328–9), and probably also in
P.Oxy. 604 descriptum (II CE-Oxyrhynchos) (Yiftach-Firanko pp. 331–2), where we
find in line 3 the participle προσφερομένην, which (see infra note 19) is a typical
component of the *ekdosis*-clause.

[6] First published by H. Cotton in *JRS* 84 (1994) 64–86. Possibly also P.Yadin
37 = P.Hever 65. See discussion infra in text at notes 39–42.

[7] H.J. Wolff, "Eherecht und Familienverfassung in Athen," *Beiträge zur Rechtsgeschichte
Altgriechenlands und des hellenistisch-römischen Ägyptens* (Weimar 1961) 155–242 at 158;
Mélèze (supra note 4) 47–9.

The Egyptian *ekdosis* was from its very beginnings of a completely different nature. The reference to the begetting of children was completely dispensed with,[8] and the rule that the delivery of the bride had to be carried out by a male relative was overridden.[9] In the case where both parents were alive, the deliverer was either the bride's father or both the father and the mother; if one of them was dead, the remaining one alone.[10]

If both parents were dead and provided the girl was still a παρθένος, that is "young girl," she would be delivered by a third person.[11] If she was not a παρθένος, and especially if she had already been married before, the most likely scenario would be auto-*ekdosis*, that is, the bride delivering herself into marriage.[12]

---

[8] Not, however, in Clem. Al. *Strom.* 2.23.1 referred to by Mélèze (supra note 4) 63 no. 115.

[9] The mother functions as the deliverer of the bride as early as the fourth century BCE (P.Eleph. 1-310 BCE) and in the third-century P.Petrie² I 25.25–27 (226–25 BCE-Crocodilopolis). The latter case is especially striking, since the testator and his wife expect their eldest son to come of age in the near future. In that case, Athenian law would prescribe the performance of the *ekdosis* by him. This is not, however, the arrangement made in P.Petrie² I 25. For the origins of the *ekdosis* performed by the mother, see W. Erdmann, "Die Rolle der Mutter bei Verheiratung der Tochter nach griechischem Recht," *ZSav* 59 (1939) 544–6.

[10] The father is recorded as the deliverer of the bride in altogether five cases: the marriage documents P.Oxy. III 496 = MChr 287; 497; VI 905 and the Judaean P.Yadin 18. In P.Oxy. III 496 = MChr 287 the father is attested to have delivered his daughter alone, but following (line 5) is a clause in which his mother— the grandmother of the bride—declares that she has delivered the bride as well. An *ekdosis* conducted by the father is also attested in the petition P.Ryl. IV 706, if we accept the highly sound restoration by Youtie (*ZPE* 21 [1976] 199–201) to line 3. In four cases the *ekdosis* is performed by both parents: the marriage documents P.Eleph. 1 = MChr 283; BGU IV 1100 (a documentation of the act of *ekdosis* in a dowry receipt); P.Oxy. XLIX 3491; BGU IV 1105 (a petition). In nine cases the sole deliverer is the mother: P.Oxy. II 372 descriptum (Yiftach-Firanko [supra note 4] pp. 328–9); P.Oxy. X 1273 = Sel.Pap. I 5); P.Vind.Bosw. 5; PSI Congr.XX 10 recto 14–28 and probably also in the Judaean P.Hever 69, as well as in the petitions P.Cair.Preis. 2+3; P.Oxy. LIV 3770; UPZ I 2 = P.Lond. I 24 p. 31 and the will P.Petrie² I 25.

[11] By other relatives: in P.Amst. I 40 (a dowry receipt) the brother-in-law, in P. Oxy. III 496 = MChr 287 the grandmother. A delivery by the paternal uncle, acting as the bride's guardian, is referred to in P.Oxy. XVII 2133; in CPR I 27 = Stud.Pal. XX 15 (dowry-receipt) it is the guardian; in P.Lips. I 41 = MChr 300 it is a *curator*. For the translation of παρθένος as "young girl" see infra note 36.

[12] See W. Erdmann, "Die Eheschließung im Rechte der gräko-ägyptischen Papyri von der Besetzung bis in die Kaiserzeit," *ZSav* 60 (1940) 151–84 at 158. Auto-*ekdosis* is attested in P.Giss. 2; P.Oxy. XLIX 3500; P.Dura I 30, possibly also in P.Mur. 115 = SB X 10305. Only in the last two cases are we directly informed that the auto-*ekdosis* took place on the occasion of the wife's second marriage.

The *ekdosis*-clause is usually opened with the blessing ἀγαθῇ τύχῃ.[13] The most common formulation of the clause is objective, the act of *ekdosis* usually being reported as a *fait accompli* in the aorist tense.[14] If the act is reported from the deliverer's point of view, the verb used to signify it is the medial form of ἐκδίδωμι, and in one case, third-century P.Dura 30 from Dura-Europos, the active form of παραδίδωμι; if described from the point of view of the receiver, the verb used would be λαμβάνω.[15]

Since a person could be handed over for other purposes as well, including into non-matrimonial types of cohabitation,[16] it was indispensable to mention that marriage was the purpose of the delivery. This purpose was expressed either as a change in the legal position of the bride—εἶναι γυναῖκα γαμετήν[17]—or as the creation of marriage—εἰς γάμου κοινωνίαν.[18]

---

[13] P.Dura. I 30.5; P.Giss. 2.8; P.Oxy. III 496.1 = MChr 287; P.Oxy. X 1273.1= Sel.Pap. I 5; P.Oxy. XLIX 3500.1; P.Vind.Bosw. 5.1; PSI Congr.XX 10 recto 14–28 at line 15. This invocation appears in only one marriage document that does not contain the *ekdosis*-clause—the Ptolemaic BGU VI 1283.7 (216/5 BCE-Oxyrhynchites). See H.J. Wolff, *Written and Unwritten Marriages in Hellenistic and Postclassical Roman Law* (Haverford 1939) 21.

[14] Objective + aorist in: P.Giss. I 2; P.Oxy. II 372 descriptum (Yiftach-Firanko [supra note 4] pp. 328–9); III 496 = MChr 287; [VI 905]; X 1273 = Sel.Pap. I 5; XLIX 3491; 3500; PSI Congr.XX 10 recto 14–28; P.Yadin. 18; P.Hever 69. Objective + present tense in P.Eleph. 1 = MChr 283 = Jur.Pap. 18 = PapPrimer⁴ 25 = Pestman, *Primer* 1. Subjective in the "additional delivery" performed by the grandmother of the bride in P.Oxy. 496 = MChr 287 1.5; P.Vind.Bosw. 5; P.Mur. 115 = SB X 10305; P.Dura I 30.

[15] In P.Mur 115 = SB X 10305 the verb προσλαμβάνω probably signifies the retaking of the wife, that is, the renewal of a dissolved marriage (infra note 45). Ἐκδίδωμι and παραδίδωμι could be used interchangeably. See Wolff (supra note 7) 164. The verb λαμβάνω could be used in a much less technical sense as well. See P.Cair.Masp. II 67092.9–10 (553 CE-Aphrodito).

[16] Is. 3.39: οἱ ἐπὶ παλλακίᾳ διδόντες τὰς ἑαυτῶν. See E. Grzybek, "Die griechische Konkubine und ihre 'Mitgift' (P.Eleph. 3 und 4)," *ZPE* 76 (1989) 206–12.

[17] P.Eleph. 1.3 = MChr 283: γυναῖκα γνησίαν; P.Giss. 2.11: [εἶναι] γυναῖκα γαμετήν; P.Oxy. XLIX 3491.5: . . .] γ(υναῖκα) γαμετήν; P.Mur. III 115.5 = SB X 10305: εἰ[ς γυναῖ]κα γαμετήν.

[18] P.Oxy. VI 905.4–5: πρὸς γάμου κοι[νωνίαν]; P.Oxy. X 1273.4 = Sel.Pap. I 5: πρὸς γάμον; P.Vind.Bosw. 5.11–12: πρὸς γάμου [κοινωνίαν τέκνων γνησίων σπορᾶς - -]| ἕνεκεν κατὰ νόμον Πάπιον Ποππαῖον; P.Dura. I 30.10–11: πρὸς γάμ[ο]υ κοιγων{ε} [ίαν]; BGU IV 1100.10: πρὸς βίου κοινωνίαν; CPR I 27.30–31 = Stud.Pal. XX 15: πρὸς γάμου κοινωνίαν; no reference to the purpose of marriage in P.Oxy. III 496 = MChr 287; P.Oxy. XLIX 3500. Unique is P.Yadin 18, the only clause in which both formulas appear together (lines 6–7): γυναῖκα | γαμετὴν πρὸς γάμου κοινωγ[ία]ν κατὰ τοὺς νόμους; see also the outer text lines 37–39. The general reference to the νόμοι is not found in any other marriage document.

Equally essential is the linkage between the act of *ekdosis* and the delivery of a dowry. The delivery of the dowry is attested either in the same sentence as the *ekdosis*-clause, connected with it by the medial present participle of the verb προσφέρω with the bride generally as subject and the dowry as object, or, in a later period, in a separate sentence in which the connection between the delivery of the dowry and the delivery of the bride is made clear.[19] This connection was so close that any family member who gave the bride a substantial piece of property could be described as performing the *ekdosis*, even in cases where it is clear that he did not do so.[20] The connection between the *ekdosis* and the delivery of the dowry will later prove to be essential for the understanding of the evolution of the act of *ekdosis* in the Roman period.

Most documents attesting marital arrangements in the Roman period do not contain the *ekdosis*-clause. Eight of the nine documents which do contain it in this period (31 BCE–400 CE) originate from Oxyrhynchos, whereas the rest of Egypt provides us with one single document of this kind, P.Vind.Bosw. 5 from 305 CE Hermopolis.[21]

---

[19] Προσφερομένην: P.Eleph. 1.4 = MChr 283; P.Giss. 2.12; P.Yadin 18.7, 39; P.Dura. I 30.12.

In P.Vind.Bosw. 5.6 the mother delivers the dowry (καὶ προσενηνοχέναι); in BGU IV 1100.11 both parents (προσενηνεγμέγροι). P.Oxy. III 496.2–3 = MChr 287: ἀ[πέχει δὲ ὁ γαμῶν παρὰ Σαραπίωνος τοῦ πατρὸς] | [κ]αὶ ἐκδότου καὶ δίδωσι κτλ.; P.Oxy. VI 905.5: ἡ δ' ἔκδοτ]ος φέρει τῷ ἀνδρὶ [εἰς φε]ρνήν; P.Oxy. X 1273.5 = Sel. Pap. I 5: ᾧ προσφέρει ἡ αὐτὴ ἐκδότις. Also possible is a simple reference to the dowry within the *ekdosis*-clause as in P.Mur. 115.5 = SB X 10305: σὺν προικὶ (δραχμῶν). It is worth mentioning that the verb φέρω with its various compounds is used in marriage documents mainly to denote the delivery of the dowry in connection with the act of *ekdosis* (see Wolff [supra note 13] 16–7). There is no apparent connection between the two acts in P.Oxy. XLIX 3491.5: ἐφ' ᾗ ἔσχ[η(κεν) ?] ὁ γαμῶν, perhaps because in this case the dowry was handed over sometime after the performance of the *ekdosis*.

[20] P.Oxy. III 496.5–6 = MChr 287. A skeptical attitude toward the *ekdosis*, allegedly performed by the grandmother of the bride, may be expressed in the subjective formulation ([ὁ]μολογεῖ ἐγδοῦναι), which stands in apparent contrast to the objective formulation in the description of the *ekdosis* performed by the father (line 2).

[21] Among the documents of marriage from Oxyrhynchos (apart from the descripta whose form we do not know) the *ekdosis*-documents form roughly a half: 8 out of 18. The rest are formulated as dowry-receipts (8 documents), as a simple promissory note (1 case), or as a declaration of an oath made by the wife (1 case). See Yiftach-Firanko (supra note 4) 17. P.Vind.Bosw. 5, which has recently been reedited and discussed by N. Kruit and K. Worp in *Analecta Papyrologica* 13 (2001) 81–90, is the only marriage document from the Hermopolites preserved. We cannot establish, however, on the base of this single document, whether the *ekdosis* documents were as popular in this nome as they were in the Oxyrhynchites.

This situation has given rise to numerous theories as to the evolution of Greek marriage customs in Egypt in the Roman period. W. Erdmann and J. Mélèze interpret it as a sign of diminishing interest in the documentation of the *ekdosis*, but neither claims that the performance of the act was dispensed with as a rule. Mélèze even regards the act of *ekdosis* as one of the most essential features of the Greek marriage throughout the Ptolemaic and Roman periods.[22]

H.J. Wolff, on the other hand, interprets the absence of the *ekdosis*-clause in most marriage documents as a sign that the *act* of *ekdosis* itself was dispensed with, as people started to form marriages through the de-facto joining of life;[23] in his view, the survival of the *ekdosis*-clause in Oxyrhynchos proves that in this region alone people held on to the old act of marriage. And finally, the most radical of all in denying the *ekdosis* any practical role is E. Kutzner, who in his 1989 study "Untersuchungen zur Stellung der Frau im römischen Oxyrhynchos" regards the *ekdosis*-clause even in this region as a "Formularbestandteil, der . . . kaum noch praktische Bedeutung besessen haben dürfte."[24]

There is no doubt that the *ekdosis*-clause rarely appears in documents dealing with matrimonial arrangements during the Roman period. But does this necessarily imply that the act of *ekdosis* itself was less frequently practiced than before, or that it was gradually abandoned in favor of another act of marriage? Does it imply, moreover, that the *ekdosis*, if performed, had lost its legal significance and that, in consequence, people showed little interest in documenting it?

I believe that the answer to all these questions should be no. It is true that documents that contain the *ekdosis*-clause originate in the Roman period primarily from Oxyrhynchos. Yet, according to the information gathered from other types of papyrological sources, as well as non-papyrological ones, the act of *ekdosis* itself seems to have been practiced during the Roman period in Oxyrhynchos no more than in any other part of Egypt: two occurrences in Alexandrian sources, two in sources from the Arsinoite nome, three from Oxyrhyn-

---

[22] Erdmann (supra note 12) 161; Mélèze (supra note 4) 57, 68.
[23] Wolff (supra note 7) 174–75; idem (supra note 13) 27–28.
[24] E. Kutzner, *Untersuchungen zur Stellung der Frau im römischen Oxyrhynchos* (Frankfurt 1989) 42.

chos, two from Hermopolis, one from Antinoopolis, and, finally, one of unknown provenance.[25]

The conclusion that the act of *ekdosis* was just as common in other parts of Egypt as in Oxyrhynchos finds further support in the famous P.Oxy. II 237 (186 CE). This is a petition submitted to the prefect Pomponius Faustianus by a woman named Dionysia, who claims that her father Chairemon should not be allowed to dissolve her marriage against her will.[26] In order to support her claim, she cites four precedents, in two of which (VII 19–29, VIII 4–7) it is argued that if a father performed the *ekdosis* of his daughter he should not be allowed henceforth to dissolve her marriage. In one of these two cases, the minutes of a hearing that took place before the prefect Flavius Titianus in 128, we find mentioned an epistrategos named Bassus, identified by J.D. Thomas as the M. Aemilius Bassus who served in this office either in Pelusium or in the Thebaid around 128 CE. We may therefore regard this case as referring to a legal situation in one of these epistrategies, and in any case not in Oxyrhynchos.[27]

As these two precedents show, in the second century CE the *ekdosis* was a living institution to the extent that legal representatives could use it as a corner-stone for their reasoning. If we accept the opinions expressed in these two precedents as correct (and we do not have to), the question of the performance of the *ekdosis*, and even more that of the identity of its performer, were decisive for the legal position of the bride. In any case, we may not regard the *ekdosis* as an "inhaltlos gewordene Formalität", as Erdmann does.[28]

---

[25] Alexandria: BGU IV 1100.7–11; 1105.5–6 and also Clemens Alexandrinus frg. 64 (ed. O. Staehlin) III 228, dealt with by Mélèze (supra note 4) 62 note 108. Fayum: CPR I 27.29–30 = Stud.Pal. XX 15; P.Flor. I 36.24–25 = P.Sakaon 38. Oxyrhynchos: P.Oxy. III 497.21; XVII 2133.14–15; LIV 3770.2–4. Hermopolis: P.Cair.Preis. 2+3.13–14; P.Lips. I 41.4 (?) = MChr 300 (ἄγεσθαι βο[ύ]λεσθαι τὴν παῖδα). Antinoopolis: P.Ryl. IV 706.3—according to Youtie's restoration, published in *ZPE* 21 (1976) 199–201. Unknown provenance: P.Amst. I 40.7–9.

[26] See now, at length, Yiftach-Firanko (supra note 4) 47–9, 84–91.

[27] J.D. Thomas, *The Epistrategos in Ptolemaic and Roman Egypt. Part 2—The Roman Epistrategos* (Cologne-1982) 186 no. 16, 194–5. Oxyrhynchos is occasionally said to be 'in the Thebaid'. This is however a geographic rather than an administrative designation. See J.D. Thomas, "The Administrative Divisions of Egypt," in D.H. Samuel (ed.), *Proceedings of the 12th International Congress of Papyrology* (Toronto 1970) 465–9 at 466.

[28] Erdmann (supra note 12) 161.

It is also noteworthy that we do not find in the source material any act of marriage other than the *ekdosis*. When the formation of marriage is referred to with no mention of the *ekdosis*, it is described in general terms, as, for example, in the Alexandrian *synchoresis*-documents from the Augustan period: συνεληλυθέναι ἀλλήλοις πρὸς βίου κοινωνίαν—"we have joined each other in partnership of life", not hinting at any other act that could have been used to constitute the bond other than the act of *ekdosis*.[29] This lack of reference to any other act of marriage among more than 300 Egyptian documents relating directly or indirectly to marriage customs suggests that the act of *ekdosis* was the only form of marriage the Greek population of Egypt was ever acquainted with.[30]

I have thus reached the following conclusions: (1) Although documents which contain the *ekdosis*-clause are rare outside Oxyrhynchos, other sources suggest that the act of *ekdosis* itself was widely practiced in Roman Egypt. (2) As shown by P.Oxy. II 237, this act had a legal significance in the Roman period. (3) It is the only act of marriage attested by the source material. Yet, if the act of *ekdosis* was so significant for the formation of marriage, how can we explain the fact that the documents that contain the *ekdosis*-clause are so rare and so unevenly distributed?

We should first of all pay attention to the fact that—apart from these "*ekdosis*-documents"—almost all the documents that are referred to in many modern studies as "marriage documents" were in both the Ptolemaic and the Roman period nothing more than dowry receipts. As such they were focused at settling the material aspects of the marriage rather than at reporting the way in which it was created.[31] In most of these dowry receipts, the person who was

---

[29] E.g. BGU 1050.6 = MChr 286. Cf. W. Erdmann (supra note 12) 177, who believes that in the Alexandrian documents it was the *mutuus consensus* that created the marriage.

[30] A possible exception is P.Berol. inv. 25423 = SB XXIV 16072 + 16073 (W. Brashear, "An Alexandrian Marriage Contract," in R. Katzoff, D. Schaps, and J. Petroff [eds.], *Classical Studies in Honor of David Sohlberg* [Ramat-Gan 1996] 367–84), where the husband is said (lines 9–11 of the final copy) to be πεπο⟨ι⟩ημένος ⟨ε⟩ἰς τὴν [Θαυβάριον] | ἣν διέχουσιν διϰ.[στηρίω . . . . . .] | [τ]ὴν χ⟨ε⟩ῖρα{ν}.

[31] This fact is exemplified by a plea from the time of Marcus Aurelius, P.Mil.Vogl. II 71, which was submitted by a wife to the *exegetes*, and by which she requested him to appoint a *kyrios ad hoc* for her for the composition of such a dowry receipt. She explains (lines 21–23) that she wants to draw up the document "since I wish to carry along to Ammonas, my long-married husband from the same village, as

reported to have delivered the dowry was also the one who performed, or was entitled to perform, the *ekdosis*—that is, the bride or
one of her parents. Since the act of *ekdosis* and the delivery of the
dowry were so closely connected, the explicit documentation of the
former was not considered necessary as long as the latter was
recorded.[32] If, on the other hand, the person who delivered the dowry
was not one who would under normal circumstances perform the
ekdosis, one would be inclined to refer to the act of *ekdosis* explicitly.
Accordingly, this act is recorded in only one out of the seventy-five
dowry receipts in which the dowry is delivered by the bride, one of
her parents or both—BGU IV 1100 (Alexandria-Augustan period),
whereas of the four documents in which the deliverer of the dowry
is a different person, it is documented in two: CPR I 27 = Stud.Pal
XX 15 (190 CE-Ptolemais Euergetis) and P.Amst. I 40 (first century
CE-origin unknown).[33]

A consideration of P.Amst. I 40 may explain this tendency:

[ὁμολογεῖ Δίδυμος - - τῷ Βακχύλῳ - - ἔχειν παρὰ Βακχύλου - - ἐπὶ τῇ τῆς
γυ]|ναῖκος| [αὐτο]ῦ| Θαισοῦτο[ς]| τῆς |καὶ Διδυ[μα]ρίου | ἀδελφῇ{ς}[34]
[Ν]ιννοῦ|τι τῇ καὶ Σεραπιάδι | παρθένῳ οὔσῃ | ἐγδεδομένη ὑ|π᾽ αὐτοῦ
Βακχύλου | καὶ συνερχομένου[35] | αὐτῷ Διδύμῳ πρὸς | γάμον φερνή⟨ν⟩
ἀρ|[γυρίου - -]

[Didymos . . . acknowledges to Bakkhylos . . . the receipt of] a dowry
[   ] in favor of Ninnous also known as Serapias, the sister of his wife

---

addition to the dowry, two quarters of approved gold in jewellery and clothing in
value of 40 drachmae. And on my own account to register Eudaimonis, a daughter born to us jointly." The woman shows no particular interest in documenting
the formation of the marriage per se.

[32] See supra text at notes 19–20.

[33] Besides CPR I 27 = Stud.Pal. XX 15 and P.Amst. I 40 we find a brother
delivering the dowry in P.Mich. V 343 (54–55 CE-Tebtunis), and a foster-father in
SB VI 9372 (2nd century CE-Oxyrhynchos). We count (leaving out the documents
containing the *ekdosis*-clause) in the Ptolemaic and Roman period (4th century
BCE–4th century CE) fifty-one cases in which the wife delivers the dowry herself,
eleven in which the father delivers the dowry and thirteen in which the wife's
mother does. In three to five cases the dowry is delivered by both parents. See
Yiftach-Firanko (supra note 4) 276–80.

[34] In P.Amst. I 40, we have difficulties in seeing in the photograph the ς of
ἀδελφῆς in line 5. But even if the very small spot of ink after the ἀδελφῇ is ς, it
is still possible to consider the genitive as mistakenly used for the dative, just as is
the case in line 25 of the same document. We propose therefore the reading ἀδελφῇ
or ἀδελφῇ{ς}.

[35] Read συνερχομένῃ.

Thaisous also known as Didymarion, who, being a young girl, is delivered by the same Bakkhylos and joins the same Didymos in marriage.

We assume that the bride, Ninnous, was an orphan at the time of
her marriage. She did not, however, reach the age at which she
would be financially independent and could contract her own marital arrangement. She was specifically a παρθένος—a "young girl."[36]
In this situation the person who "gave her out" and furnished her
with a dowry was Bakkhylos, her brother-in-law. Since, however,
brothers-in-law would not usually perform these acts, the very validity of the union as a lawful marriage might later be challenged, and
recording its formation, that is the act of *ekdosis*, became advisable
in order to forestall such a challenge. A reference of this kind was,
on the other hand, hardly necessary if the person who delivered the
dowry was the one who usually would perform the *ekdosis*. In such
a case the marriage was presumed to have been created properly, and
an explicit reference to the act of *ekdosis* could be dispensed with.[37]

The fact that the *ekdosis*-clause was incorporated in the Oxyrhynchite
documents has, according to this explanation, no bearing on the
question of the performance or non-performance of the act of *ekdosis* per se. It does indeed, as Wolff claims, suggest conservative tendencies in Oxyrhynchos. Not, however, because the *ekdosis* was
performed in this nome alone, but because people here still felt it
necessary to insert into their marriage documents a clause that would
officially attest its performance.

The Ekdosis *in the Greek Marriage Documents from the Judaean Desert*

Among the papyri from the Judaean Desert, the act of *ekdosis* may
well have been documented in all the Greek marriage documents

---

[36] The term παρθένος is often translated as *virgin*—see Lewis' translation to P.Yadin
18 (p. 85), or Sijpesteijn's translation to P.Lond. II 294 descr., *ZPE* 111 (1996)
163–70 at 169. This is however only one of the meanings of this word, which could
be occasionally used for any young, unmarried girl (See LSJ⁹ 1339, Preisigke, WB
II 269). Sexual inexperience formed no doubt an important aspect of this term, but
just as much the social, legal and financial dependency of the bride, which, I think,
plays a more important role in this context. Cf. also P.Ryl. II 125.23 where παρθένος
is translated by the editors as "*unmarried*".

[37] See in particular P.Flor. 36 = P.Sakaon 38 (312 CE-Theadelphia); see also
Yiftach-Firanko (supra note 4) 51–2.

whose upper part was to some extent preserved. This clause undoubtedly appears in P.Hever 69: a mother is reported to have delivered her daughter Shelamzion. The *ekdosis* is reported in an objective form (third person–aorist) in close connection with the delivery of the dowry[38]—all in conformity with the source material from Egypt.

In another document, P.Yadin 37, republished by Hannah Cotton as P.Hever 65, the existence of an *ekdosis*-clause is controversial. According to Lewis' restoration of lines 4–5,[39] Jesus son of Menachem acknowledges that he has taken Salome Komaïse to be his wedded wife. According to Cotton's restoration, all that we face here is a simple dowry receipt, in which Menachem acknowledges to Salome the receipt of 96 denarii as her dowry.[40] The formula ὥστε αὐτούς, which we regard as the beginning of the "designation of purpose" found in almost all the Greek *ekdosis*-documents from Egypt as well as in P.Yadin 18, leads us to prefer Lewis' restoration of these particular lines. True, the use of the subjective formulation (ὁμολογεῖ εἰληφέναι) differs from that of the two clear *ekdosis* formulas in P.Yadin 18 and P.Hever 69, and the fact that the couple is said to have lived together may speak against such an interpretation. But neither counter-argument is insurmountable. The subjective formulation is well attested;[41] as to the fact that the couple lived together earlier, nowhere is it said that the *ekdosis* took place on the occasion of the composition of the present document. It is just as likely that an *ekdosis* that took place on the occasion of the beginning of joint life would be documented also in a later instrument.[42]

---

[38] The *ekdosis* is attested in lines 3–5, the delivery of the dowry and the other financial arrangements in connection with the formation of marriage in lines 6–9. Cotton's suggestion that the participle προσφερομένην may be restored at the end of line 5 is no doubt acceptable—this is of course if we assume that the wife "brought along" the dowry herself. Other formulas are possible as well—see supra note 19.

[39] εἰληφέναι Σ]αλώμην καλουμένην Κο[μαῒν ± 12] | γυναῖκα Μ[α]ωζηνὴν ὥστε αὐτούς {ὥστε α[ὐτοὺς] - -

[40] H. Cotton and A. Yardeni, *Discoveries in the Judaean Desert XVII* (Oxford 1997) (= *P.Hever*) 228–9. Cotton assumes the formula: ὁμολογεῖ Ἰησοῦς πρὸς Σαλώμην ἀπεσχηκέναι καὶ ὀφείλειν τὴν προῖκα κτλ., and regards the composition of the dowry receipt after a period of cohabitation as equivalent to the alleged Greek transformation of ἄγραφος γάμος into ἔγγραφος γάμος. See Yiftach-Firanko (supra note 4) 94–102.

[41] See supra note 14.

[42] Similar situation in P.Oxy. XLIX 3491.1–5.

P.Mur. II 115 is just as problematic.

νυν{ε}ὶ ὁμολογεῖ ὁ αὐτὸς Ἐλαῖος Σίμω[νος] | ἐξ ἀνανεώσεος[43] καταλλάξαι κ[αὶ] προσλαβέσθαι τὴν αὐτὴν Σαλώ[μην Ἰω]άγ[ο]υ Γ[αλγο]υλὰ εἰ[ς γυναῖ]κα γαμετὴν σὺν προικὶ (δραχμῶν) ͞σ κτλ.[44]

... now the same Elaios son of Simon acknowledges that by renewal he reconciled and retook the same Salome daughter of Johannes-Galgula to be his wedded wife, with a dowry amounting to 200 drachmai ...

The verb used to denote the act of marriage, προσλαμβάνω, reminds us of the λαμβάνω used to describe the *ekdosis* from the point of view of the groom in P.Eleph. 1 (λαμβάνω). The prefix προσ- emphasizes the fact that it is the couple's second marriage and that Elaios *re*took Salome.[45] The identification of the above-cited lines as an *ekdosis*-clause is also supported by two further features: (1) the designation of purpose (εἰ[ς γυναῖ]κα γαμετήν), and (2) the connection made in it between the act of delivery (or rather receipt) of the bride and the delivery of the dowry.

Yet this is a unique kind of *ekdosis*. A couple, who had lived together earlier, has dissolved its marriage, and now, after reconciliation, restores it. How ambiguous this situation was we learn both from papyrological as well as other legal sources.[46] We do not know, therefore, what formulaic form the *ekdosis* would assume on such an occasion. As in other cases of the wife's remarriage, we may assume an auto-*ekdosis*. This is possibly what we have here: an *ekdosis*-clause attesting an act of auto-*ekdosis*, which was modified by, and adapted to, the peculiar situation in which the couple found itself on the occasion of its reunion.

In the fourth marriage document, P.Yadin 18, we find the most comprehensive and well preserved *ekdosis*-clause among the Judaean documents (lines 3–7):

---

[43] Read: ἀνανεώσεως.

[44] Lines 4–5.

[45] This translation appears neither in *LSJ*[9] 1518–9 nor in Preisigke, *WB* II 407. This is, however, how Benoit, *P.Mur.* p. 250, translated this verb ("reprendre la même femme").

[46] We know, for example, that no special clauses were developed within the Greek formulaic tradition to deal with such a reunion, as in the case of 'the declaration of joint life' in P.Oxy. XII 1473.10–11, and in the case of the ἀσφαλείαι composed in similar circumstances according to P.Oxy. L 3581.8–11. See Dig. 23.3.33.

ἐξέδοτο Ἰούδας Ἐ]λεα[ζ]άρου το[ῦ καὶ] | Χθουσίωνος Σ[ελα]μψιώγην [τὴν ἰδίαν θυγατέρα α]ὐτοῦ παρθένον Ἰούδα[τι υἱῷ] | Ἀναγίου Σωμαλα καλουμένῳ [Κίμβερι, ἀμφότεροι ἀπὸ κώμης Ἐνγαδῶν τ]ῆς Ἰουδαί | [ας ἐ]νθάδε καταμέν-οντες, εἶναι τὴν Σελαμψιώγην⟨ν⟩ Ἰούδατι Κίμβερι γυναῖκα | γαμετὴν πρὸς γάμου κοινων[ία]ν κατὰ τοὺς νόμους, προσφερομένην κτλ.

Judah son of Eleazar, also known as Khthusion, gave over Shelamzion, his very own daughter, a young girl, to Judah surnamed Cimber son of Ananias son of Somalas, both of the village of En-gedi in Judaea residing here, for Shelamzion to be wedded wife to Judah Cimber for the partnership of marriage according to the customs.

It is unanimously agreed that this clause belongs to the Greek for-mulaic tradition.[47] The clause in P.Yadin 18 shares four of the five characteristics of the Egyptian *ekdosis*: objective formulation used of the verb ἐκδίδωμι; the designation of marriage as the purpose of the delivery; and the linkage between the act of *ekdosis* and the delivery of the dowry that is signified through the participle προσφερομένη, whose subject is the bride and whose object is the dowry.[48]

The clause of P.Yadin 18 shows, however, some peculiarities. The first one is the designation of the bride as a παρθένος—"a young girl". In no contemporary Egyptian *ekdosis*-clause is the bride reported to be a παρθένος, and in the two documents that mention the *partheneia* of the bride in connection with the act of *ekdosis* this should proba-bly be attributed to the fact that the *ekdosis* was performed by an outsider. We know that this designation was generally dispensed with if the marriage was transacted by the father or the mother.[49]

This finding may prima facie be used as an argument in favor of Katzoff's *interpretatio hebraica* of this document, according to which the *ekdosis*-clause of P.Yadin 18 reflects a Jewish contemporary custom, attested in the Rabbinic sources, of fathers giving their minor daugh-ters into marriage. This is not, however, strong confirmation. According to the Egyptian material as well, even if the father or mother of the

---

[47] See supra note 3.

[48] The omission of the invocation ἀγαθῇ τύχῃ is not crucial. It is omitted in P.Eleph. 1 = MChr 283, P.Oxy. VI 905, and P.Oxy. XLIX 3491 as well.

[49] Παρθένος appears in Egypt in only 3 out of 84 documents in which the mar-riage is transacted by the bride or by one of her parents (CPR I 24.4–5 = Stud.Pal. XX 5; P.Lond. II 294.5, published in full by P.J. Sijpesteijn in *ZPE* 111 (1996) 163–70; P.Stras. VIII 764.19). Of the four cases in which the marriage is trans-acted by another person, this designation appears in two (CPR I 27 = Stud.Pal. XX 15; P.Amst. I 40).

wife transacted the marriage, a reference to the *partheneia* of the bride was not unthinkable.[50] If such a reference is known in Egypt, we may not exclude the possibility that it was also made among the non-Jewish Greek population of early second-century CE Judaea and Arabia. In any case, the designation of the bride as a παρθένος in the framework of the *ekdosis*-clause is not proven to be a Jewish peculiarity.[51]

It is the second peculiarity that leads us to prefer the *interpretatio graeca* of the *ekdosis*-clause in P.Yadin 18. While the declared purpose of the *ekdosis* is, according to the Egyptian documents, either the formation of marriage (εἰς γάμου κοινωνίαν) or the change of the status of the bride into that of a wedded wife (εἶναι γυναῖκα γαμετήν), we find in P.Yadin 18 an awkward pleonasm:

(1) εἶναι τὴν Σελαμψιώνη(ν) Ἰούδατι Κίμβερι γυναῖκα γαμετήν
(2) πρὸς γάμου κοινωγ[ία]ν
(3) κατὰ τοὺς γόμους

The statement that the marriage is "according to the customs" *per se* can be used to support both the *interpretatio hebraica* and the *interpretatio graeca*, depending on the supposed identity of these "customs."[52] The reference further down in the document to the νόμος ἱλληνικός in the framework of the maintenance-clause (lines 16, 51) cannot promote a Greek identity of the customs of the *ekdosis*-clause, as there is no proven connection between the νόμοι in the two clauses. What does seem to support it, however, is the very context in which the reference to "our" νόμοι is made—in the framework of a distinct Greek clause, in which the author endeavors, so it seems, to cast aside any doubt as to the "Griechentum" of the act, stressing accordingly in any possible way that what has been performed here is the good old Greek *ekdosis*.

In conclusion, the appearance of the *ekdosis*-clause is likely in all four Judaean Desert Greek marriage documents whose initial part

---

[50] See supra note 49.

[51] Katzoff (supra note 1) 240 and also (supra note 2, 1991) 173–4. Documents in which the bride is designated as παρθένος and the dowry is delivered by her natural *ekdotes* are: CPR I 24.4–5 = Stud.Pal. XX 5; P.Stras. VIII 764.19; P.Lond. II 294.5 published in full by P.J. Sijpesteijn in *ZPE* 111 (1996) 163–70.

[52] Katzoff (supra note 1) 241; Wasserstein (supra note 2) 113. As Katzoff points out (*ibid.*, p. 240), νόμοι should be translated as *customs* rather than as *laws*.

is preserved. In P.Yadin 18 and P.Hever 69 it is undisputed. In P.Yadin 37 = P.Hever 65 we tend to accept its restoration, as suggested by N. Lewis, because of the ὥστε αὐτούς in line 5, which seems to us to be the designation of purpose known from other *ekdosis*-clauses. In P.Mur. II 115, we suggest that lines 4–5 form an *ekdosis*-clause adapted to the peculiar situation of the restoration of a dissolved union.[53]

This finding has two implications: First, it shows that *ekdosis* was the only attested Greek act of marriage not only in Egypt, but also in the Greek documents from the Judaean Desert.[54] Second, it shows that in the Judaean Desert, even more than in Oxyrhynchos, one did not dispense with the incorporation of the *ekdosis*-clause in the marriage documents even when the dowry was delivered by the bride or one of her parents (see pages 10–11). In other words, the very documentation of the delivery of the dowry did not suffice to establish the presumption that the *ekdosis* had taken place and it therefore had to be recorded explicitly.

This phenomenon may be attributed to the conservative tendencies of the Greek scribes in this province of Arabia as compared with their Egyptian counterparts. Yet we would consider another explanation. Considering the financial transactions brought about by the marriage, we find a completely different mechanism in the Judaean documents from that known in the contemporary Greek papyri from Egypt.

Some similarities are undeniable. Both in the Judaean documents and in those originating from Egypt we find the same terms denoting various types of property conveyed in connections to the marriage: προίξ, φερνή, προσφορά. In addition, the προσφορά—the dowry brought along by Shelamzion in P.Yadin 18 on the occasion of her marriage—is essentially the same institution as the Egyptian φερνή—both consist of "silver, gold and clothing."[55]

Yet the Judaean documents show two crucial peculiarities. First is the husband's obligation to the bride of 150% of the value of her dowry, documented in line 13–15 of P.Yadin 18. A contribution on

---

[53] The verb ἐκδίδωμι appears in P.Mur. 116.4 = SB X 10306, but the document is so mutilated that no inference is possible concerning the circumstances.

[54] Possibly the same situation in P.Dura I 30 from 232 CE Dura-Europos.

[55] Lines 8–9, 40–1. Cf. e.g. P.Eleph. 1.4 = MChr 283; BGU IV 1099.8–9; 1100.12–13.

the part of the husband is not evident in Egypt before the fourth century CE.[56] It seems that even in Arabia it was not a well-known institution, for the author of P.Yadin 18 does not seem to have been able to find an appropriate legal term for it.

Second, the terms used to denote the various categories of property in the Judaean document do not correspond to those found in their Egyptian counterparts. Φερνή, which appears in contemporary Greek documents from Egypt to denote clothing, jewels and cash brought by the bride as her dowry, is used in P.Yadin 18 l. 71 to designate the whole property for which the husband is liable.[57] Προσφορά is used in the Judaean documents to designate the dowry and is identical with regard to its components (as just pointed out) with the Egyptian φερνή, whereas the προσφορά in Egypt is any kind of property brought by the wife after the marriage was created— and more technically for landed property and slaves delivered on such an occasion.[58] Προίξ denotes in P.Yadin 18.6 the total amount of the dowry of the bride together with the amount of money that the groom is obliged to pay. In P.Yadin 37.6 and P.Hever 69, on the other hand, it relates to the wife's dowry alone. In Roman Egypt it is used to denote the Roman *dos*, but may occasionally designate any other type of dowry that cannot fit into any other category.[59] Striking is the lack of any designation of the 300 *denarii* promised by the husband in P.Yadin 18.[60]

In Egypt, the documentation of the act of *ekdosis* was thought, according to our explanation, to be dispensable, since a dowry—a Greek dowry—was documented as having been delivered. In the Judaean documents, by contrast, even though such a Greek dowry is evident, it is woven into the non-Greek material mechanism to such an extent that through its documentation alone the *ekdosis* could

---

[56] Yiftach-Firanko (supra note 4) 217.

[57] In P.Mur. 116 = SB X 10306 fr. 1 line 6, its position is not clear: G. Häge, *Ehegüterrechtliche Verhältnisse in den griechischen Papyri Ägyptens bis Diokletian* (Cologne-Graz 1968) 60–1, 141. The φερνή in P.Yadin 18 does, however, resemble in this respect the institution of the φερνή as recorded in the Ptolemaic source material. See Yiftach-Firanko (supra note 4) 107–16.

[58] Häge, (supra fn. 57) 257–9, 282–5; Yiftach-Firanko (supra note 4) 164–75. P.Yadin 18.8, 40 and possibly also in P.Hever 69.6.

[59] See SB VI 9065. See Häge (supra fn. 57) 209.

[60] The term προίξ in line 15 refers to the whole 500 denarii (πάντα εἰς λόγον προι{ο}κός).

not be presumed to have taken place, but rather had to be attested explicitly. Paradoxically, then, the appearance of the *ekdosis*-clause of the second-century Judaean Desert may serve as an indication that the marriage recorded in these documents was of non-Greek nature. What we have here is another example of the attempt to formulate in Greek terms and according to the Greek formulaic tradition institutions and customs of non-Greek origin.

Conclusions

In Egypt the *ekdosis* was the only attested act of marriage; the bride was handed over to the groom for the purpose of marriage accompanied by a dowry. The act was performed by one of her parents, by both, or by the bride herself. In case both parents were dead or otherwise absent and the bride was still too young to form her marriage herself, she would be delivered by a third person, even by one who was not her next-of kin.

In Egypt, the *ekdosis*-clause appears almost exclusively in the Oxyhrynchite nome, whereas in other regions, if couples decided to draw up a written instrument documenting their marriages they were mainly interested in recording the arrangements concerning the dowry and not the act of marriage itself. For this reason they applied in this instrument the formula of a dowry receipt.

These dowry receipts would not in normal circumstances report the performance of *ekdosis*. This, however, was not because the *ekdosis* did not take place, but rather because through the very documentation of the delivery of the dowry the act of *ekdosis* was attested as already performed. A possible exception to this rule were the cases in which the dowry was not delivered by a person who would under normal circumstances perform the *ekdosis*—that is, either the bride or one of her parents. In this event, the *ekdosis* tended to be recorded in the dowry receipts as well, in order to prevent any future doubts as to the validity of the marriage.

In the Judaean Desert, the *ekdosis*-clause was probably incorporated in all four documents whose upper part was preserved. This fact may be attributed to the conservatism of the scribes in this region. A more profound explanation, however, would be the differences between the material mechanism of the marriage here and in the Egyptian documents. In Egypt the delivery of a dowry created the presumption of the performance of the act of *ekdosis*. In the documents of the Judaean Desert the same Greek dowry was woven into an essentially non-Greek financial arrangement to such an extent that from the acknowledgment of receipt of such a dowry the performance of the *ekdosis* could no more be presumed, and had therefore to be attested explicitly. This is, I think, a probable explanation why the *ekdosis*-clause is never dispensed with in the Greek marriage documents from Judaea.

THE WIDOW BABATHA AND THE POOR ORPHAN BOY

Ann Ellis Hanson

Papyrologists who work with the Greek documents from Roman Egypt have found in Babatha and other provincials of the eastern Mediterranean confirmation for our belief that Egypt was by no means a unique province within the Roman system.[1] The texts discovered in Palestine, Syria, and north-western Mesopotamia closely resemble the documents from Egypt and are similar in content—family papers concerned with property and inheritance, private letters, dealings with the Roman bureaucracy through the mechanics of the census, taxation, and military affairs. Like the papyri from Roman Egypt, the documents represent ancient quotidian lives in all their long-ago, yet still vivid, pettiness. The Greek in which they were written is also similar in paleography, in morphology and syntax, in formulae, and in the habit of incorporating expressions and proper names from the various native languages that continued to dominate oral exchanges throughout the region. Writing served essentially the same functions in the Roman Near East as it did in Roman Egypt, and the societies the documents reflect give the feel of being literate ones, even if the numbers who read and wrote as we understand the terms were few. The Jewess Babatha had much in common with many women in Roman Egypt—young mother, young widow, illiterate owner of property. Not only did Babatha share specific life experiences with her Graeco-Egyptian counterparts, but for the most part she seems to have responded to many of them in

[1] The theme animates R.S. Bagnall, *Reading Papyri, Writing Ancient History* (London-New York 1995) and H.M. Cotton, W.E.H. Cockle and F.G.B. Millar, "The Papyrology of the Roman Near East: A Survey," *JRS* 85 (1995) 214–35. See also H.M. Cotton, "The Guardianship of Jesus son of Babatha: Roman and Local Law in the Province of Arabia," *JRS* 83 (1993) 94–108, and *eadem*, "A Canceled Marriage Contract from the Judaean Desert (XHev/Se Gr. 2)," *JRS* 84 (1994) 64–86.

For help in the preparation of this paper, I thank the following and hope they can approve of the use made here of their generous advice and encouragement: Professors R. Katzoff and H. Eshel (both of Bar Ilan University, Ramat-Gan); H.M. Cotton (Hebrew University, Jerusalem); T. Chiusi (Universität München); V. Grimm, R. Wilson, and S. Fraade (all of Yale University, New Haven).

similar fashion. It is the similarities and differences which, I believe,
are pertinent to the themes of this conference, and to them I turn.

When Naphtali Lewis edited Babatha's Greek documents, demog-
raphers of the classical world had not yet focused their attention
upon the census declarations submitted by heads of households in
Roman Egypt between 11 and 257 CE, and social historians of the
ancient Mediterranean still believed that most fertile young widows
returned successfully to the marriage market.[2] The census data, however, reveal not only the harsh mortality functions operative within
the population at large, with life expectancy at birth hovering in the
lower twenties for females and nearly half the infants born dying
before a fifth birthday, but also the early marriage expected for girls,
with the youngest brides about 13 years old and virtually all women
married by age 20, and the fact that a significant number of youngish
widows did not remarry. The majority of the men of the census declarations married for a first time in their mid-twenties, yielding a
mean gap in age between husband and wife at the time of first marriage of about seven and one-half years, although nearly one-quar-
ter of grooms acquired brides some 17 to 18 years their junior.
However much the traditional society preferred to position the sex-
ually active young woman as wife and mother, mistress of her husband's household, prevailing marriage patterns worked against this
preference: the percentage of females who had married and were
still married reaches its high point for women around age 30 and
declines steadily thereafter, while the percentage of males who had
married and were still married continues to climb for men in their
thirties to reach its high point only for those in their mid-forties.[3]
The men of the census declarations married and, if necessary, remarried, with aggressive determination and obvious success, despite their

---

[2] For demographic profiles from the census documents, see, e.g., R.S. Bagnall
and B.W. Frier, *The Demography of Roman Egypt* (Cambridge 1994); J.-U. Krause,
Verwitwung und Wiederverheiratung (Witwen und Waisen im römischen Reich I, Stuttgart
1994); R. Saller, *Patriarchy, Property and Death in the Roman Family* (Cambridge 1994).
Krause, *Verwitwung* 2–3, lists those social historians who either assumed the number of unmarried women in the Roman populations to be small, or who felt they
had established remarriage as common for a particular population within the late
Republic or Empire. Particularly important for the wide acceptance of the proposition that young widows usually remarried was the study by M. Humbert, *Le
remariage à Rome. Étude d'histoire juridique et sociale* (Milan 1972).
[3] Bagnall and Frier (supra note 2) 121–6.

increasing age, while only some younger widows and divorcées were successful when they reentered the marriage market. Being propertied and well-dowered for a second time around, as well as less than 30 years of age, enhanced the likelihood that a widow might find a new husband.[4]

Babatha's life pattern is one frequently encountered in Roman Egypt: early marriage, perhaps a bride between 13 and 16 years; pregnancy not long thereafter, bringing the birth of the desired son and heir, followed by at least 18 months to two and one-half years for nursing her baby.[5] Her son Jesus, the child of her first marriage, not only required the guardians (*epitropoi*) appointed for him by the council of Petra in the first half of 124 CE, but still required the guardians eight years later.[6] The fact that the Petran council undertook such action at some point between 27 February and 28 June 124 demonstrates that the baby's father was dead and Babatha herself already a widow for the first time. Although additional pregnancies cannot be ruled out for the first marriage, no other child survived to be mentioned in Babatha's documents. Thus her first marriage was apparently of short duration and widowhood probably came when the child of that union was still a toddler, perhaps yet a nursling.[7] However old her first husband Jesus may have been, Babatha's second husband, Judah, son of Eleazar Khthousion, was certainly older than she, for the daughter of his first marriage, Shelamzion, was old enough to become the bride of Judah Cimber through a written contract of marriage on 5 April 128 (P.Yadin =

---

[4] In P.Coll.Youtie II 67 (Oxyrhynchus 260/1 CE), the prominent and wealthy Aurelia Dioscuriaena not only acknowledged the return of the very substantial dowry her recently widowed daughter Aurelia Apollinarion had brought her groom in their original marriage contract, but announced her intention to bestow the returned items upon her daughter once again, whenever she was to be married to a new husband.

[5] For a collection of nursing contracts from Roman Egypt, the majority of which specify a period of between 18 and 39 months, see M.M. Masciadri, and O. Montevecchi, *I contratti di baliatico* (= *CPGr* I, Milan 1984) 32–35.

[6] P.Yadin **27**, and cf. H.M. Cotton and J.C. Greenfield, "Babatha's Property and the Law of Succession in the Babatha Archive," *ZPE* 104 (1994) 211–24, especially 221–2.

[7] Women of the census documents continued to bear children throughout their fertile lives, although lactation had a dampening effect on their fertility: B.W. Frier, "Natural Fertility and Family Limitation in Roman Marriage," *CP* 89 (1994) 318–33, especially 322–3, 332.

P.Babatha **18**).[8] Judah, son of Eleazar Khthousion, died at some
point between April 128 (**19**) and June 130 (**20**), leaving Babatha a
widow for the second time. As Naphtali Lewis suggested, Babatha
was likely to have been about 30 years old at the time of her death.[9]

Lewis also suggested that Babatha's second marriage probably took
place in 124 or 125 CE and considered this union "the best that a
widow—even a young, well-to-do widow—could expect in Babatha's
situation" (22).[10] I believe that her marriage to Judah, son of Eleazar
Khthousion, was likely to have taken place several years later and
further that Babatha viewed the union as advantageous for her interests. Judah had served as Babatha's transactional guardian (*epitropos*)
as early as October 125 for two documents drawn up on the same
day in Maoza: she summoned one of the guardians for her orphaned
son—John, son of Joseph Eglas[11]—to appear before the governor's
court at Petra on the charge that the latter was not supplying his
share of the boy's maintenance (**14**) and she filed a deposition against
both John and the boy's other guardian, 'Abdoöbdas, son of Ellouthas,
outlining their deficiencies in greater detail and suggesting that they
turn the boy's assets over to her (**15**). Judah again served Babatha
in the same capacity in the first days of December 127, when she
submitted to Roman authorities in Rabbath-Moab a declaration of
property, her date palm groves at Maoza, and he also affixed Babatha's

---

[8] Henceforth, the Greek papyri published in N. Lewis, *The Documents from the
Bar-Kokhba Period in the Cave of Letters: Greek Papyri* (Jerusalem 1989), and the Aramaic
papyri published in Y. Yadin, J.C. Greenfield, A. Yardeni, and B. Levine, eds., *The
Documents from the Bar Kokhba Period in the Cave of Letters. Hebrew, Aramaic and Nabatean-
Aramaic Papyri* (Jerusalem 2002) will be cited in both text and notes only by bold-
faced numerals, with line numbers when pertinent.

[9] Lewis (supra note 8) 22 placed Babatha's death "*in or soon after AD 132.*"
Babatha probably perished near the end of the revolt in summer of 135 CE. Babatha
was already married by 120 CE—see Cotton and Greenfield (supra note 6) 217, citing the then unpublished Aramaic bequest of property from Babatha's father Simon
to her mother Miriam (**7**); for further quotations from **7**, see H.M. Cotton, "Deeds
of Gift and the Law of Succession in the Documents from the Judaean Desert,"
Akten des 21. Internationalen Papyrologenkongresses, Berlin 1995 (= *ArchPF* Beiheft 3) 179–86,
especially 179–80. If her age at this first marriage was about 13–16 years, she
would have been at most around 20 when first widowed in 124 and still little more
than 30 some 11 years later.

[10] Lewis (supra note 8) 29 implied an even earlier date for the marriage in the
"Table of Papyri," attributing Babatha's *ketubba* (**10**) to between 122 and 125.

[11] That is, "a man from . . . 'Egaltein," for which, see G.W. Bowersock, "The
Babatha papyri, Masada, and Rome," *JRA* 4 (1991) 336–44, especially 340–1, and
H.M. Cotton and J.C. Greenfield, "Babatha's *Patria*: Maḥoza, Maḥoz 'Eglatain and
Ẓo'ar," *ZPE* 107 (1995) 126–34, especially 130–4.

signature in Aramaic on the back of the return (**16**). Nonetheless, the earliest document to name Babatha as Judah's wife is dated 21 February 128 (**17**.4, 22), and for this transaction Jacob, son of Jesus (perhaps the brother of Babatha's first husband), served as her guardian, no doubt because Judah himself was party to the agreement, acknowledging that he received from Babatha, his wife, a deposit-loan of 300 denarii.[12] As Ranon Katzoff has pointed out, if Judah were Babatha's husband, he would be likely to serve as her guardian, yet serving as her guardian by no means proves he was at the same time her husband.[13] Babatha required a guardian in order to conduct transactions that were valid in the Roman courts, and her habits after Judah's death show she had recourse to three different men to act in the role of *epitropos*, but married none of them: on 11 September 130, John, son of Makhouthas, a Jew from Maoza (**22**);[14] on 9 July 131, Maras, son of Abdalgos, a Nabataean from Petra (**25**);[15] and on 19 August 132, Babelis, son of Menahem, another Jew from Maoza (**27**).

Whether or not Judah was still married to Miriam, mother of Shelamzion, when he and Babatha became husband and wife, remains under discussion.[16] Lewis motivated Judah's execution of a deed of gift on 16 April 128 (**19**), in which he named Shelamzion heir to his property in En-Gedi, half being transferred now and half after his death, as in accordance with Jewish marriage customs as they are recorded in the *Book of Tobit*, and/or due to ill health on the part of Judah, since he died within the next two years.[17] Katzoff amplified the connection between the father's illness, his gift, and his daughter's marriage by underscoring Judah's explicit exclusion of the "small old courtyard" as the means to make his donation to

---

[12] For a similar marriage practice in early Roman Egypt, see L. Koenen et al., "A First Century Archive from Oxyrhynchos: Oxyrhynchite Loan Contracts and Egyptian Marriage," in J.H. Johnson, ed., *Life in a Multi-cultural Society: Egypt from Cambyses to Constantine and Beyond* (= Studies in Ancient Oriental Civilization 51, Chicago 1992) 181–205.

[13] R. Katzoff, "Polygamy in P.Yadin?," *ZPE* 109 (1995) 128–32, especially 130 and no. 14.

[14] John earlier functioned as a witness for Babatha's summons to the guardians of her orphan son Jesus (**14**) and cf. **5b**, in which John's role is less clear.

[15] Cf. H.M. Cotton, "The Guardian (ΕΠΙΤΡΟΠΟΣ) of a Woman in the Documents from the Judaean Desert," *ZPE* 118 (1997) 267–73.

[16] Cf. Lewis (supra note 8) 22–4; Katzoff (supra note 13) 128–32.

[17] Lewis (supra note 8) 83.

Shelamzion permanent and unassailable in accordance with Mishnaic
interpretation,[18] and he too emphasized the gift's role as an integral
part of Shelamzion's marriage settlement concluded 11 days previously on 5 April 128 (**18**).[19] Judah's deed of gift was, naturally enough,
concerned with events that would take place after his death, although
the half of the gift that came now would be of use to Shelamzion
in the new household the marriage established.[20] The marriage contract he wrote out for Babatha, however, looked to the future, assur-
ing her with phrases customary in contemporary *ketubbot* from Palestine
that, should he die first, male children born to them would inherit
her *ketubba* money (as well as Judah's estate) and females would be
provided for out of that estate (**10**).[21] As Hannah Cotton has noted,
both Judah's gift to Shelamzion (**19**) and the deed of gift from Salome
Grapte (or Gropte) in favor of her daughter Salome Komaise (P.Hever
64) intersected not only with the daughter's marriage, but also with
the second marriage of the parent endowing the daughter. Such
deeds of gift may, then, have been motivated as much by the parent's anticipation of the birth of a male child in the subsequent marriage, who would deprive a daughter from the previous marriage of
her right to inherit unless specific steps were undertaken, as by the
fact of the daughter's own marriage.[22] If Judah were a recent bride-
groom himself, making Babatha his wife after early December 127
(**16**) and before 21 February 128 (**17**), his hopes for a son from the
new union rested, naturally enough, with the young Babatha's proven
fertility and the fact that she had already produced a male heir for

---

[18] "A dying man who wrote over his property to others [as a gift] but left himself a piece of land of any size whatever—his gift is valid," M. Bava Batra 9.6
(Neusner 3.108).
[19] R. Katzoff, "An Interpretation of P.Yadin 19: A Jewish Gift after Death," in
A. Bülow-Jacobsen, ed., *Proceedings of the 20th International Congress of Papyrology, Copenhagen,
23–29 August 1992* (Copenhagen 1994) 562–5.
[20] H.M. Cotton, "The Law of Succession in the Documents from the Judaean
Desert Again," *SCI* 17 (1998) 115–22, especially 117. Cotton (supra note 9) 183
argues against Lewis' supposition that the given courtyard in **19** was the same courtyard conceded to Shelamazion in **20**.
[21] Y. Yadin et al., "Babatha's *Ketubba*," *IEJ* 44 (1994) 75–101, especially 78–9
and 92–4.
[22] H.M. Cotton and A. Yardeni, *Aramaic, Hebrew and Greek Documentary Texts from
Naḥal Ḥever and Other Sites* (Oxford 1997) 204, introduction to P.Hever 64, Maoza,
9 November 129 CE. For the inheritance strategies involved, see Cotton and Greenfield
(supra note 6) 211–24, modified somewhat in Cotton (supra note 9) and *eadem* (supra
note 20).

her first husband.[23] This additional motive by no means negates the suggestion that Shelamzion and her groom Judah Cimber, as well as her mother Miriam, may also have pressed Judah to make the donation only 11 days after the young couple's marriage contract was signed. Renewed hope for offspring, especially a son as *suus heres*, compromised Judah's existing obligations to and affection for the daughter of his first marriage, perhaps precipitating her marriage to Judah Cimber (**18**), as well as the deed of gift (**19**).[24]

Anticipation of a male heir coupled with the failure to engender one, so far as is known, likewise impacts on the length of time Judah and Babatha were husband and wife, implying that their marriage endured only a short time—perhaps a matter of months, or, at most, a little over two years, for Judah was dead before June 130 and Babatha once again a widow.

Both John and Babelis, transactional guardians for Babatha during her second widowhood, also served as subscribers when the illiterate widow's signature was required on her documents, and, like the guardians and subscribers of Roman Egypt, the men who assisted the widow and whose hand she borrowed for the signing apparently occupied a special position in her trust.[25] One thing the two guardians had in common with her second husband Judah was literacy in Aramaic. Babatha herself was literate in no language, neither Aramaic, nor Greek, yet despite her inability to read, or even to sign her name, she clearly understood the role written documents played in

---

[23] Procreation seems to have become an obligation for Jewish men during the Yavnean period. J. Cohen, *Be Fertile and Increase, Fill the Earth and Master It: The Ancient and Medieval Career of a Biblical Text* (Ithaca-London 1989) 110, cites t. Yevamot. 8.7, ed. Lieberman, 3.20. D. Daube, *The Duty of Procreation* (Edinburgh 1977) 35–7, argued that the transformation was a response to the Great Revolt, but Cohen, 109–61, suggests more persuasively that it was due to the Bar Kokhba revolt and its aftermath. For having borne a son to a previous husband as an important attraction in a potential wife, see Poppaea Sabina to Nero, Tac. *Ann.* 14.1.

[24] The practice of a man setting his affairs in order on the occasion of his marriage may have been a fairly common phenomenon in Greek and Roman Egypt: see W. Clarysse, "Le mariage et le testament de Dryton en 150 avant J.-C.," *ChrEg* 61 (1986) 99–103. New fragments published as Text 2 in K. Vandorpe, *The Bilingual Family Archive of Dryton, his Wife Apollonia, and their Daughter Senmouthis* (Brussels, 2002) 59–68.

[25] H.C. Youtie, "ΥΠΟΓΡΑΦΕΥΣ: The Social Impact of Illiteracy in Graeco-Roman Egypt," *ZPE* 17 (1975) 201–21 = *Scriptiunculae posteriores* I (Bonn 1981) 179–99. See also H.M. Cotton, "Subscriptions and Signatures in the Papyri from the Judaean Desert: the ΧΕΙΡΟΧΡΗΣΤΗΣ," *JJurP* 25 (1995) 29–40, who compares, among other things, a contract made on Rhodes, P.Oxy. L 3593 i. 18 and ii. 45–6, with the phrase χῖρα χρησάμενος (*cheira chresamenos*).

protecting her many assets.[26] Not only did she apparently insist on having Greek documents translated for her (cf. below), but she also gives every indication of having chosen those who acted in her behalf judiciously, repeatedly employing, for example, the Greek scribe Germanos, son of Judah, for the drafting of her documents in Maoza.[27] Germanos made his earliest appearance in the archive as scribe for the concession of rights that Besas and Julia Crispina, representing the claims of the orphans of Judah's brother Jesus, sent to Shelamzion in mid-June 130 (**20**), and, as opponents of Babatha, they employed him for three other texts between mid-November 130 and July 131 (**23–25**), summoning her to the court of the Roman *legatus Augusti pro praetore* in Petra and deposing against her in behalf of the orphans. By mid-September of 130 Babatha too was employing Germanos to write her transactions involving the sale of a date crop (**21–22**), and he continued to serve her in this capacity in the documents involving disputes over the deceased Judah's properties (**26–27, 34**). The latest of these, dated to 19 August 132, shows her still resident in Maoza (**27**). It is, of course, not improbable that the number of people able to draft a text in Greek was limited in the recently constituted province of Arabia, and perhaps as limited as in Ptolemaic Pathyris, southwest of Thebes, when in 126 BCE the Greek cavalryman Dryton made use of four witnesses who signed with Egyptian letters out of the total of six witnesses, "because," as the document noted, "there were not in the place a sufficient number of Greeks" (P.Batav. 4). This third will was presumably the last will Dryton wrote, now dividing his assets between the son of his first marriage and the five daughters born to him from the second marriage.[28] Germanos' continued presence as scribe of Babatha's own papers suggests that once she encountered him, she placed sufficient confidence in his ability to record her wishes and protect her interests, despite the "limited mastery of Greek morphology and accordance" that impressed the editor of the documents Germanos drafted.[29]

---

[26] Cf. Cotton (supra note 15) 270; A.E. Hanson, "Ancient Illiteracy," in J. Humphrey, ed., *Literacy in the Roman world* (= *JRA* Supplement 3) (Ann Arbor 1991) 159–98.

[27] On Germanos' title λιβλάριος = *libellarius*, see Bowersock (supra note 11) 339.

[28] Dryton registered his second will on the same day he registered the marriage to his second wife (supra note 24).

[29] Lewis (supra note 8) 88; cf. infra note 51.

Whatever his personal qualities, Judah, son of Eleazar Khthousion, could offer the young widow Babatha literacy in Aramaic, and this was surely an attractive feature in her eyes, an additional protection for her property and the interests of her minor son. Judah's editors have praised his hand as exhibiting the fluidity of an experienced writer,[30] and being an experienced writer insured that he was also an accurate reader of Aramaic documents. Samples of Judah's writing and his signatures are known in the Greek documents dated from October 125 to April 128 (**15, 17, 18, 19**); he also wrote Babatha's *ketubba* (**10**)[31] and functioned as guardian and subscriber in the registration of her land for Roman authorities (**16**). Babatha kept her papers in an attractive leather purse, and when she deposited the purse in a crevice of the cave's wall for safe-keeping, she first placed the purse within a water-skin filled with balls of flaxen thread. While the contents of the purse reveal her business acumen, the balls of threads served the illiterate young woman not only as raw materials for making clothing, but provided her with the strings and cloths that organized the texts she could not herself read. In addition, documents of particular interest to Babatha and Shelamzion—Simon's deed of gift to Babatha's mother (**7**),[32] the *ketubba* of her marriage to Judah (**10**) and Shelamzion's marriage contract (**18**)—were individually wrapped.[33]

The papers of the Graeco-Egyptian Aurelia Sarapias, also a young widow with a minor child, her daughter Paulina, offer interesting parallels to Babatha's leather purse and its contents. Sarapias and her deceased husband Paulus were citizens of the Greek city of Antinoopolis, although papers concerning the family were found at the Fayum village of Tebtunis in 1899/1900 by the Oxford papyrologists B.P. Grenfell and A.S. Hunt "tied up in a bundle" (introduction to

---

[30] Y. Yadin and J.C. Greenfield, "Aramaic and Nabatean Signatures and Subscriptions," in Lewis (supra note 8) 136.

[31] Yadin et al. (supra note 21) 75–101.

[32] Y. Yadin et al., "A Deed of Gift in Aramaic Found in Naḥal Ḥever: *Papyrus Yadin 7*," *ErIsr* 25 (1996) 383–403 (Hebrew); English summary in Cotton (supra note 9) 179–80.

[33] For a reconstruction of the purse, Y. Yadin, *The Finds from the Bar Kokhba Period in the Cave of Letters* (*Judaean Desert Studies* 1, Jerusalem 1963) 258–9, and fig. 158; for description of the Babatha finds in Locus 61, near the south-western corner of Hall C, 38–40. Photos of the purse and the wrapped papyri in Y. Yadin, *Bar-Kokhba* (London 1971) 222–8; Lewis (supra note 8) 3–4, quotes from Y. Yadin, "Expedition D—The Cave of the Letters," *IEJ* 12 (1962) 227–57, especially 231–6.

P.Tebt. II 326).[34] Arthur Verhoogt has persuasively divided the texts
into two groups—those concerning Sarapammon, dating between
248 and 265 CE,[35] and those concerning Sarapias that cluster around
the death of her husband Paulus at some point between 264 and
270 CE.[36] Sarapias' petition to the prefect, asking that her brother
Aurelius Sarapion alias Alexander be named Paulina's guardian and
administrator of her child's property, now that the father and husband Paulus was dead, demonstrates that Sarapias expected Paulina
to inherit from him, despite the fact that he died intestate (P.Tebt.
II 326). Nonetheless, Paulus' estate was subsequently turned over to
his brother Pasigenes (P.Tebt. II 406, 590), not to his daughter. The
fact that Paulina did not become her father's heir also explains the
presence in Aurelia Sarapias' bundle of a rescript from the emperor
Gordian III (P.Tebt. II 285) dated to 238 CE, but copied at some
point after Gordian's death in 244. The emperor was responding to
a question involving legitimacy of children and he declared that registration was not legal cause for establishing either their legitimacy
or illegitimacy. Pasigenes had apparently questioned Paulina's legal
status, offering proof to authorities that she was illegitimate and not
her father's legal heir. Verhoogt joined the Sarapias documents to
the Sarapammon documents by suggesting that Sarapammon was
her male relative, probably her father, and that his papers came into
her hands when, after she returned to the family home upon her
husband's death, Sarapammon also died.

Aurelia Sarapias' papers give no indication that she was literate,
neither her petition to the prefect (P.Tebt. II 326), written throughout by the same professional hand, nor the two copies of the inven-
tories of Paulus' property and personal effects (406 and 590), each
written by a different and practiced hand. Her habit of fastening

---

[34] The texts are: P.Tebt. II 285, 319, 326, 335 (recto text, with 404 and 424 on
verso), 378, 406, 588 (a copy of 378); Grenfell and Hunt imply that 590, a copy
of 406, was not within the bundle, but it is clearly related. Sarapias' documents
have been studied by A.M.F.W. Verhoogt, "Family Papers from Tebtunis," in
A.M.F.W. Verhoogt and S.P. Vleeming, eds., *The Two Faces of Graeco-Roman Egypt:
Greek and Demotic and Greek-Demotic Texts and Studies Presented to P.W. Pestman* (= *P.Lug.Bat.*
30, Leiden-Boston-Köln 1998) 141–54.
[35] P.Tebt. II 319, 378 (588, copy of 378), 424 (335 and 404 were written on the
same sheet of papyrus). In the latest of his papers Sarapammon is said to be "past
his prime" (378.1: *parêlix*, παρῆλιξ).
[36] P.Tebt. II 326, 406 (and 590).

together papers important to her suggests that, like Babatha, she too was illiterate and relied on non-verbal signals of arrangement in order to distinguish one document from another. Also like Babatha, she was by no means unsophisticated about the worth of her husband's possessions. The meticulous accounting of the items and slaves she surrendered to Pasigenes included remarks on the condition and value of individual pieces, and some details would have been best known only to the wife of the deceased: "A complete lamp-stand with a Cupid and lamp, valued at [.]6 drachmas"; "a tunic new from the fuller, with a Laconian stripe, worth a stater"; "white linen cloths, 12 in number, worth eight drachmas each, 96 drachmas" (P.Tebt. II 406.12, 14, 18; cf. II 590). That one copy of the inventory (406) was kept within the bundle and the other (590) outside, but nearby, may represent a deliberate and mnemonic ordering of papers by another young widow who did not know letters.[37]

The two young widows, both with dependent children and both careful arrangers of their documents, overcoming their inability to read them through ordering, separating, and combining, share another characteristic. Both retained copies of official Roman pronouncements that addressed the legal matter lying at the center of their struggles to safeguard the financial welfare of their children. Aurelia Sarapias retained the rescript of Gordian on the relation of a child's registration to its legitimacy, and Babatha retained three copies, written out by two different hands, of a Greek version of one of the Roman praetor's *actiones* dealing with guardianship of orphans (**28–30**, ca. 125 CE).[38] Some four months after the appointment of guardians for her orphaned son, Babatha was petitioning the

---

[37] Details of the find-spots at Tebtunis supplied by Grenfell and Hunt are jejune, but for the evidence from the "T" numbers, see Verhoogt (supra note 34) 142–4, and A.E. Hanson, "Text and Context for the Illustrated Herbal from Tebtunis," in I. Andorlini et al., eds., *Atti del XXII Congresso Internazionale de Papirologia, Firenze, 23–29 Agosto 1998* (Florence 2001) I, 585–604. Although Verhoogt ultimately concluded that Sarapias bundled her papers for disposal, rather than for further use (153–4), this seems unlikely, since, as he earlier admitted, "The inventory of things delivered to Paulus' brother may well imply that Sarapias had hope of getting it back and therefore wanted to carefully register it" (151 and no. 56).

[38] The appropriateness of the praetor's pronouncement to Babatha's case against the guardians of her son, prior to termination of the tutelage, has been much discussed: see, Cotton, "Guardianship," (supra note 1) 104–8, and T. Chiusi, "Babatha vs. the Guardians of her Son: a Struggle for Guardianship—Legal and Practical Aspects of P.Yadin 12—15, 27," in this volume.

governor, explaining the family's financial situation, the niggard-
liness of a male kinsman, who, "though he had sufficient funds,
neither paid family debts, nor contributed to the orphan's maintenance," and the paltry sum the guardians were providing (**13**.17–24).
In October 125, Babatha continued her efforts with a summons
against one of the guardians (**14**) and a deposition against them both,
charging them with not supplying "maintenance money commensurate with the income from the interest on his money and property
and commensurate in particular with a style of life which befits (?)
him" (**15**.20–24). Babatha suggested that the guardians allow her to
manage the boy's assets, secured by a mortgage of an equivalent
amount of her own property. She would then increase threefold the
money that came for his support—interest of one and one-half
denarius per 100 denarii, rather than the half-denarius per 100
denarii the guardians were providing. Babatha seems to have been
hardly more successful than Aurelia Sarapias in manipulating into
tangible results the copies of the official ruling they acquired and
diligently preserved. The latest dated document in Babatha's purse,
from mid-August 132, was the receipt she issued to Simon the hunchback, who succeeded his father John, son of Joseph Eglas, as guardian
of Jesus, indicating she was receiving the same amount of money
per month as eight years previously (**27**).

Documents from Roman Egypt also suggest that a principal thrust
in the young widow's strategy to secure financial resources to support herself and her orphaned child was the recovery of dowry.[39]
The marriage contracts of Roman Egypt, whether involving a Roman
citizen bride or a Graeco-Egyptian one, listed dower goods with their
monetary values and often stipulated the terms under which return
was to be made to the woman, or to her family in the event a child-
less marriage terminated in her death. Shelamzion's marriage contract to Judah Cimber evaluated the feminine adornment and clothing
she brought as bride gift at 200 *denarii* of silver, and spelled out the
terms of return (**18**); so too the marriage contract of Salome alias
Komaise with its 96 *denarii* of silver (P.Hever 65, 7 August 131). For
some young widows of Roman Egypt, the return of dowry from the

---

[39] A.E. Hanson, "Widows too young in their Widowhood," in D.E.E. Kleiner
and S. Matheson, eds., *I Claudia II. Women in Roman Art and Society* (Austin 2000)
149–65.

deceased husband's heirs was not easily effected, and they were compelled by rival heirs to sign away their own claims and those of their
children to the deceased's estate, merely to get the dowry back. A
poignant example from early Roman Alexandria is offered by the
young and pregnant widow Dionysarion who acknowledged to her
mother-in-law Hermione that her dowry, consisting of clothing worth
240 drachmas, earrings and a finger-ring, and 100 silver drachmas,
had been returned; that neither she nor her unborn child retained
any claim on her dead husband's estate; that she renounced further
litigation, even with regard to expenses for delivery of her child. The
agreement also permitted Dionysarion to remarry whomsoever she
wished and to expose the baby posthumously born (BGU IV 1104,
8 BCE). A half century later in the metropolis of Oxyrhynchus the
widow Ammonarion acknowledged that she had received back her
dowry of 800 drachmas from her husband's heir, his nephew
Antiphanes, and that Ophelous, the daughter from her marriage,
likewise resigned to the nephew her claims to a share of her deceased
father's property (P.Oxy. II 268 + BL VII 129, 58 CE).[40]

Babatha and other Jewish widows were likewise entitled to the
return of dowry, or at least to maintenance at the expense of a
deceased husband's estate. The unnamed mother-in-law of Babatha's
first marriage apparently received her marriage money back without
incident after the death of her husband Jesus, son of Joseph surnamed Zaboudos, for its return to her was noted in the receipt of
deposit the son of her marriage, Jesus (Babatha's first husband),
received from his paternal uncle Joseph (5).[41] This same family apparently returned Babatha's dowry after the death of Jesus, since no
papers in her archive mention it being withheld, nor any action

---

[40] More vigorous in defending the rights of her child to inherit from its deceased
father was Petronilla (P.Gen. II 103–104, + BL VIII 136, 147 CE), for which see
text 224 in J. Rowlandson, ed., *Women & Society in Greek & Roman Egypt: A source-
book* (Cambridge 1998), pages 289–91.

[41] Cf. Bowersock (supra note 11) 341–2, where he suggested that "blacks" most
likely refers to silver issues of the old Nabataean coinage; for the assertion that "one
black" equals a half denarius, see W. Weiser and H.M. Cotton, "Gebt dem Kaiser,
was des Kaisers ist: Die Geldwährungen der Griechen, Juden, Nabatäer und Römer
im syrisch-nabatäischen Raum unter besonderer Berücksichtigung des Kurses von
Sela'/Melaina und Lepton nach der Annexion des Königreiches der Nabatäer durch
Rom," *ZPE* 114 (1997) 237–87.

against the estate of Jesus by Babatha, or by another acting in her behalf. By contrast the dowry Babatha brought her second husband Judah, son of Eleazar Khthousion, was apparently not returned to her satisfaction, and a group of seven documents, dated between mid-130 and mid-131 (**20–26**), reveal the legal maneuvers to which the various parties resorted. Babatha certainly took possession of three productive date orchards and in 130 CE sold the year's crop, with contracts of the sale explaining that she did so "in lieu of the dowry and debts [owed to her]" (**21**.11–12; **22**.9–10). Among the rival claimants to Judah's property in addition to Babatha were the orphans of Judah's brother Jesus, represented by their guardian Besas, son of Jesus, and by Julia Crispina.[42] Besas issued a summons to Babatha and then deposed against her in November 130, because she had seized a date orchard (**23, 24**), and after Besas became ill some eight months later, Julia Crispina continued to press the orphans' claim that Babatha held properties belonging to them (**25**, and below). By this time, Babatha was also accusing Judah's first wife, Miriam, of having wrongfully seized property from Judah's house (**26**).

The younger unattached women of the census documents who found themselves without a husband showed a preference for living either in the household of a male kinsman—father, if he were alive, brother, or paternal uncle—or in a predominantly female household that often included minor children; the woman's mother or sister, if she too be unattached; additional kin, who, if male, tended to be young; even a family of lodgers (but only rarely an unattached male lodger); and perhaps a complement of female slaves.[43] Such preferences among the younger women without husbands imply a concern for reputation, perhaps in the hope of enhancing prospects for remarriage. Some time after August 132 Babatha left Maoza in the territory of Zoar in Arabia[44] for En-Gedi, across the Dead Sea in Judaea and a principal center of the Bar Kokhba revolt. Others took

---

[42] For Julia Crispina, see Bowersock (supra note 11) 341: her father Ber(e)nicianus (**25**.2) was likely to have been cos. suf. in 116 CE and a descendant of the house of Herod Agrippa. Crispina was called the orphans' "supervisor" (*episkopos*), for which see N. Lewis, "The Babatha Archive: A Response," *IEJ* 44 (1994) 243–6, especially 245, and Cotton, "Guardianship" (supra note 1) 97.

[43] Hanson (supra note 39).

[44] H.M. Cotton, "Introduction to the Greek Documentary Texts," *DJD* XXVII (Oxford 1997) 151–2.

the same path, and Babatha was not alone in her flight to the refuge of the cave, as the uprising drew to its bloody conclusion, probably in the summer of 135. Her stepdaughter Shelamzion, and an acquaintance, or even close friend, Salome alias Komaise, were with her, as the presence of their documents in the Cave of the Letters makes clear. These women whose husbands were either dead or occupied elsewhere clustered together in the hope of surviving to more peaceful times, of taking up the lives they left behind, or forging new ties.[45] The papers they brought with them to the cave would play a vital role in reestablishing their position as respectable women and owners of property. Babatha brought with her not only her precious documents, but also keys, bowls and other implements, clothing, and a mirror.[46] Although the latter was useless in the darkness of the cave, the fact that she brought a mirror highlights a naiveté not otherwise apparent in the shrewdness of her business dealings, and perhaps even her hopes for yet another husband.

No dossier or archive from Roman Egypt, so far as I am aware, displays a young widow so energetically defending her own rights to a deceased husband's property and the rights of her orphan child to what she considered his due and, at the same time, aggressively proceeding against another widow, Miriam, and another set of orphans, those of Jesus, son of Eleazar Khthousion. Babatha was well able to manipulate the intricate judicial machinery the representatives of Rome provided for the new province of Arabia, and though young, illiterate, and often without a close male kinsman upon whom to rely, her sophistication is evident—not only in her careful choices of male representatives and scribes, but also in matters of detail, such as her flattering flourish for the Roman governor when deposing against her son's guardians that extolled "the most blessed times of the governorship of Julius Julianus" (**15**.26–28), or in her retaining

---

[45] For the likelihood that Babatha and Salome knew one another in Maoza, see H.M. Cotton, "The Archive of Salome Komaise, Daughter of Levi: Another Archive from the Cave of the Letters," *ZPE* 105 (1995) 171–208 at 171–2, and *eadem* (supra note 44) 158–60. The majority of the 17 skulls found in the burial niche in Hall C belonged to women and children (six children, eight females between 15 and 30 years of age, as opposed to three males between 14 and 40), Yadin, *The Finds* (supra note 33) 34.

[46] 61.3.4 in Yadin, *The Finds* (supra note 33), 39–40, and, for the mirror, 125 and fig. 48.

copies of a Greek version of one of the Roman praetor's *actiones* on guardianship of orphan children (**28–30**).

The widows of Greek and Roman Egypt frequently resorted in their petitions to what can be labeled "a rhetoric of widows," appealing to the helplessness of the woman alone (*monê*), without a husband or other helper (*aboêthos*), a creature endowed with a weak female nature (*physis gynaikeia*), whose hope for redress lay in the hands of the official addressed.[47] The plaintive phrases were clearly thought to heighten the likelihood that the widow's case would receive the desired hearing in the magistrate's court, even though, when presiding, magistrates were known to dismiss special pleading as irrelevant to the case and without bearing on whether or not a wrong had been committed.[48] In her depositions and summons, however, Babatha did not use widows' rhetoric, emphasizing instead the fact that she was more capable of managing her son's assets than were the guardians appointed by the council of Petra. The orphans of Greek and Roman Egypt likewise rehearsed the violent wrongs kinsmen committed against them, underage and helpless, when, as adults, they petitioned government officials to aid them in regaining a lost inheritance.[49] Roman authorities in Egypt did, in fact, come to require that guardians of orphaned minor children submit yearly accounts of their management of the child's property as early as the beginning of the third century CE (P.Oxy. LVIII 3921, 219 CE). Yet even in her efforts to compel Jesus' guardians into providing more income, Babatha did not introduce her child's privations, but again accented the positive results additional income would produce for the boy, "wherewith my son may be maintained splendidly" (**15**.10, 26–27). In this latter instance an allusion to what her son lacked due to his less than splendid maintenance would not have diminished her own stature as the more fit manager for his assets.

It is, of course, impossible to know whether Babatha's eschewing the rhetoric of widows and orphans was due to ignorance on her

---

[47] See e.g. P.Mich. I 29, 256 BCE; P.Oxy. L 3555, first-second century CE.

[48] Cf. e.g. A.E. Hanson, "A Petition and Court Proceedings: P.Michigan inv. 6060," *ZPE* 111 (1996) 175–82.

[49] E.g. UPZ I 9, 161/60 BCE; SB V 7558.12–31, as reedited by H.C. Youtie, "P.Mich. inv. 2922 = *Sammelbuch* V 7558," *ZPE* 13 (1974) 241–8 (= *Scriptiunculae Posteriores* I [supra note 25] 97–104) 172/73 CE; P.Oxy. XXXIV 2713 (+ *BL* VI 111, VIII 261), ca. 297 CE.

part of phrases popular in petitions from the widows and orphans of Egypt, or whether such rhetoric was known to her, but was dispositionally displeasing. A small hint that Babatha was perhaps unaware of the rhetorical strategies to which the petitions from the widowed and orphaned had recourse may come from her reaction to a summons from Besas and a later one from Julia Crispina which claimed that Babatha was holding *through force* the date orchard, or orchards, belonging to the orphans of Jesus, son of Eleazar Khthousion (**23**.6, 17; **25**.10). In Babatha's countersummons her guardian Maras, son of Abdalgos, gave voice to her objection to the charge she resorted to violence (*bian moi chrômenê sykophantousa moi*, **25**.18–19, 51–52).[50] Her objection reveals that the accusation had been translated from Greek in her hearing, even if the explanation of the word *bia* given her in her own tongue is lost to us. We have only her protest—that the claim was, in her view, unseemly, inappropriate, calumnious. She might have instructed Maras, for example, to reiterate her right to the property previously enunciated in the sale of the date crop: she distrained the orchards "in lieu of the dowry and debts [owed to her]." The documents from both Babatha and the buyer of the crop did signal an awareness that the property was under dispute: Babatha, when she promised to clear the orchards of counterclaims and to refund the buyer for labors and expenses, should she fail to do so (**22**.20–25); and the buyer, when he echoed Babatha's assertion of ownership, yet qualified it with "as you say" (ὡς λέγ⟨ε⟩ις, **21**.11). In a subsequent deposition against her Besas questioned Babatha's claim that Judah, son of Eleazar Khthousion, had registered the date orchards under her name (**24** a.4–12), and he notified her that if he were not satisfied with the document that proved her right of possession, he intended to register the orchards in the name of the orphans. But, as Lewis noted, much remains unclear about this entire matter, and while neither party appears to have an

---

[50] The scribe Germanos ought to have written *bia* (βίᾳ), dative case with *chrômenê*, instead of the accusative *bian*. Further, at **25**.42, the first written outer text, Germanos omitted the phrase found in the inner text "[properties . . .] you hold by force which did not devolve to you" (βίᾳ διακρατ⟨ε⟩ῖς ἃ οὐκ ἀνῆκέν σοι **25**.10). Given the fact that Babatha's objection to Crispina's charge that she was using force appeared in both inner and outer text, the omission seems an inadvertent one on Germanos' part, rather than Lewis' "epexegetical afterthought"—see Lewis (supra note 8) 112, note *ad* **25**. 10 and 42.

incontestable right, the claims and counter-claims of both parties contain suspicious elements: on Babatha's part, the lack of a document among her papers to prove the orchards belonged to Judah and were then subsequently transferred to her;[51] on Besas' and Crispina's part, the fact that the earliest summons spoke only of a single date orchard (**23**.5–6, 16), but the subsequent depositions increased the orphans' claim to "orchards" (**24**.5–6; **25**.9, 41). As Lewis suggested, Besas may have been falsely laying an additional claim to orchards that were, in fact, Babatha's own, mentioned in her census declaration of 127 (**16**).[52]

Wherever the right of possession lay and whatever properties were in dispute, Babatha's objection to the use of *bia* would seem unsophisticated to litigants familiar with Greek and Roman practice. Forms of the noun (*bia*), the adjective (*biaios*), and the verb (*biazô*) were common in papyri from Egypt, occurring more than 450 times, most often in petitions to government officials and in accusations hurled at opponents during judicial hearings.[53] Emphasizing the violent behavior of an opponent was an accepted rhetorical strategy in the litigious climate of Egypt, although this usage was apparently less familiar to the Jews of Maoza in the province of Arabia, recently incorporated into the Roman system.[54] By contrast, Julia Crispina

---

[51] Lewis (supra note 8) 107, notes ad **24**.4–6. Cotton and Greenfield (supra note 6) 212–3 argue that ἀπεγράψατο . . . ἐν τῇ ἀπογραφῇ, **24**.4–5, refers to land registration, and not the Roman census.

[52] These vineyards had come to Babatha from her father; see Cotton and Greenfield (supra note 6) 211–24.

[53] Forms of *bia*- appear in Greek petitions from the earliest (e.g. P.Cair.Zeno. II 59275.3, 251 BCE; P.Enteux. 12.3, 244 BCE) to the latest (e.g. P.Cair.Masp. I 67006. recto 3, ca. 522 CE).

[54] Of the some 50 appearances of the various forms of the root *bia*- in the Septuagint, it seems worthwhile to note that as many as half are employed in the meaning "strength of natural forces" (Bauer-Arndt-Gingrich, s.v. 1a; cf. *LSJ*, s.v. I); many occur in the poetic books Wisdom of Solomon and Psalms, qualifying winds, hail, fire, floods, thunder and lightning. To be sure, the remaining passages involve the meaning "use of force" (Bauer-Arndt-Gingrich, s.v. 2) or "act of violence" (*LSJ*, s.v. II), describing actions by men in war (e.g. Egyptians in Exodus; Antiochus and other Greeks in Maccabees) or against women (e.g. Deuteronomy 22:25, 28; Esther 7:8; Sirach 20:4). By contrast, the Hellenized authors Philo Judaeus and Josephus employed *bia*- forms to qualify actions of men in the vast majority of the occurrences: Josephus, for example, introduced 15 *bia*- forms into his retelling of Genesis, although none occurred in the Septuagint, and only Josephus' paraphrases of violence against women in the laws on marriage (Deuteronomy 22:25, 28, and *AJ* 4.252) and in Haman's assault on Esther (Esther 7:8 and *AJ* 11.265) find echoes in the Septuagint.

was born into a more sophisticated environment: not only was her father Ber(e)nicianus a descendant of Herod Agrippa, but her mother was from a wealthy and powerful family of landholders in Egypt. Crispina herself certainly knew more of the vituperative flourishes employed in the accusations and court cases of the Roman world than did Babatha, her cadre of guardians and subscribers, and the scribes employed to turn her texts into Greek.[55] Had Babatha, an otherwise competent young widow, been aware of the rhetorical devices artfully deployed elsewhere, she too would have been likely to have embellished some of the charges and counter-charges she made against her opponents. Yet even without Crispina's exposure to rhetorical flourishes and exaggerations, Babatha was a vigorous champion of the rights she deemed hers. Babatha remained a formidable opponent.

---

[55] For Crispina's mother, see Bowersock (supra note 11) 341. For interference by scribes, despite their commission to represent the words spoken to them by illiterates, see J. Rowlandson, ed. (supra n. 40), chapter 3, archive B, pages 98–105, and archive K, pages 147–51.

BABATHA VS. THE GUARDIANS OF HER SON: A STRUGGLE FOR GUARDIANSHIP—LEGAL AND PRACTICAL ASPECTS OF P.YADIN 12–15, 27

Tiziana J. Chiusi

I

In accordance with the focal point of our congress I would like to explore the coexistence of different legal traditions that are reflected in P.Yadin 12–15.[1] I advisedly speak of 'coexistence' or, even better, of 'combination' rather than of 'influence.' For 'influence' presupposes the search for something original and something which follows, the search for what was in the beginning and what became successful later. Such exact separations, however, are difficult in the field of law, especially in antiquity, where the idea of a state in the modern sense and the claim for legal unity derived from that idea were unknown. In our case we must add that the dominating people had, in general, no specific interest to impose their own law upon the provincials, and rather tended to leave more or less autonomy in internal affairs to them, as far as the strategic and political interests of Rome were not affected. For this reason my exploration of P.Yadin 12–15 and 27 will not start from an abstract idea of Roman law whose traces might be found in the papyri. On the contrary, I would like to examine whether and and to what extent it is possible to find traces of interaction among different legal traditions. We shall see this in the discussion of P.Yadin 15, which will be the focus of this paper.

---

[1] I would like to thank Prof. R. Katzoff very much for giving me the opportunity to attend the very interesting, stimulating and perfectly organized conference. Furthermore, I would like to thank Prof. H.M. Cotton for her valuable advice and suggestions. Last but not least, I wish to thank my colleague Prof. H.-D. Spengler for his assistance in the English version of this paper. In this paper the papyri will be considered only with regard to the theme of the volume. For a general and comprehensive analysis of the texts, in particular their importance for the Roman law of guardianship, see H. Cotton, "The Guardianship of Jesus Son of Babatha: Roman and Local Law in the Province of Arabia," *JRS* 83 (1993) 94–108, and T.J. Chiusi, "Zur Vormundschaft der Mutter," *ZSav* 111 (1994) 155–96.

II

1. The first document, P.Yadin 12, written between 27 February and 28 June 124 CE, is a copy from the minutes of the town council of Petra, the metropolis of the former Nabatean kingdom,[2] a copy which was issued to Babatha, a Jewish woman who lived in Maoza, a village at the southern coast of the Dead Sea.[3]

Inner Text

1. ἐγγεγραμμένον καὶ ἀντιβεβλημένον κεφαλαίου ἑνὸς ἀπὸ ἄκτων βουλῆς Πετραίων
2. τῆς μητροπόλεως προκειμένω⟨ν⟩ ἐν τῷ ἐν Πέτρᾳ Ἀφροδεισίῳ καὶ ἔστιν καθὼς
3. ὑποτέτακται ἐν τοῖ⟨ς⟩ ἐξωτέροις.

Outer Text

4. ἐγ⟨γ⟩εγραμμένον καὶ ἀντιβεβλημένον κεφαλαίου ἑνὸς ʽἐπιτροπῆςʼ ἀπὸ ἄκτων
5. βουλῆς Πετραίων τῆς μητροπόλεως προκειμένω⟨ν⟩ ἐν τῷ
6. ἐν Πέτρᾳ Ἀφροδεισίῳ καὶ ἔστιν καθὼς ὑποτέτακται· καὶ Ἰασσού-
7. ου Ἰουδαίου υἱοῦ Ἰασσούου κώμης Μαωζα⟨ς⟩ Αβδοβδας
8. Ἰλλουθα καὶ Ἰωάνης Ἐγλα. ἐπράχθη ἐν Πέτρᾳ μητρο-
9. πόλει τῆς Ἀραβ[ία]ς πρ]ὸ τεσσ]άρων καλανδῶν [±4 ἰ]-
10. ων ἐπὶ ὑπάτων [Μ]αγ[ί]ου Ἀκειλίου Γλαβρίωνος καὶ Γα-
11. ίου Βελλικ⟨ί⟩ου Τ[ο]ρκουάτου .. σ[.] .. τουου vac

On the back, individual signatures

‏12. נובי בר ולת שהד‎
‏13. ואלו בר קיננ/חד/ר.. שהד‎
‏14. עבדעבדת [ב]ר ש[ה]ירו שהד‎
‏15. ע[....]חו בר עבדאיסי שהד‎

---

[2] On the Nabateans see A. Negev, "The Nabateans and the Provincia Arabia," *ANRW* II 8 (1977) 520–686.

[3] M. Goodman, "Babatha's Story," *JRS* 81 (1991) 169–75 at 170 doubts the Jewish origin of Babatha with unconvincing onomastic arguments; see also Cotton (supra note 1) 94 n. 5.

16. Ἀβδερεὺς Σουμα[ί]ου
17. μά(ρτυς)[4]

> Inner text: "Verified exact copy of one item from the minutes of the council of Petra the metropolis, minutes displayed in the temple of Aphrodite in Petra, and it is as appended below in the outer text." Outer text: "Verified exact copy of one item from the minutes of the council of Petra the metropolis, minutes displayed in the temple of Aphrodite in Petra and it is as appended below: 'And of Jesus, a Jew, son of Jesus, of the village Maoza, Abdobdas son of Illouthas and John son of Eglas [are appointed guardians].' Done in Petra, metropolis of Arabia, four days before the kalends of . . ., in the consulship of Manius Acilius Glabrio and Gaius Bellicius Torquatus . . .
>
> On the back, individual signatures: "Nubi son of Walat, witness; Walu son of . . ., witness; Abdobdath son of Šuheiru, witness; . . . son of Abd'isay, witness; Abdereus son of Soumaios, witness."

From this papyrus we can see that two guardians had been appointed for the orphan Jesus, son of Jesus of the village Maoza, Babatha's son. They were Abdobdas, son of Illouthas and Johannes, son of Eglas. As we can see from his name, Abdobdas seems to have been a Nabatean. That in P.Yadin 15 his subscription is written in a clear Nabatean cursive,[5] a fact which could indicate his Nabatean origin, speaks against the hypothesis that Abdobdas was a Jew with a Nabatean name.

I doubt, however, whether the note of the editor N. Lewis is correct that the number of the guardians was presumably dictated by local custom, on the grounds that in Greek and Roman practice generally only one person was appointed guardian.[6] In Rome the number of guardians was not legally fixed, and we can often find several *tutores* (as the office of a tutor also was an office with high appreciation).

It is remarkable that the council as a whole and not the municipal magistrates nominated the *tutores*. That might be due to the organization of the city, of which we do not know much. One could associate the information given by P.Yadin 12 (and also by P.Yadin

---

[4] The translation of papyri is that of N. Lewis, in N. Lewis, Y. Yadin, B. Greenfield, *Judean Desert Studies. The Documents from the Bar Kokhba Period in the Cave of Letters. Greek Papyri* (Jerusalem 1989).
[5] See Greenfield (supra note 4) 139.
[6] Lewis (supra note 4) 48.

13.19–21) with the evidence of the *lex Irnitana*, the *lex Salpensana* and two Herculaneum wax tablets.[7] There the appointment of the *tutores* for children under age is done *ex decreto decurionum*. H. Cotton argues that (*katastathentes epitropoi*) *hypo boules ton Petraion* in P.Yadin 13 is not incompatible with *ex decreto decurionum*.[8] However, the epigraphic evidence deals with *civitates Romanae*, and it is very improbable that Petra possessed such a status. With respect to the insufficient level of our information on the administrative structures of the city of Petra, two models of explanation could be offerred: 1) The appointment by the boule was in accordance with the law of the town of Petra and was not affected by Romanization. This opinion presupposes a municipal structure, which the Romans left unchanged. 2) Alternatively, Petra may have been administrated in a manner (e.g. directly by the King) that did not fit the municipal organization familiar to the Romans. In this case there would have been no administrative structures which could be adopted. On the contrary the Romans would have had to invent adequate structures. It seems likely that in this case the Romans would have tended to make use of the forms of the Roman municipal organization.

According to Jewish law in case the father had not nominated a tutor, a local court took his place (b. Gittin 37a) and appointed a tutor (m. Gittin 5.4). Furthermore, it was not impossible for a mother to be guardian of her children if she was a widow and the father had not disposed otherwise.[9] Falk thinks that the *boulê tôn Petraiôn* had taken over the competence which the relatives and, later, the orphan's court had had before the destruction of the temple.[10] In this view, this transfer of competence to a municipal institution could be regarded as an indication of a loss of autonomy for the Jewish community, which leads to the old opinion of Mommsen.[11]

---

[7] See V. Arangio-Ruiz's reconstruction and his basic arguments with regard to the question of the nomination of guardians in the provinces in "Due nuove Tavolette di Ercolano relative alla nomina di tutori muliebri," in *Studi in onore di P. de Francisci* I (1954) 3–17 at 3–12.

[8] H. Cotton (supra note 1) 95 f. On the problems of the nomination of *tutores* in the municipal laws cited see recently F. Lamberti, *Tabulae Irnitanae* (Naples 1993) 57–64 (with a summary of the considerable literature on the topic).

[9] Gen. 24:55; I Kings 17:12; II Kings 4:1; 4:7; 8:1–6; on this see Z. Falk, *Hebrew Law in Biblical Times* (Jerusalem 1964) 112 and 158.

[10] Z. Falk, *Introduction to Jewish Law of the Second Commonwealth* (Leiden 1978) 328.

[11] See Th. Mommsen, "Der Religionsfrevel nach römischem Recht," in *Gesammelte*

The expression *apo aktôn* (without article) suggests that it is a Greek transliteration of a Latin formula, which might have read *ex actis* (*senatus Petraeorum*).[12] In the outer text, contrary to the version of the inner text, the word *epitropes* was added above line 4 between *kefalaiou enos* and *apo aktôn*.[13] This addition presumably was made by the scribe himself.[14] It does not change the sense of the text, but it is interesting to ask about the reason for the addition. One could think that, in accordance with the custom of posting documents at temples, which is attested for the Nabatean culture, the papyrus reproduces a section *epitropes* or *epitropai* from the record which was put up at the temple of Aphrodite, and from which the scribe made an extract for Babatha.[15] The reference to this might have been regarded as superfluous for the inner text, which is, indeed, only an abridged version, and therefore it was added only in the outer text. But a convincing reason for the addendum (or for its initial absence) can no longer be found.

It also would be interesting to investigate whether *henos* is an indefinite article or an ordinal number. If we assume that the wording of the papyrus is based on a Latin model, the Latin retroversion would be: *descriptum et recognitum capitis unius tutelae ex actis senatus Petraeorum*. In this formula *unius* sounds a bit strange, because there is no reason for stressing the "singularity" of the *caput*.

Schriften III (Berlin 1907) 389–422. Mommsen's theory is opposed by J. Juster, *Les Juifs dans l'Empire Romain II* (Paris 1914) 9 ff. On this discussion see A.M. Rabello, "The Legal Condition of the Jews in the Roman Empire," *ANRW* II 13 (1980) 662–762 at 725–6. On the delegation of the appointment and supervision of the tutors to the magistrates, especially in Roman Egypt, see M. Kaser – K. Hackl, *Das römische Zivilprozeßrecht* 2nd ed. (Munich 1996) 471; E. Sachers, "tutela," *RE* VII A 2 (1948) 1497–1599 at 1514; L. Mitteis, *Grundzüge der Papyruskunde* (Leipzig 1912) 254; R. Taubenschlag, *The Law of Greco-Roman Egypt in the Light of the Papyri 332 BC–640 AD* 2nd ed. (Warsaw 1955) 161.

[12] See Lewis (supra note 4) 48 and 50.

[13] See the facsimile pl. V.

[14] Lewis (supra note 4) 50 does not deal with this question in his commentary to line 4.

[15] See A. Grohmann, "Nabataioi," *RE* XVI 2 (1935) 1453–68 at 1465. See also H. Cotton (supra note 1) 95, who thinks that the minutes contained a list of similar appointments and as a whole could be described as a "register of guardians". See also H.J. Polotsky, "The Greek papyri from the Cave of the Letters," *IEJ* 12 (1962) 258–62 at 260.

2. The record of the appointment of the guardians is followed by the very fragmentary P.Yadin 13, our second text.

17. τιν[α ὀ]νομάσαι τὰς δι᾽ οἴ-
18. κ[ου] ὀφειλ[ὰς] ἐξορθώ[σασθ]αι καὶ τοῦτο τὸ ἀργύριον ἐν ἱ[κ]ανῷ
19. ἀξιοχρέῳ ἔχοντα, οὐδέποτε τροφῖα Ἰη[σ]ούου ἔδωκεν, καὶ οἱ
20. πρὸ μηνῶν τεσσ[ά]ρων κ[α]ὶ πλείω κατασταθέντες ἐπίτροποι
21. [ὑπ]ὸ βουλῆς τῶ[ν] Πετρα[ί]ων Αβδοοβδα⟨ς⟩ Ελλουθα καὶ Ἰωάνης
22. [᾽Εγλ]α οὐδ[ὲ] α[ὐτοὶ τρ]οφῖα το[ῦ ὀρ]φανοῦ ἔδωκα[ν] εἰ μὴ μ[όν]ον
23. δηνάρια δυω (read δύο) [κατὰ μ]ῆνα, κα[ὶ δι]ὰ τὸ μ[ὴ] ἀρκεῖ[ν]
  ταῦ[τα εἰ]ς
24. τρ[ο]φὴν κατ[± 7]κε[..]..παρ[ὰ] τῶ[ν ..] .ιο[..]ω
25. κι..δ..νο[± 7]τοα[....] ἐπιταξ.[. πρὸ]ς τὴν δύ-
26. ναμιν τῶν [ὑπαρ]χ[ό]ν[τω]ν [αὐτο]ῦ τροφη[± 9] ἀξιοῦ-
27. σι [τῷ] ὀρφα[νῷ] αιτ..[..] σοι ὥστ[ε - -]
28. [- -].[..].[.].. ἀργυ[ριο - -]
29. [..].ε[- -]...ν[.]ι[....]τ.ε..[- -]
30. [..]ριον π[- -]
31. (2nd hand) διευτύχει κύριε.

This document is an *axioma*, a petition from Babatha to the provincial governor, which dates from the second half of the year 124. Babatha's name is not preserved, but the legible remains of the papyrus make clear that the petition came from her.[16] Only a few traces of the content of the document can be detected in the first part of the poorly conserved text. One may assume that Babatha told some details of the economic situation of her family or of her late husband's family in the first part of the petition, because the text mentions the fortune of Joseph, her late husband's brother, the shares of Babatha's son Jesus in the family property, a *chirographon* and a receipt of business affairs. The context of this enumeration of topics cannot be reconstructed. One might assume that Babatha wanted to explain the circumstances of her economic situation to the provincial governor.

The second part of the text mentions another person, not identifiable. This person was to pay the family debts, as he had enough money. Babatha complains that he never contributed anything to the orphan's maintenance. If the complaints refer to the uncle Joseph,

---

16 Lewis (supra note 4) 51.

this might be the reason why the town appointed other persons rather than him as tutor even though he was the next agnate. However, it could be that he had been tutor and that the town had deprived him of the guardianship because of his failures and appointed Abdobdas and Johannes as guardians.[17]

Above all, however, she complains about the guardians appointed by the city council four months ago, who are said to give only two *denarii* a month, an amount insufficient for the maintenance of her son. It is very difficult to reconstruct Babatha's intention from the fragmentary text of the papyrus.[18] Thinking of Roman practice as a background I would like to propose the hypothesis that she is applying to the governor to fix a sum adequate to the financial resources of the orphan's estate, as the sum of two *denarii*, which might have been paid voluntarily by the guardians, is insufficient in her opinion. Let me refer to Ulpian (1 de omn. trib.)[19] D.27.2.3.pr.: *Ius alimentorum decernendorum pupillis praetori competit, ut ipse moderetur, quam summam tutores vel curatores ad alimenta pupillis vel adulescentibus praestare debeant.* (The right of determining the level of provision for *pupilli* is the praetor's; he himself should fix what amount tutors or curators ought to

---

[17] In respect to this uncle there was a misunderstanding in the literature. From a communication of Polotsky (supra note 15) 258 that in a document of the year 110, now P.Yadin 5, a Joseph son of Joseph acknowledged liabilities to a Jesus the son of his brother, H.J. Wolff, "Römisches Provinzialrecht in der Provinz Arabia (Rechtspolitik als Instrument der Beherrschung)," *ANRW* II 13 (1980) 763–806 at 779 n. 33 concluded that the orphan Jesus was the nephew of Joseph. This led Wolff to the question of why Jesus was still under *tutela* in 132, and to the hypothesis that Jesus was under a kind of *cura furiosi*. The same problem arises for A. Biscardi, "Nuove testimonianze di un papiro arabo-giudaico per la storia del processo provinciale romano," in *Studi in onore di Gaetano Scherillo* I (Milan 1972) 111–52 at 114. But from the edition of Lewis (supra note 4) 25 we can learn that the grandfather of the orphan Jesus himself was also called Jesus, and that he had a brother called Joseph. The Joseph of P.Yadin 5 (from 2nd June 110) is the uncle of the father of our orphan Jesus. In the light of the publication of P.Yadin 12, which contains the appointment of the guardians by the Petra town council in 124, a guardianship for Jesus in 132 is no longer strange.

[18] The badly damaged text of ll. 27–30 does not allow decisive conclusions.

[19] This work is regarded by F. Schulz, *History of Roman Legal Science* (Oxford 1946) 256 as likely to be a postclassical compilation of excerpts from Ulpian, with alterations and additions. For classicity see now T. Honoré, *Ulpian* (Oxford 1982) 96–7; D. Liebs in K. Sallman, ed., *Die Literatur des Umbruchs. Von der römischen zur christlichen Literatur, 117 bis 284 n. Chr.*, Handbuch der lateinischen Literatur der Antike IV (Munich 1977) (= Handbuch der Altertumswissenschaft VIII.4) 183 f. On the controversy concerning its contents cf. on the one side A. Pernice, "Parerga," *ZSav* 14 (1893) 135–82 at 136 ff. and on the other side M. Wlassak, *Zum römischen Provinzialprozeß* (Vienna 1919) 70 ff.

expend on the provisions of their *pupilli* or adolescents). And in section 1 of this fragment Ulpian states: He (the praetor) must take into account the size of the inheritance when he determines the provision.[20] (*Modum autem patrimonii spectare debet, cum alimenta decernit.*) The question, in which form the governor could do so, must remain open. One may think of a legal procedure instituted by this petition or of a decision made by the governor himself on the basis of his *cognitio.*

3. If we understand P.Yadin 13 in this way, then we must interpret P.Yadin 14 differently from the first editor's opinion.

Outer Text

15. ἔτους ἐνάτου Αὐτοκράτ[ορος Τραιανοῦ Ἀδριανοῦ Καίσαρος]
16. Σεβαστοῦ, ἐπὶ ὑπάτων Μάρκ[ου] Οὐαλερίου Ἀσιατικοῦ τὸ [β κα]ὶ
17. Τιτίου Ἀκυλείνου πρὸ τεσσάρων εἰδῶν Ὀκτωβρίω[ν, κατὰ]
18. δὲ τὸν ἀριθμὸν τῆς [ἐπαρχείας Ἀραβίας ἔτους εἰκοστοῦ]
19. μηνὸς Ὑπερβερεταίου λεγ[ομένου Θεσρεὶ τετάρτῃ καὶ εἰ]-
20. κας (read εἰκάδι), ἐν Μαωζᾳ περὶ Ζ[οαραν, ἐπὶ τῶν ἐπιβεβ-
    λημένων]
21. μαρτύρων παρήγγει[λεν Βαβαθα Σίμωνος τοῦ Μανα]-
22. ήμου, διὰ ἐπιτρόπου αὐτ[ῆς τ]οῦδε τοῦ πράγμ[ατος]
23. Ἰούδα Χθουσίωνος, Ἰωάνη Ἰωσήπου τοῦ Ἔγλα ἑ[νὶ τῶν]
24. κατασταθέντων ἐπιτρ[όπ]ων Ἰησοῦ [υἱῷ αὐτῆς ὄντι]
25. [ὀρ]φανῷ τοῦ Ἰησοῦ ὑπὸ βο[υλ]ῆς τῶν Πετραίω[ν, λέγου]-
26. [σ]α · διὰ τό σε μὴ δε[δωκέναι τῷ] υ[ἱ]ῷ μου ± 10 τῷ]
27. αὐτῷ ὀρφανῷ ἐξ οὗ .[. .].[. . .].εστ.[- -]
28. καθάπερ δέδωκεν Ἀβδοοβδας Ἑλλο[υ]θα ὁ κολλή[γας σου]
29. δι' ἀποχῆς, διὸ παραγγέλλω σοι παρεδρεῦσαι [ἐπὶ βῆμα]-
30. τος Ἰουλίου Ἰουλιανοῦ ἡγεμώνος (read ἡγεμόνος) ἐν Πέτρᾳ
    [μητροπόλει]
31. [τῆ]ς Ἀραβίας [μέχρι οὗ διακουσθῶμεν ἐ]ν τῷ ἐν Πέ[τρᾳ τρι-
    βουναλίῳ]
32. [τῆ]ς δευτέρας ἡμέρας τ[οῦ Δίου μηνὸς ἢ εἰς τὴν αὐτοῦ ἔγγιστα]
33. [. .]ι ἐν Πέ[τρᾳ π]αρου[σίαν - -]
34. [κ]αιπερ [. . . .] . .[- -]

---

[20] The translation follows A. Lewis, in A. Watson, ed., *The Digest of Justinian* II (Philadelphia 1985) 794.

35.] . [
36. [ο]ἱ ἐπ[ιβε]β[λ]ημένοι μάρτυρ[ε]ς · Ἰωάνης Μακ[ου]θ[α]
37. Σαμμοῦος Μαναήμου
38. Θαδδαῖος Θαδδαίου
39. Ἰώσηπος Ἀνανία
40. [. . .]ας Λιβανοῦ traces of ink (Greek)
    [Traces of two or three lines in Aramaic?]
    ἔ[γρ]αψα.

On the back, individual signatures

44. יותנא בר מכותא שהד
45. שמוע בר מנתם שהד

46. Θαδαῖος Θα[δαίου] μάρ(τυς)

47. יוהסף [בר] תניה שהד

Outer text: In the ninth year of Imperator Traianus Hadrianus Caesar
Augustus, in the consulship of Marcus Valerius Asiaticus for the 2nd
time and Titius Aquilinus four days before the ides of October, and
according to the compute of the province of Arabia year twentieth
on the twenty-fourth of month Hyperberetaios called Thesrei, in
Maoza, Zoara district, before the attending witnesses Babatha daughter of Simon son of Menaham—through her guardian for this matter, Judah son of Khthousion—summoned John son of Joseph Eglas,
one of the guardians appointed by the council of Petra for her son
Jesus the orphan of Jesus, saying: On account of your not having
given . . . to my son, the said orphan . . . just as ʿAbdoöbdas son of
Ellouthas, your colleague, has given by receipt, therefore I summon
you to attend at the court of the governor Julius Julianus in Petra
the metropolis of Arabia until we are heard in the tribunal in Petra
[the inner text adds: before Julianus, governor] on the second day
of the month Dios (?) or at his next sitting in Petra . . . The attending witnesses: John son of Makhouthas, Sammouos son of Menahem,
Thaddeus son of Thaddeus, Joseph son of Ananias, Jesus (?) son of
Libanos (?).

On the back, individual signatures: Yoḥana son of Makhouta, witness; Shammuʿa son of Menaḥem, witness; Thaddeus son of Thaddeus,
witness; Yehosef son of Ḥananiah, witness

Lewis assumes that P.Yadin 13 contains complaints of Babatha
that the guardians pay too little maintenance, and that these complaints are continued in P.Yadin 14, which dates from the 11th or

12th October 125.[21] This, however, is not true. In P.Yadin 13
Babatha's main purpose was that the governor should fix the adequate sum. She did not want to institute proceedings against any-
body; otherwise she would not have used the form of a petition, an
axioma. That she complained in this context about the insufficiency
of the money that the guardians paid is self-evident, for otherwise
there would not have been a reason for addressing the provincial
governor. In P.Yadin 14, however, Babatha complains that one of
the two guardians, Johannes, son of Joseph Eglas, is not paying his
share, whereas his colleague is fulfilling his obligations. P.Yadin 14
deals not with the low level of the amount due to Babatha, but only
with the failure of payment by the co-guardian Johannes. The law-
suit is directed against him alone, and he is summoned by Babatha
by means of *parangelia* to appear at the court of the governor.

This *parangelia* is executed by Babatha herself without the participation of an authority.[22] In Egyptian papyri, however, the plaintiff
addressed the *strategos* in order that the strategos should hand down
the summons to the defendant.[23] It is remarkable that Babatha summons Johannes through a tutor who is appointed just for this purpose (see lines 22/23). The Greek term used for him is *epitropos*,
which corresponds to Roman terminology, not *kyrios*, the expression
used in Greek legal systems. In Roman legal terminology the expression *tutor* is used both for the guardian of minors and of women.
Wolff[24] has argued that Roman terminology generally prevailed over
Greek terminology. The Roman *tutor* of a woman, however, was
normally appointed permanently, not *tou pragmatos*. The *epitropos tou
pragmatos* resembles a Roman *curator unius rei* or pretorian *tutor*.[25] They,
however, were appointed only for specific transactions in which the

---

[21] Lewis (supra note 4) 54 (to line 23 and 57).

[22] H.J. Wolff (supra note 17) 778 already thought of this possibility on the basis
of (now) P.Yadin 15; P.Yadin 14 had not been published at that time. On the
problems of the *parangelia* made with the participation of the *strategos* or by the party
himself see G. Foti Talamanca, *Ricerche sul processo nel Egitto greco-romano II: L'introduzione
del giudizio* (Milan 1979) 79–102, with extensive exegesis of texts.

[23] Cf. Mitteis (supra note 11) 36–7; Taubenschlag (supra note 11) 500; Kaser/Hackl
(supra note 11) 475; A. Steinwenter, *Studien zum römischen Versäumnisverfahren* (Munich
1914) 73–91; A.J. Boyé, *La denuntiatio introductive d'instance sous le principat* (Bordeaux
1922) 23 ff.

[24] H.J. Wolff (supra note 17) 796.

[25] For the *epitropos tou pragmatos* there is other papyrological evidence. See e.g.
P.Hamb. IV 270, where a woman applies for such a guardian because she has

permanent guardian was not allowed to carry out his duties (because he himself was a party in the controversy with the woman or the ward) or was not able to do so (because he was absent).[26] That is not the case here, since Babatha's guardian is her (second) husband, Judah son of Khthousion.[27]

The papyrus mentions the defendant's duty to attend the *conventus* until the proceedings took place (line 29). This corresponds to the normal course of a *conventus*, where the parties appeared at its opening and waited for their case to be called.[28] But the fragmentary end of the papyrus as restored by the editor shows two alternative dates (see lines 32/33). Of the first date the first words are preserved (line 32: "on the second day"). The second date might have referred to

---

neither husband nor son. For other examples see H.A. Rupprecht, "Zur Frage der Frauentutel im römischen Ägypten," in *Festschrift für Arnold Kränzlein* (Graz 1986) 95–102.

[26] Inst. 1.21.3; Gai. 1.184; Ulp. ep. 11.24; D.26.1.3.2–4. See M. Kaser, *Das römische Privatrecht*[2] I (Munich 1971) 359. We have an example for this from the material of the Judaean Desert in P.Yadin 17 and P.Hever 65. In this context H.M. Cotton, "The Guardian (ἐπίτροπος) of a Woman in the Documents from the Judaean Desert," *ZPE* 118 (1997) 267–73 at 269 ff. has rightly put the question what the actual function of the *epitropos* was. She has pointed out that in some documents (P.Yadin 16 lines 35–6; P.Yadin 22 line 29; P.Yadin 27 lines 4–5) the *epitropos* has also the function of the *cheirochrestes*, the subscriber for Babatha, who being illiterate can not subscribe by herself, whereas in P.Yadin 15 line 34 the subscriber for Babatha is Eleazar son of Eleazar and not Judah, her *epitropos tou pragmatos*, who is able to write, and subscribes this document as *epitropos* (see also P.Yadin 16, where he is both an *epitropos* and subscriber for Babatha). Further, there are documents in which no guardian is involved at all (P.Yadin 19; 21; 23; 24; 26). Since a guardian does not appear in the Semitic documents from the Judaean Desert, one could think that the presence of a guardian depended on the nature of the anticipated court. For Roman institutions a guardian was necessary and for this reason present; for other institutions this was not the case and he could be absent. However, the analysis of the papyri in which a tutor is lacking also allows the hypothesis, as Cotton goes on to say, that in these cases the guardian was superfluous, even under Roman legal procedures. With regard to the number of Babatha's various *epitropoi* occurring in the archive (for a detailed list see H. Cotton, *ibid.* 267 ff.), I have the impression that the presence of a guardian seems to be rather a formal element which has something to do with procedural matters. Whether this suffices for the hypothesis that the presence of an *epitropos* was required by the application of Roman patterns cannot be said with certainty.

[27] It cannot be said for certain that Babatha and Judah were already married at the time when P.Yadin 14 was written, because Babatha's Ketubba in P.Yadin 10 does not preserve the date of the marriage. See Y. Yadin, J.C. Greenfield, A. Yardeni, "Babatha's Ketubba," *IEJ* 44 (1994) 75–101 at 77 and H. Cotton (supra note 26) 269. The mention of Judah as a guardian in P.Yadin 15 could be used to date P.Yadin 10 if one presumes that a husband generally is the *epitropos* of his wife.

[28] See Mitteis (supra note 11) 37.

the next *conventus*.[29] Lewis completes the missing name of the month with the name of the following month Dios and he seems to think that this date is the time of the proceedings before the provincial governor.[30] He regards it as probable that the summons was written after the parties had known the date for the hearing. But the first date could also denote only the opening of the *conventus*. This would fit better the summons to wait for the case to be called. As to the question of the process available to Babatha, the use of *parangelia* to start the proceedings points to the *cognitio* procedure;[31] but the presence of a Greek translation of the *formula* of the *actio tutelae* induces me to take into account also the possibility of some kind of *formula* procedure. The more basic question, however, of whether there existed an edict of the provincial governor containing the procedural formulas or at least an official collection of the *formulae* to which the mentioned formula of the *actio tutelae* might go back, cannot be answered for the province of Arabia from the extant sources.

4. In response to Babatha's petition the governor might well have fixed the sum of money demanded from Johannes. The amount might have remained the same (two *denarii*). As Lewis notes, this is supported by P.Yadin 27 from 19th August 132, in which Babatha issues a receipt for two *denarii* to one of the two guardians. But it is possible that the governor fixed an amount of two *denarii* per guardian. This could explain the fact that Babatha issued the receipt only to one guardian. The text does not exclude this possibility, but we cannot substantiate this hypothesis by other documentary evidence.[32]

---

[29] This date, almost completely damaged in the outer text, can be reconstructed from line 14 of the inner text.

[30] Lewis (supra note 4) 57.

[31] On this see Wolff (supra note 17) 784 ff. and Biscardi (supra note 17) 114 ff. Both authors see the proceedings in the Province of Arabia as *cognitio*, "in welcher der Formel lediglich die Funktion der Instruktion des delegierten Unterrichters zugekommen sei." (Wolff, 805); contra E. Seidl, "Ein Papyrusfund zum klassischen Zivilprozeßrecht," in *Studi in onore di Giuseppe Grosso II* (Turin 1968) 345–61 at 351 f. Interesting but unproven is Biscardi's opinion (142), according to which this draft of the *actio tutelae* was copied by a private person from some "*repertorio di formule processuali destinato all'uso forense.*" On the topic see now D. Nörr, "Prozessuales aus dem Babatha-Archiv," in *Hommage à la mémoire de André Magdelein* (Paris 1998) 317–41.

[32] Less plausible seems the presumption that the Jew Johannes was engaged with the administration, whereas his co-tutor Abdobdas was only a co-tutor without

1. ἐπὶ ὑπάτων Γαΐου Σερρίου Αὐγορείγου καὶ Πουπλίου Τρεβίο[υ
   Σεργ]ι̣[ανο]ῦ̣ [π]ρ̣ὸ

2. δεκατεσσάρων καλανδῶν Σεπτεμ[β]ρίων, κατὰ τὸν τῆς νέας
   ἐ[πα]ρχίας Ἀραβί-

3. ας ἀριθμὸν ἔτους ἑβδόμου εἰκοστο̣[ῦ] μηνὸς Γορπιαίου πρώτ̣[η,
   ἐ]ν Μαωζα

4. περιμέτρῳ Ζοορων. Βαβαθας Σίμω[ν]ος, συμπαρόντος αὐτῇ
   [ἐπιτρόπου] κ̣[α]ὶ̣

5. ὑπὲρ αὐτῆς ὑπογράφοντος Βαβελι̣[ς] Μαναήμου, ἀμφότε[ροι τ]ῆ̣[ς]
   α̣ὐτῆς Μαω-

6. ζας, Σίμωνι κυρτῷ Ἰωάνου Ἐγλα [τῆ]ς αὐτ̣[ῆ]ς Μαωζας χαίρι̣[ν]·
   ϛ̣ου̣ δευτέρου ἐπι-

7. τρόπου κατασταθέντο̣ς [± 16] ὑπ̣[ὸ βουλῆς Πετρ]αίων Ἰησο̣[ύ]-

8. ου Ἰησούου ὀρφανοῦ υ[ἱοῦ] μου, ἀπ[έσχ]ο̣ν π̣[αρ]ά σ̣[ο]υ ⟨ε⟩ἰς
   λό̣γο̣[ν τρ]οφίων καί αμφι-

9. αζμου (read ἀμφιασμοῦ) τοῦ αὐτοῦ Ἰησούο̣υ υ[ἱοῦ] μ̣[ου] ἀργυρίου
   δηναριων̣ (read δηνάρια) [ἐ̣ξ] ἀ̣[π]ὸ̣ μηνὸς

10. Πανήμου πρώτη⟨ς⟩ τοῦ αὐτοῦ ἔτου⟨ς⟩ ἑβδόμου εἰκοστοῦ μέχρι
    Γορπι[αίο]υ τριακα-

11. δι (read τριακάδος), μηνῶν τελίων τρις (read τριῶν) בבתיה ברת

    שמעון אתקבליה מן שמעון נ[בי]חיה בר

12. יהנ. אפ[טרפא] ישוע ברי לכסות [ו]מ[ז]ון דישוע [ברי כס]ף
    ד[י]נרן שתיה מחד/בתמוז ועדי

13. תלח‹ל›ין באלולא שנת עשרין ושבע [די ליר]חי. תלח‹ל›
    שוו די בבלי בר מנחם כתביה

14. על דבר ..[ ].. ר

15. ἑρμηνία{ς} Βαβαθας Σίμωνος· ἀπέσχον παρὰ Σιμωνι (read
    Σίμωνος) κυρτω (read κυρτοῦ) Ἰωάγου

16. επιτροπος (read ἐπιτρόπου) Ἰησούου υιω (read υἱοῦ) μου ⟨ε⟩ἰς
    λό[γ]ο̣ν τ[ρο]φίων κ̣αὶ αμφιαζμου (read ἀμφιασμοῦ) αὐτοῦ

17. ἀργυρίου δηναριων (read δηνάρια) ἐξ ἀπὸ μηνὸς Παγήμου πρώτης
    μέχρι Γορπιαίου τριακαδι (read τριακάδος) ἔτους

18. ἑβδόμου εἰκοστοῦ, αι (read οἵ) εἰσιν μῆγες [τέλειοι τρε]ῖ̣ς. [διὰ
    ἐπιτ]ρ̣ό̣που αὐτῆς Βαβελις Μαναήμου

19. Γερμαγ[ὸ]ς Ἰούδ[ο]υ ἔγραψα.

---

specific duties. E. Koffmann, *Die Doppelurkunden aus der Wüste Juda* (Leiden 1968) 100
thinks of the second tutor as evidence for Roman influence. This view, however,
is not compelling, for the number of *tutores* was not fixed in Rome.

In the consulship of Gaius Serrius Augurinus and Publius Trebius
Sergianus fourteen days before the kalends of September, according
to the compute of the new province of Arabia year twenty-seventh
on the first of the month Gorpiaios, in Maoza in the district of
Zoöra. Babathas (sic) daughter of Simon, being present with her as
guardian and subscribing for her, Babelis son of Menahem, both of
the said Maoza, to Simon the hunchback, son of John son of Eglas,
of the said Maoza, greeting. You having been appointed by the
council of Petra to be [in place of your father?] the second guardian
of my orphan son Jesus son of Jesus, I have received from you,
toward the account of maintenance and clothing of the said Jesus
my son, six denarii of silver [for the period] from the first of the
month Panemos of the said twenty-seventh year up to the thirtieth
of Gorpiaios, three full months.
[2nd hand, Aramaic] Babatha the daughter of Shimʿon: I have
received from Shimʿon the hunchback, son of Yoḥanan the guardian
of Yeshuʿa my son for clothing and food for Yeshuʿa my son six
silver denars from the first of Tammuz until the thirtieth of Elul
year twenty-seven, which equals three months. This is what Babeli
the son of Menaḥem wrote.
[1st hand] Translation of [the attestation of] Babatha daughter of
Simon: I have received from Simon the hunchback son of John,
guardian of Jesus my son, toward the account of his maintenance
and clothing, six denarii of silver [for the period] from the first of
the month Panemos up to the thirtieth of Gorpiaios of the twenty-
seventh year, which are three full months. By her guardian Babelis
son of Menaḥem.
I, Germanos son of Judah, wrote [it].

The guardian in P.Yadin 27 is Simon the hunchback, the son of
the guardian Johannes. He probably took the place of his father in
consequence of his nomination by the council of Petra. The reasons
for the replacement of the guardian Johannes are not mentioned in
the papyrus. Presumably Johannes had died in the meantime, because
in between the summons to the governor's court and the receipt lies
a period of seven years. It is precisely this long period that contra-
dicts the assumption of a substitution of Johannes on the occasion
of the procedure before the court of the provincial governor which
Babatha instituted against him according to P.Yadin 14.

III

With respect to the central question of our workshop I now want to draw special attention to P.Yadin 15, a text which is the most telling for the problems of guardianship. The papyrus' date is the same as the date of the summons before the governor's court, the 11th or 12th of October 125. The text contains Babatha's complaint against the guardians of her son Jesus, who are reproached with negligent and selfish administration of the orphan's fortune.

Outer Text

14. ἔτου[ς ἐνάτου Αὐτοκράτορος] Τραιανοῦ Ἀδριανοῦ Καίσαρος
    Σεβαστοῦ, ἐπὶ ὑπάτ[ω]ν [Μάρκου Οὐαλερίου]

15. [Ἀσιατικοῦ τὸ β̅ καὶ Τιτίου Ἀκυλεί]νου πρὸ τ[εσσάρων] εἰδῶν
    [Ὀκ]τ[ωβρίων, κατὰ δὲ τὸν ἀριθμὸν τῆς ἐπαρχείας]

16. [Ἀραβίας ἔτους εἰκοστοῦ μηνὸς Ὑ]περ[βε]ρ[εταίου λεγομένου
    Θεσρε]ὶ̣ [τ]ε̣[τά]ρ[τη καὶ εἰκάς, ἐν Μαωζᾳ περὶ]

17. [Ζοαραν, ἐπὶ τῶν ἐπιβεβλη]μένων μαρτύρων ἐμαρτυροποιήσατ̣ο̣
    Βαβαθα Σίμωνος τοῦ Μανα-

18. [ήμου κατὰ Ἰωάνου Ἰωσή]που τοῦ Ἐγλα καὶ Ἀβδοοβδα Ἑλλουθα
    ἐπιτρόπων Ἰησοῦ Ἰησοῦτος

19. [υἱοῦ αὐτῆς ὀρφανοῦ κατασ]ταθέντων τῷ αὐτῷ ὀρφανῷ ὑπὸ
    βουλῆς τῶν Πετραίων, παρόντω[ν]

20. [τῶν αὐτῶν ἐπιτρόπων,] λέγουσα· διὰ τὸ ὑμᾶς μὴ δεδωκέναι τῷ
    υἱῷ [μου ὀρ]φα̣νῷ δ.[.]ε-

21. [... τρο]φεῖα πρὸς τὴν δύν]αμιν τόκου [ἀ]ργυρίου [αὐ]τοῦ [κ]αὶ
    [τῶν] λοιπῶ[ν] ὑ̣[παρχόντων αὐτοῦ]

22. [κ]α̣[ὶ μ]ά̣λ̣[ιστα πρὸς ὁμιλία]ν̣ ἣν̣ [..]...[.]α̣[..]..[..]. [. καὶ μὴ
    χορηγεῖν αὐτῷ τόκον]

23. τῷ[ῦ] ἀρ[γυρ]ίου ε[ἰ μὴ [τροπαι]εικὸν ἕν̣α εἰς ἑκατὸν δηνάρια,
    ἔ̣[χουσ]α̣ ὑπάρχο[ντα] ἀ̣ξι[όχρεα]

24. τῷ[ύτ]ου [τοῦ ἀργυρίου] οὗ ἔχετε τοῦ ὀρφανοῦ, διὸ προεμαρ-
    τυροποίησα ἵνα εἰ δοκεῖ

25. ὑμεῖν δ̣ο̣ῦναί μ[οι τὸ] ἀργύριον δι᾿ ἀσφαλίας `.....´ περὶ ὑποθήκης
    τῶν ὑπαρχόντων μου, χορη-

26. [γ]οῦσα τ̣όκον τ̣οῦ [ἀργυρίο]υ ὡς ἑκατὸν δηναρίων δηνάριν ἓν
    ἥμισυ, ὅθεν λαμπρῶς διασω-

27. θ[ῆ μου] ὁ̣ υἱὸς εὐχαριστῶν τοῖς μακαριωτάτοις καιροῖς ἡγεμωνε-
    [ιας] (read ἡγεμονίας) Ἰουλ̣[ί]ο̣υ Ἰουλιανοῦ

28. ηγεμωνος (read ἡγεμόνος), ἐπὶ οὗ περὶ τῆς ἀπειθαρχείας ἀποδόσεως τῶν τροφίων παρήνγειλα ἐγὼ Βα-

29. βαθα Ἰωάνῃ τῷ προγεγραμμένῳ ἐνεὶ τῶν ἐπιτρόπων τοῦ ὀρφανοῦ. εἰ δὲ μή, ἔσται

30. τοῦτο [τὸ μαρτυρο]πρίημα εἰς δικαίωμα κέρδους ἀργυρίου τοῦ ὀρφανοῦ εἰ διδόντες

31. .....[.].... [ἐμαρ]τυροποιήσατο ἡ Βαβαθα ὡς προγέγραπται διὰ ἐπιτρόπου αὐτῆς τοῦδε

32. τοῦ πράγματο[ς Ἰούδου Χ]θουσίωνος ὃς παρὼν ὑπέγραψεν. (2nd hand) Βαβαθας Σίμωνος ἐμαρτυροποιησάμη⟨ν⟩

33. κᾳτᾲ Ἰωάνου Ἐγλα Ἀ⟨βδ⟩αοβδα Ἐλλουθα επιτρωπων (read ἐπιτρόπων) ησους (read Ἰησοῦ) υ⟨ἱ⟩ο⟨ῦ⟩ μου ὀρφανοῦ δι’ ἐπιτρόπου μου Ἰούδα

34. Χαθουσίωνος ἀκοͅλ[ο]ύθῳς τες (read ταῖς) προγεγραμμενες (read προγεγραμμέναις) ερεσασιν (read αἱρέσεσιν). Ἐλεάζαρος Ἐλεαζάρου ἔγραψα ὑπὲρ αὐτῆς

35. ἐρωτηθεὶς διὰ τὸ αυτης (read αὐτὴν) μὴ ε⟨ἰ⟩δένα⟨ι⟩ γράμματα. vac

36. (1st hand) καὶ ἐπεβάλοντο μάρτυρες ἑπτά.

37. יהודה בר כתושין אדון בבתה בקמי השרת בבתה ככל די על
כתב יהודה כתבה

38. עבדעבדת בר אילותא במקמי ובמקם יוחנה חברי בר ענלא
כתיבת שהדתא דא כדי עלא כתיב עבדעבדת כתבה

39. יהוחנן בר אלכס ביד יהוסף ברה   ὁ δὲ γράψας τοῦτο Θεενας
Σίμωνος λιβλάριος.

On the back, individual signatures

                             [   ]
                             [   ]
                         [   ] שהד
              יהוסף בר חננ[י]ה [ש]הֹד
                תֹומֹה בר שמע[ון ש]הד
                [י]שֹוע בר ישוע [שהד]

According to Lewis' translation the outer text, after the dating, reads:[33]

> ... before the attending witnesses Babatha daughter of Simon son of
> Menahem deposed against John son of Joseph Eglas and 'Abdoöbdas
> son of Ellouthas, guardians of her orphan son Jesus son of Jesus,
> appointed guardians for the said orphan by the council of Petra, in
> the presence of the said guardians, saying:

---

[33] Lewis (supra note 4) 61.

On account of your not having given my orphan son generous(?) maintenance money commensurate with the income from the interest on his money and the rest of his property, and commensurate in particular with a style of life which befits(?) him, and you contribute for him as interest on the money only one half-denarius per hundred denarii [per month],[34] as I have property equivalent in value to this money of the orphan's that you have, therefore I previously deposed in order that you might decide to give me the money on security involving a hypothec of my property, with me contributing interest on the money at the rate of a denarius and a half per hundred denarii, wherewith my son may be raised in splendid style, rendering thanks to the[se] most blessed times of the governorship of Julius Julianus, our governor, before whom I, Babatha, summoned the aforesaid John, one of the guardians of the orphan, for his refusal of disbursement of the [appropriate] maintenance money. Otherwise this deposition will serve as documentary evidence of [your] profiteering from the money of the orphan by giving . . .

Babatha deposed as aforestated through her guardian for this matter, Judah son of Khthousion, who was present and subscribed. [2nd hand] I, Babatha daughter of Simon, have deposed through my guardian Judah son of Khthousion against John son of Eglas and ʿAbdoöbdas son of Ellouthas, guardians of my orphan son Jesus, according to the aforestated conditions. I, Eleazar son of Eleazar, wrote for her by request, because of her being illiterate.

[1st hand] And there were at hand seven witnesses.

[3rd hand, Aramaic] Yehudah son of Khthousion "lord" of Babatha: In my presence Babatha confirmed all that is written above. Yehudah wrote it.

[4th hand, Nabatean] ʿAbdʿobdath son of Elloutha: In my presence and in the presence of Yohana, my colleague, son of ʿEgla, this testimony is written according to what is written above. ʿAbdʿobdath wrote it.

[5th hand, Aramaic] Yehoḥanan son of Aleks, by the hand of Yehoseph his son.

[1st hand] The writer of this [is] Theënas son of Simon, *librarius*.

The facts of the case underlying this deposition are not very clear.[35] First of all: what is the legal nature and the purpose of the document?

---

[34] This would amount to 24 *denarii* (6% p.a.) for an estimated ward's estate of 400 *denarii*. For the reconstruction of the ward's estate see Lewis (supra note 4) 24, 53 (to l. 23).

[35] This document was presented to the scholarly world first by H.J. Polotsky, "The Greek Papyri fron the Cave of the Letters", *IEJ* 12 (1962) 258–62 and Y. Yadin, "Expedition D—The Cave of the Letters," *IEJ* 12 (1962) 227–57. Since that time the papyrus has been dealt with by Koffmann (supra note 32) 99 ff.; E. Seidl (supra note 31); id. "Nachträge zu 'La preuve dans l'Antiquité'," in *Études offertes à*

Seidl regarded P.Yadin 15 as an *editio actionis*.[36] Wolff,[37] Biscardi[38] and Lemosse[39] have pointed out that this interpretation is incorrect. In addition to this I just want to note that Babatha could not sue the guardians solely on the grounds that they did not accept her offer contained in P.Yadin 15.

For reasons of the identical dating there should be a connection between P.Yadin 15 and the summons before the court of the provincial governor. But P.Yadin 14 is to institute legal proceedings, whereas P.Yadin 15 constitutes a declaration of Babatha (*testatio*), attested by witnesses, made in presence of the guardians concerned. Furthermore, P.Yadin 14 is addressed to only one of the guardians, whereas P.Yadin 15 is addressed to both. Johannes is summoned for not having paid, a fact repeated by P.Yadin 15. Noteworthy is the expression by which Johannes is reproached for not having paid. Babatha uses the term *apeitharcheia*. Wolff had already suggested "disobedience against official instructions" as the meaning of this word at a time when P.Yadin 13 was not yet published.[40] Taking our interpretation of P.Yadin 13 as a basis, the term can be ascribed taken in this meaning: In consequence of Babatha's petition in P.Yadin 13 the governor may have fixed the sum of money due for the ward's maintenance. The lack of payment of one of the guardians represents an *apeitharcheia* for this reason, i.e. disobedience against an official instruction.

Both guardians, however, are accused of contributing too little to the orphan's maintenance. In respect to this Babatha uses the arguments already known from the petition: the sum paid is insufficient and does not correspond to the financial power of the boy's fortune.[41] This argument provides the opportunity for Babatha to offer

---

Jean Macqueron (Aix-en-Provence 1970) 599–603 at 601; R. Martini, *Ricerche in tema di editto provinciale* (Milan 1969) 9 n. 30, 25 n. 26, 141 n. 28; M. Lemosse, "Le procès de Babatha," in *The Irish Jurist* 3 (1968) 363–76; id., "Indications nouvelles sur le iussum iudicandi," in *RHD* 47 (1969) 291–3; Wolff (supra note 17) 767 ff.; Biscardi (supra note 17) 111; A. Markus, *Tutela impuberis. Einfluß des Volksrechts auf das klassische römische Vormundschaftsrecht unter besonderer Berücksichtigung der gräko-ägyptischen Papyri* (unpublished Diss., Marburg 1989) 57.

[36] Seidl (supra note 31) 353 ff.
[37] Wolff (supra note 17) 775 ff.
[38] Biscardi (supra note 17) 117 f.
[39] Lemosse "Le procès" (supra note 35) 372 ff.
[40] Wolff (supra note 17) 777.
[41] Wolff (supra note 17) 767 reconstructs the text differently from Lewis: *malista pros homeilian hen hekousa hymin* and translates "besonders auf das Gespräch hin, das

an agreement to the guardians that would be satisfying for all persons involved. She offers to pay her son an interest rate of one and a half *denarii* per 100, which would amount to 72 *denarii* per annum on an estimated fortune of 400, if the boy's assets are handed over to her on the security of a mortgage on her entire property, whose value is equivalent to that of the boy's fortune.

Therefore the purpose of P.Yadin 15 could be the formal submission of this offer. This can be assumed from the alternative mentioned in the papyrus that in case the guardians reject Babatha's offer the document should serve as evidence for the income of the boy's money.[42]

Johannes and Abdobdas are said to have invested the money of Jesus and to have realized a profit. Babatha insists that they pay too low an interest rate per 100 *denarii* and offers a higher interest rate in order to obtain the administration of her son's property. That makes sense if we assume an economic use of the ward's property.[43]

Furthermore, Johannes is said not to have carried out his duties. This is the reason for the simultaneity of P.Yadin 14 and 15. At the same time as Johannes was summoned because he had not paid he was offered a compromise which would have made the task easier for him and his co-guardian and, if he had accepted, he would have been able to avoid the proceedings which Babatha intended in P.Yadin 14. Besides, P.Yadin 15 could help Babatha for her proceedings in P.Yadin 14 against Johannes before the provincial governor, because it demonstrates that she is willing to negotiate.

On the other hand, Babatha left other legal options open against the negligent and selfish administration of the orphan's fortune. She had the Greek version of the *actio tutelae* in her archive (P.Yadin 28–30). Presumably Babatha, who pursues her interests in the preserved

---

ich (zu euch) kommend mit euch hatte" (770). With regard to the reading of the papyrus (ll. 6–7, 22) Lewis (supra note 4) is right when saying (63): "although the tops of the letters after ην are lost, enough remains to rule out eta as a possible reading before kappa." His argument that the translation of *pros homeilian* with "auf das Gespräch hin" does not provide an appropriate parallel to *pros ten dynamin* of the previous line is convincing as well.

[42] Lemosse (supra note 35) 374 translates *eis dikaioma* with *apud acta*. But Lewis (supra note 4) 63 has rightly pointed out that *dikaioma* does not mean *actum* and cannot be interpreted in this way. Similarly Wolff (supra note 17) 779 ff.

[43] This *martyropoiema* does not deal with the quota of the maintenance costs, as might be the case in P.Yadin 13 and 14, but only with the interest which is or can be realized from the ward's property.

documents so vigorously, planned to induce her son to sue the guardians with the *actio tutelae* after the end of the guardianship. For this purpose she had to give evidence for the possible income of the ward's fortune by offering a corresponding interest rate by herself. This was done by the *martyropoiema* of P.Yadin 15.

IV

1. P.Yadin 28–30 have been looked upon as evidence of Roman influence. Dieter Nörr has studied the procedural aspects of this opinion.[44] We have seen that the papyri examined here, P.Yadin 12–15, 27 could confirm this view in various points.[45] A particular role in this context is played by P.Yadin 15.

We have Roman legal texts from which we can infer that the mother administers the ward's property *de facto* without giving security and without authorization from the guardians.[46] I limit myself to mention of the rescript of Septimius Severus in D.26.6.2.2, where it is surprising to see what great importance is attached to the appointment of guardians for wards. Mothers who administered their childrens' property without applying for a tutor, or who tried to achieve this *de facto* by proposing unsuitable persons as guardians or by not making a second proposal as soon as the first was rejected, certainly

---

[44] D. Nörr, "Römisches Zivilprozeßrecht nach Max Kaser: Prozeßrecht und Prozeßpraxis in der Provinz Arabia," *ZSav* 115 (1998) 80–98; id. (supra note 31); "Zur condemnatio cum taxatione im römischen Zivilprozeß," *ZSav* 112 (1995) 51–90; "The *Xenokritai* in Babatha's Archive (P.Yadin 28–30)," *Israel Law Review* 29 (1995) 83–94.

[45] By this I do not mean the political aspects of Roman influence, e.g. the fact rightly noted by Goodman (supra note 3) 169 ff. that in this part of the province Arabia the use of the calendar based on dating by the consuls of the year is an indication of Romanization: "What was significant was the desire to behave in Roman fashion". Already Wolff (supra note 17) 790 ff. had regarded the fact that in all these documents the date is at the beginning of the document and that the dating follows the Roman consuls and the Roman calendar as an argument for the influence of Roman law. Also the fact that Babatha addresses the governor so often could be an indication of the confidence that justice was to be obtained from the Roman administration. However, the mention of the "most blessed times of the governorship of Iulius Iulianus, our governor" in P.Yadin 15 l. 27 f. seems to be a rhetorical and, in this kind of document, a recurrent topical argument *ad captandam benevolentiam*.

[46] E.g. D.3.5.30.6; D.26.2.26.pr.; D.26.7.5.8; D.46.3.88; C.5.45.1; P.S.1.4.4.

were not isolated cases, as the emperor so vehemently turned against them.[47]

But we also have texts in which the mother herself took the initiative for the administration of the ward's property by undertaking the risk of the administration and exempting the official guardians from liability to the ward by means of warranty clauses. I want to discuss those texts that describe a situation similar to P.Yadin 15.

First, a constitution of Alexander Severus from the year 228, C.4.29.6. The legal frame of this text is the *senatus consultum Velleianum* which prohibited the intercession of women, that is, the intervention by incurring liabilities for the benefit of others.

> *Si mater, cum filiorum suorum patrimonium gereret, tutoribus eorum securitatem promiserit et fideiussorem praestiterit vel pignora dederit, quoniam quodammodo suum negotium gessisse videtur, senatus consulti auxilio neque ipsa neque fideiussor ab ea praestitus neque res eius pigneratae adiuvantur. 1 Sin autem tutore se excusare volente ipsa se interposuit indemnitatem ei repromittens, auxilio senatusconsulti uti minime prohibetur. 2 Si vero tutores petiit, et sponte periculum suscepit, quominus teneatur, auctoritate iuris tuetur.*

When a mother, while transacting the business of her children, gives security to their guardians by furnishing a security, or delivering pledges, as she is considered, to a certain extent, as having attended to her own affairs, neither she nor the surety furnished by her can take advantage of the senatusconsult, nor will she derive any benefit from the fact that her own property was pledged. (1) When the guardian desired to excuse himself, and the mother interposed to prevent it, and promised him an indemnity, she will by no means be prevented from availing herself of the aid of the senatusconsult. (2) If, however, she demanded guardians, and voluntarily assumed responsibility she will be protected by the authority of the law from being liable.[48]

---

[47] D.26.6.2.2. *Divus Severus Cuspio Rufino. Omnem me rationem adhibere subveniendis pupillis, cum ad curam publicam pertineat, liquere omnibus volo. Et ideo quae mater vel non petierit tutores idoneos filiis suis vel prioribus excusatis reiectisve non confestim aliorum nomina dederit, ius non habeat vindicandorum sibi bonorum intestatorum filiorum.* "The deified Severus to Cuspius Rufinus. I wish it to be clear to everyone that I take all possible care to help *pupilli*, since this is a matter of public concern. And, therefore, any mother who does not request suitable tutors for her sons or who does not without delay put forward the names of others when the previous tutors have been exempted or rejected, will have no right of *vindicatio* over the propety of her sons if they die intestate." On the mother's guardianship in Roman law see recently T.J. Chiusi (supra note 1) 155–96 with comprehensive bibliography on the topic.

[48] Translation of passages from the Code of Justinian follows S.P. Scott, *The Civil Law* (Cincinnati 1932) with some corrections.

The text mentions three situations. In the first alternative the *senatus consultum Velleianum* cannot be applied, because the mother, as the emperor says, has promised securities to the guardians in order to take over the administration of the fortune. Doing so she seems to have managed her own affairs. In the second case she could avoid the *excusatio* of the guardian only by promising a guarantee of indemnity against the ward's claims. Third comes a case in which the mother applied for guardians and simultaneously took over the risk of their administration. In the latter cases the *senatusconsultum Velleianum* is applicable, because the mother in both cases took over liability for the debts of the guardians.

The direct administration of property by the mother, which is the case of the *principium*, should be noticed. This manner of administration was only possible if she undertook liability to the *tutores*. But there are different cases of liability: the liability of the *tutores* towards the ward by means of *actio tutelae* and the liability of the mother towards the *tutores* if they are sued by the ward. In sections 1 and 2 the mother does not administer the ward's property directly, but she has influence on the administration as she secures the *tutores* against financial loss and because of her role in the selection of the guardians. In section 2 the mother applies for certain guardians (this is my understanding of *petiit*) and she takes over the risk of their administration.

2. The applicability of the *senatusconsultum Velleianum* is also denied in Pauli Sententiae 2.11.2:

> *Mulier, quae pro tutoribus filiorum suorum indemnitatem promisit, ad beneficium senatus consulti non pertinet.*

> A woman who promised indemnity to the guardians of her children does not receive the benefit of the senatusconsult.

The words *pro tutoribus . . . promisit* of this controversially interpreted text[49] indicate a promise the mother made for the guardians of her children. One could think of the *satisdatio rem pupilli salvam fore*.[50] By means of this stipulation the administration of the property was given to that co-guardian who offered security to his colleagues. In this

---

[49] See the references in H.H. Seiler, *Der Tatbestand der negotiorum gestio im römischen Recht* (Köln – Graz 1968) 243.

[50] Cf. P. Frezza, "La capacità delle donne all'esercizio della tutela nel diritto romano classico e nei papiri greco-egizi," *Aegyptus* 11 (1930–1931) 363–85 at 374.

text the mother offered the *cautio* to the guardians in order to obtain
the administration of the property. That is basically what Babatha
offers in P.Yadin 15.

3. A case which corresponds to the *principium* of C.4.29.6 is found
in C.5.51.9 (Diocl. Max., a. 293).

> *Tutorem quondam, ut tam rationem, quam si quid reliquorum nomine debet, red-*
> *dat, apud praetorem convenire potes. quamvis enim matrem tuam, susceptis bonis*
> *vestris, indemnitatem pro hac administratione tutori se praestituram promisisse pro-*
> *ponatur, tamen adversus tutorem tibi tutelae, non adversus matris successores ex*
> *stipulatu competit actio.*

> You can sue your former guardian before the praetor to compel him
> both to render an account, and to return what he owes you by way
> of balance. For although it is alleged that your mother, having taken
> over your property, promised to indemnify your guardian for any loss
> due to this administration, nonetheless you have a right of action based
> on guardianship against the guardian, but not an action based on the
> stipulation against your mother's heirs.

A son asks the emperor by which action he can sue his and his
siblings' guardian. The second sentence tells us that the guardian
pointed out to the emperor that the mother had promised him
indemnity. Hence the son should sue the late mother's heirs. The
emperor answers the son that he should sue the guardian for rendering of account and payment of possible outstanding debts. The
son can bring the *actio tutelae* against the guardian, but not an *actio
ex stipulatu* against his mother's heirs. In fact it is only the guardian
who can sue the mother's heirs by an *actio ex stipulatu*. The words
susceptis bonis show that the mother had taken over the administration of the property. In this case, too, the mother had to promise
indemnity to the guardian in order to obtain the administration. The
fact that an *actio ex stipulatu* is not possible does not exclude, however, another action against the mother or her heirs, the *actio negotiorum gestorum*.

4. The problem of how to sue the mother who had accepted liability also arises in the last text I want to mention. It is a constitution of Philip the Arab and his son from the year 246, C.5.46.2:

> *Quaedam pupillorum vestrorum a matre itemque avo paterno administrata, eorumque*
> *nomine indemnitatem vobis promissam esse adseveratis. Quae si ita sunt, et iidem*
> *pupilli, legitimae aetatis effecti non adversus matrem suam itemque avum, sed contra*

vos congredi malunt, non immerito indemnitatem ab his praestari desiderabitis, quos et administrationem suo periculo pridem suscepisse proponitis.

You allege that some of the property of your wards was administered by their mother and paternal grandfather, and that indemnity was promised to you in their name. If that is the case, and the said wards, having reached lawful age, prefer to proceed against you legally and not against their mother or their grandfather, it is not without reason that you ask to receive idemnity from those who you say at that time also undertook the administration at their own risk.

According to the guardians the mother and the paternal grandfather had administered a part of the fortune of their wards and had promised indemnity to them. When after the end of the guardianship the wards prefer to raise claims against the *tutores* instead of suing the mother and the grandfather, the emperor replies to the guardians that they now can rightly demand indemnity from those who had administered the fortune at their risk, i.e that the *tutores* can have recourse against the mother and the grandfather.

Again the ward's property is administered by the mother, in this case, however, only partly, as the mother acts together with the grandfather. Apparently an action against the mother was possible, but finally the "normal" way to sue the guardians by the *actio tutelae* was preferred (*congredi malunt*). In my opinion there is no contradiction between this text and the aforementioned constitution of Diocletian, for C.5.51.9 denies the ward the possibility of an *actio ex stipulatu* against the mother or her heirs. There the *stipulatio* took place between the *tutor* and the mother, and therefore the *actio ex stipulatu* was open only to the *tutor*. C.5.46.2 does not mention the particular action which could be instituted against the mother, and one could think of the *actio negotiorum gestorum* as well.

From the mention of the *actio ex stipulatu* we can deduce that the *stipulatio* was the means for promising indemnity to the guardians. The *satisdatio rem pupilli salvam fore* is also made in form of a stipulation.

5. All these texts describe the situation we can see in P.Yadin 15: a mother demands the administration of her child's property and offers her own property as security for this purpose, without, however, asserting a legal claim. This is important for the discussion of the question of Roman law in the archive of Babatha: A mother's offer to encumber her own property with a mortgage in order to get the administration of the ward's property is, as far as I know,

only found in Roman sources. Wolff[51] observed that this formulation does not have linguistic parallels in the Greek evidence. For
him Babatha's manner of proceeding is inexplicable.[52] But in the
light of the background of the Roman sources Babatha's manner of
proceeding becomes clearer. She offers her own property as security
and stresses that it is equivalent to that of the orphan. By this she
shows that the boy's fortune will not suffer damages in case of mal-
administration and she meets the concern that her administration
might negatively affect the interest of the ward.[53] Babatha's intention may have been to administer her son's property by herself and
to obligate herself to the payment of a certain interest rate per month
to the ward in order to obtain the administration. If she were to fail
her duties or diminish the orphan's fortune, the guardians would
have the mortgaged property of Babatha, equivalent to that of the
ward, as security in case of action by the ward. Even in this case
the guardians would bear the risk of the guardianship.

V

Taking into account that all the Roman legal texts I referred to are
100 or 150 years later than P.Yadin 15, it is difficult to regard this
as evidence for Roman influence. One could argue that in those
cases the provincial practice was adopted by Roman law. In view
of the Roman sources in which the mother's administration of or
influence on the administration of the child's property is revealed,
Leopold Wenger had already assumed this sort of movement from
the provinces to Rome with respect to Greek papyri from Egypt

---

[51] Wolff (supra note 17) 768.

[52] Babatha's document cannot be compared with texts such as D.3.5.30.6,
D.26.2.26.pr. or D.26.7.5.8, in which the widow is appointed guardian by will.
Papinian's point is that this cannot be regarded as guardianship *de iure*. Babatha,
however, is neither a guardian by will nor is she charged with any other task. She
wants to administer the ward's property by herself and is willing to pay a price for
this. These circumstances correspond to the cited texts from the Codex and the
Pauli Sententiae.

[53] From the willingness of the mother to mortgage her property Wolff (supra
note 17) 801 concludes that she only took care of the maintenance costs and that
the reason for her request to obtain the ward's property was not the wish to replace
the guardians as administrator of the estate. The exact meaning of this remark is
not clear. Being administrator of the ward's property and taking care of the son
are not contradictory tasks—quite the opposite!

dealing with the assumption of guardianship and the administration of a ward's property by the mother or the grandmother.[54] Nevertheless the question of mutual influence cannot be answered with mere chronological arguments.[55] Roman sources from the first century onwards attest the tendency to hand over the administration of the ward's property to the mother, both by de facto approval of her administration and by appointment of the woman as heir under a *fideicommissum*. It could have originated in Rome itself for various social and juridical factors. The social factors can be seen in the dissolution of the agnatic bonds at the end of the Roman Republic and, consequently, the loss of importance of the legal guardianship of the agnates and the increasing independence of women. The juridical factor was mainly the progressive liberation of women from *tutela mulierum*, which made them in fact independent administrators of their own property.

Surely, in contrast to Roman law, the Hellenistic legal tradition of Egypt knew mother's guardianship.[56] The papyri, however, show mothers as *epitropoi* only until the second half of the second century. From this time on mothers no longer appear as *epitropos*. What is more, in papyri from the third century mothers appear together with a guardian as *epakolouthetria*. The inference seems likely that this may be a consequence of the *constitutio Antoniniana*. The grant of Roman citizenship with the consequence of the general applicability of Roman law could have made the guardianship of a woman legally impossible in the eastern provinces as well, and it could have necessitated the recourse to the institution of *epakolouthetria* in order to entrust the mother with the administration of the ward's property or to let her participate in administration. Hence, in contrast to Wenger's opinion, one can consider influence of Roman law on Greek legal practice.

To my mind, P.Yadin 15 as well as the other papyri considered here give the opportunity for hypotheses on interactions. The deal offered by Babatha resembles the *satisdatio rem pupilli salvam fore*, as

---

[54] L. Wenger, "Zur Vormundschaft der Mutter," *ZSav* 26 (1905) 449–56 at 455.

[55] In "Zur Vormundschaft der Mutter" (supra note 1) 191–2 I expressed doubt about inferring an influence of Greek legal practice on the imperial constitutions from the mere chronological order. On the contrary I thought of possible effects of Roman law on the Greek practice.

[56] Cf. T.J. Chiusi (supra note 1) 175 with sources and bibliography.

pointed out. This instrument, however, was conceived for a co-guardian, not for a person who was not *tutor*. The mothers who promised indemnity to the guardians in the imperial constitutions and the Pauli Sententiae could have done so in the form of a promise which was aimed at this *satisdatio*. In these cases the reference to the guardianship in the formula of the *cautio* would have been omitted. The question which should be raised here is whether it is possible that Babatha could herself have intended a *satisdatio* when making her promise in P.Yadin 15. As mentioned above, in Babatha's archive we find a Greek translation of the *actio tutelae*. We do not know whether this translation comes from a local *nomikos* or from the governor's bureau or directly from the edict of the provincial governor (and prior to this puzzle we would have to solve the problem of whether there existed one or several edicts in the provinces or any edict at all). It is clear, however, that Babatha had the opportunity to obtain as typically Roman and rather technical an instrument as the *formula* of the *actio tutelae* and that with great probability she wanted to use the *formula* in order to raise her son's claims against the guardians. That means that she thought of the *formula* as useful for her purposes, that the Roman legal instruments were available in the province of Arabia, and that the inhabitants perhaps were receptive to Roman law. It would not be absurd, then, to imagine that Babatha had heard something of the possibility of a promise of indemnity for the guardians in order to obtain the guardianship and that she tried to make use of it.

The question remains why Babatha, being Jewish, should have made use of Roman law. Even if we do not accept Mommsen's old hypothesis that she was not allowed recourse to Jewish law[57] she might have regarded Roman legal instruments as the more appropriate means for reaching her goal. The reason for that need not be an insufficiently developed juristic technique in the former Nabatean kingdom. Rather, the chance to prevail in the proceedings before the Roman governor was presumably greater if one observed the Roman forms. Then P.Yadin would be the first document in respect to the mother's administration of her children's property that reveals a legal practice originating in Roman law. Babatha offers something which is not (and cannot be) a technical *satisdatio*, but which is

---

[57] See Mommsen (supra note 11) 389.

directed at such a model. Venturing to speculate, one may raise the question of whether the *promissio* mentioned in the Roman texts considered above, all of which are later than P.Yadin 15, could trace its origins to this practice. Seen under this aspect, to put it provocatively, the Jewess Babatha contributed to the evolution of Roman legal instruments, and simultaneously to their propagation into the provinces.

We have thus returned to the question with which we began: Roman influence on provincial legal institutions, or change of Roman institutions by contamination with provincial practice? The answer ultimately depends on one's point of view. When at the beginning of the century papyrology and "Antike Rechtsgeschichte" were flourishing, such scholars as Mitteis and Wenger took the first view. Later, in the thirties and forties, the second concept prevailed. More realistic, however, seems to be the opinion that like human beings, legal systems are not isolated entities, but always the result of various encounters and adaptations. This picture evokes a notion of interaction in which the exchange of ideas goes into both directions.

ON P.YADIN 37 = P.HEVER 65

Ranon Katzoff

P.Yadin 37, dated in 131 of this era, is a document associated with
the marriage of Salome daughter of Levi and Iesous son of Menachem.
It was first published by Naphtali Lewis in the volume conventionally known as *P.Yadin*,[1] that is the Babatha papyri, even though there
is no apparent connection with Babatha, because when Lewis received
the lot of the Babatha papyri to publish this one was in there. A
couple of years after *P.Yadin* appeared, Hannah Cotton published
several other papyri in which Salome or her relatives figured,[2] and
it became apparent that this text belonged to that group of documents. As such it was republished, with many fresh readings, at least
one quite important, by Hannah Cotton, as Number 65 in Volume
27 of *Documents of the Judaean Desert*,[3] which is the final publication
of various papyri from Nahal Hever and accordingly has the conventional title *P.Hever*.

This document has been at the center of some controversy, because
it appears that the couple, Salome and Iesous, had been living
together for some time before this document was written. Lewis' first
thought, coming at this from his perspective as a scholar of Greek
papyri from Egypt, was to connect it with the phenomenon of written and unwritten marriages, *gamos engraphos* and *gamos agraphos*, which
figures prominently in the literature on papyri from Egypt. However,
he promptly abandoned the idea in favor of an explanation in terms
of the Jewish institution of provisional marriage for orphan girls

---

[1] *The Documents from the Bar Kokhba Period in the Cave of Letters. Greek Papyri*, ed.
N. Lewis. Aramaic and Nabatean Signatures and Subscriptions, ed. Y. Yadin and
J.C. Greenfield (Jerusalem 1989).

[2] H. Cotton, "The Archive of Salome Komaise Daughter of Levi: Another Archive
from the 'Cave of Letters,'" *Zeitschrift für Papyrologie und Epigraphik* 105 (1995) 171–208.

[3] *Aramaic, Hebrew and Greek Documentary Texts from Nahal Hever and Other Sites with
an Appendix Containing Alleged Qumran Texts (The Seiyal Collection II)* ed. H.M. Cotton
and A. Yardeni (*Discoveries in the Judaean Desert XXVII*) (Oxford 1997).

younger than the legal age of majority, familiar from rabbinic literature.[4] This explanation was rejected out of hand in studies by Tal
Ilan[5] and later by Hannah Cotton[6]. Ilan argued that there indeed
was an accepted Jewish practice of young couples living together
before marriage—very contemporary—and Cotton, for her part, put
it back into the notion of the Egyptian *gamos agraphos* and *gamos
engraphos*, and sees it as one more reflection of the thoroughgoing
assimilation of the Jews to the Hellenistic world. This papyrus, then,
supplies a substantial impetus, in one direction or another, to broad
assessments of the nature of the Jewish community in the second
century and of its legal behavior.

Now I am afraid I have to take responsibility for the interpretation in terms of the minor orphan girl, because it was I who suggested it to Lewis. I thought that this was the more economical of
the two explanations, since it did not require transferring a poorly
attested institution from Egypt, making the necessary changes in it,
and somehow explaining away the absence of any rabbinic reference to it. I also thought then that the institution of the marriage
of the minor orphan girl was so well-known as not to require explanation and documentation. Clearly I was mistaken in that. So, I feel
obligated to defend the position that Lewis took on my authority,
and to examine critically the charges that were brought against it.
I suppose I should have done so as soon as Dr. Ilan's article appeared
in the 1993 *Harvard Theological Review*, but, I admit, I did not take
her article seriously. Ilan, to her credit, is candid in her article that
her interpretative choices there are made according to what is more
provocative[7]—in other words, that the article is more an exercise in
radical writing than a scholarly essay. Nonetheless, to my surprise,
her conclusions have entered the mainstream of scholarship. As prominent a scholar as John Collins has incorporated Ilan's position *in toto*
in *Families in Ancient Israel*;[8] Hannah Cotton adopted Ilan's position

---

[4] Lewis (supra note 1) page 130.

[5] T. Ilan, "Premarital Cohabitation in Ancient Judea: The Evidence of the Babatha
Archive and the Mishna (*Ketubbot* 1.4)," *Harvard Theological Review* 86:3 (1993) 247–64,
summarized in T. Ilan, *Jewish Women in Greco-Roman Palestine* (Peabody, Mass. 1995)
99–100.

[6] Cotton (supra note 3) pages 227–8.

[7] Ilan (supra note 5).

[8] J.J. Collins, "Marriage, Divorce, and Family in Second Temple Judaism," in
L.G. Perdue et al., *Families in Ancient Israel* (Louisville 1997) 113.

partially in her DJD Volume 27, as did Michael Satlow in his *Jewish Families in Antiquity*.[9]

After reading the papyrus, I will explain the general lines of the institution of the marriage of the minor orphan girl, look briefly at Ilan's critique, and finally at Cotton's. One of the new readings suggested by Cotton is central to the discussion, and I want to look at the implications of that as well.

The operative part of the document as restored and translated by Lewis, after indications of the Roman date and the place, is as follows:

> [3]Jesus son of Menahem, domiciled in the village of [4]Soffathe . . . in the district of the city of Livias of the administrative region of P[ ] acknowledged of his own free will(?) that he has taken Salome (Σοφφαθε [.] . . περὶ πόλιν Λιουιάδος τῆς π[±10 εἰληφέναι Σ]αλώμην) also called Komaïs . . . [5]a Maozene woman, for them to . . . and for Jesus to live with [6]her as also before this time . . . to the said Komaïs as her dowry [7]ninety-six denarii of silver, and the bridegroom, the said Jesus, acknowledged that he has received from her on the present day [8]feminine adornment in silver and gold and clothing and other feminine articles equivalent in appraised value [9]to the [stated sum of] money, with his undertaking of feeding and clothing both her and the children to come in accordance with Greek custom [10]and Greek manners upon the said Jesus' good faith and peril of all his possessions, [11]both those which he possesses in his home village of Soffathe . . . and those which he may in addition acquire, she having the right of execution [12]both from the said Jesus and upon all (?) his validly held possessions everywhere, in whatever manner [13]the said Komaïs or whoever acts through her (*i.e.* a successor) or for her (*i.e.* an agent) may choose to carry out the execution, regarding this [14]being thus rightly done the formal question having in good faith been asked and acknowledged in reply.

Note that in line 4 the text represented by the translation "that he has taken," εἰληφέναι, is Lewis' restoration of a lacuna. We will return to that. Note too the presence in line 14 of a Roman *stipulatio*-clause, an assertion that the parties performed the formal question and congruent answer which would create a unilateral and *stricti iuris*, though conditioned, obligation on the part of the husband.[10] The

---

[9] M. Satlow, *Jewish Marriage in Antiquity* (Princeton and Oxford 2001) 100 and 305 note 63.

[10] W.W. Buckland, *A Text-book of Roman Law from Augustus to Justinian*[3] (Cambridge 1963) 434–7.

document is thus framed by a consular date at the beginning and *stipulatio*-clause at the end, two uniquely Roman features.[11]

Before I go on, I want to get rid of a red herring, this "in accordance with Greek custom and Greek manners," νόμῳ ἑλληνικῷ καὶ ἑλληνικῷ τρόπῳ (9–10). The phrase *helleniko nomo* occurred famously in P.Yadin 18.51, the marriage contract of Shelamzion, Babatha's stepdaughter, and in reference to that, Yigael Yadin said that the Jews wrote their contracts in accordance with Greek law.[12] Even though the late Professor Wasserstein admonished us, or rather me, not to take grammar too seriously,[13] the fact remains that the way to say "according to Greek laws, or customs" is κατὰ τοὺς τῶν ἑλλήνων νομούς, that is κατὰ with accusative plural, not νόμῳ ἑλληνικῷ in dative singular.[14] If one might have had any doubt in P.Yadin 18, one can have no doubt in this document, because the writer makes crystal clear what he means by adding *helleniko tropo*, which certainly can mean neither law nor custom, but only style, fashion. It modifies not αἵρεσις, undertaking, but τροφή and ἀμφιασμός, food and clothing. It refers not to the Greek customs of law, but to their habits as consumers. The husband promises to support his wife on a Greek standard of living. It is as if an Arab in Israel promised to support his wife *Ioudaiko nomo*. He does not mean a reference to the Shulchan Aruch, but that he will support her in the standard of living of the Jews in Israel—plaster on the walls, children will wear shoes, his wife will have a washing machine, a clothes dryer, microwave oven, and all those other things that Jewish Israelis feel their newly married daughters must have. So this phrase has nothing whatever to do with Greek law. Furthermore, nothing like this clause appears in Greek marriage contracts other than those of Jews. There the support clause is almost always phrased as an obligation of the husband to support his wife "as well as he can afford."

Another detail that separates this document from the routine Greek

---

[11] So too P.Yadin 18. See R. Katzoff, "Legal Commentary" in N. Lewis, R. Katzoff, and J. Greenfield, "Papyrus Yadin 18," *IEJ* 37 (1987) 229–50.

[12] Y. Yadin, *Bar-Kokhba: the Rediscovery of the Legendary Hero of the Last Jewish Revolt Against Imperial Rome* (London 1971) 246.

[13] Orally, at my lecture on this subject to the Classics Seminar at the Hebrew University. See also A. Wasserstein, "A Marriage Contract from the Province of Arabia Nova: Notes on Papyrus Yadin 18," *Jewish Quarterly Review* 80 (1989) 93–130, at 108; R. Katzoff, "Papyrus Yadin 18 Again: A Rejoinder," *Jewish Quarterly Review* 82 (1991) 171–6 at 174–5.

[14] See Katzoff (supra note 11) at 239–40.

documents from Egypt is that the obligation is to feed not only the wife but also the children to be born. This too is hardly ever found in Greek marriage contracts, since the Greeks occasionally practiced infant exposure, and this clause forbids that. Jews were notorious in antiquity for raising all their children. Since I am counting up points of continuity in the one direction or the other, I also have to note on the other hand that there is no dowry addition from the side of the groom here, as one would expect on the basis of rabbinic literature,[15] and as one finds in P.Yadin 18. But then, the rabbis said, "one person marries off his daughter and gains money, another marries off his daughter and pays money."[16] Perhaps Salome was not a great beauty.

To return to our problem, the institution of the marriage of the minor orphan girl stems from a problem in the rules on the requirements for marriage. For Romanists it may be useful to set out the law on the subject on the background of Roman law. In Roman law the requirements for the formation of marriage are three: *conubium*, *aetas*, and *consensus*. *Conubium*: There must be the capacity for marriage, for instance, that the union is not incestuous. *Aetas*: Both parties must be of age, that is, past puberty. And finally, there must be the will to marry on both sides.[17] Jewish law also requires these things, among others. On age there is a difference between Roman and Jewish law. In Jewish law age past puberty is a requirement for the husband but not for the wife. So it was certainly in the second century. There is also a great difference between Roman and Jewish law in the matter of will. Whose will counts? In Roman law it is that of the *paterfamilias*. No matter how old the spouses, if they have a *paterfamilias*, it is his will which determines the marriage. In Jewish law on the other hand, there is no *patria potestas*. That, says Gaius, is almost uniquely Roman. In Jewish law it is the will of the spouses that makes the difference. If the spouses are adults, that is, past puberty, it is their will, and only their will, which is determinative.

---

[15] M.Ketubot 6.3. See Katzoff, "*Donatio ante nuptias* and Jewish Dowry Additions," in N. Lewis, ed., *Papyrology* (Yale Classical Studies 28) (Cambridge 1985) 231–44.

[16] T.Ketubot 6.3. ‏יש שמשיא את בתו ונוטל מעות ויש שמשיא את בתו ונותן אחריה מעות‎.

[17] Ulpian 5.2: *Iustum matrimonium est, si inter eos qui nuptias contrahunt conubium sit, et tam masculus quam femina potens sit, et utrique consentiant, si sui iuris sunt, aut etiam parentes eorum, si in potestate sunt.* "Marriage is lawful if between the parties to the marriage there is *conubium*, both the male and female partners are of age, and both consent, if they are *sui iuris*, or their parents as well, if the partners are in *potestas*." Buckland (supra note 10) 112–6.

If the spouses are not adult, then, if the husband is a minor, the marriage fails because of age. If the bride is a minor, her father's will counts, not hers; a minor is not counted as having a will.[18] Now comes the problem: What if a minor girl is an orphan, has no father? She cannot express her will to marry, because a minor has no will; and she has no father to express *his* will for her marriage. What to do? The rabbis recognized an institution by which the bride's mother or brother can express *their* will for the girl's marriage instead of the deceased father. The rabbis also recognized this marriage as provisional. The couple could live together, yet at any point, originally even after the wife reached adulthood, she, the wife, could call the marriage off by simply expressing her disapproval of it.[19]

The institution is not recherché.[20] An entire chapter of the Mishna, chapter 13 of *Yevamot*, is devoted to the matter of the "expression of disapproval," מיאון. References are ubiquitous in the Talmud.[21] It was definitely practiced at about the time of our papyrus. Two particular instances, borderline cases which raised principal issues, come to mind, instances in which named known individuals were involved, R. Yehuda ben Bava[22] and R. Yishmael. Both were contemporaries of our document; R. Yishmael was from Aziz in southeastern Judaea, only a few kilometers from the cave where our document was found. His daughter, or daughter-in-law, was married in this way.[23]

I have argued elsewhere that Jewish girls at that time commonly—I cannot be more precise than that—married at or before puberty.[24]

---

[18] M.Ketubot 4.4; T.Yevamot 13.2. M.A. Friedman, *Jewish Marriage in Palestine. A Cairo Geniza Study* I (Tel Aviv and New York 1980) 216–7. For a detailed account see H.Z. Reines, "The Marriage of Minors in the Talmud," Z. Ravid, ed., *Zvi Scharfstein Jubilee Volume* (Tel Aviv 1970) 191–200 (Hebrew). For a summary account see B.-Z. Schereschewsky, "Marriage: Legal Aspects," *Encyclopedia Judaica* XI 1045–51, and *idem*, "Child Marriage," *ibid.* V 423–6; repr. In M. Elon, ed., *The Principles of Jewish Law* (Jerusalem 1975) 356–60 and 363–6.

[19] M.Yevamot 13.2; M.Ketubot 6.6; T.Yevamot 13.1. Friedman (supra note 18) 228.

[20] *Pace* Cotton (supra note 3) page 227 note 23.

[21] A quick digital search of the Mishna, Tosefta and the two Talmudim for five inflected forms of one technical term associated with the institution, למאן, yielded 261 hits from 12 different tractates. Students with a smattering of elementary Talmud may have come across the institution in the fourth chapter of B. Berachot, often used as an introductory text, at 27a (in a quotation from M.Eduyot 6.1).

[22] M.Eduyot 6.1.

[23] B.Nidah 52a; Y.Yevamot 13.1 13c.

[24] R. Katzoff, "Age at Marriage of Jewish Girls During the Talmudic Period," in M.A. Friedman, ed., *Marriage and the Family in Halakha and Jewish Thought* = *Te'udah* 13 (1997) 9–18 (Hebrew).

Then, the demographic figures which have been worked up for the Roman world point to startlingly early mortality. Whereas in Rome this probably mitigated the rigors of *patria potestas*,[25] among Jews it would mean young orphan brides. Our Salome was definitely an orphan. P.Hever 63, dated, it appears, in 127, is a settlement of a dispute over succession to her father's property. At some point after the orphan child bride reaches majority the marriage becomes permanent, and that would be an appropriate time to write a marriage contract, to institute or to increase a dowry. That, I suggested to Lewis, is what is happening here.

Tal Ilan's criticism of this is mainly that Lewis' and my interpretation is apologetic rather than provocative. Well, Salome is not *my* daughter, so she can do whatever she wants and I can look at my friends straight in the eye. Also, to interpret a legal document in terms of the law of the community to which its writers belonged seems to me to be the correct approach. Failing that one uses other strategies.

Ilan's own interpretation is that there was in ancient Judaea a regular and legally recognized practice of trial marriage. She claims to find support for her idea not only in this papyrus—a slender reed to be sure—but mainly in Talmudic literature, where several passages indicate a practice in Judaea, in contrast to Galilee, whereby betrothed couples would מתייחד, be alone together, before marriage. Ilan takes this to mean a regular practice of pre-marital cohabitation.

Back a century ago and more there was much interest in this sort of thing. Westermarck collected reports of trial marriages from all sorts of places, Native American tribes, southern India, Pacific islands and especially from areas with strong Celtic roots—Wales, Scotland, and Ireland.[26] At that time the distinction in Greek-speaking Egypt between "written" and "unwritten" marriages was thought to reflect trial marriages.[27] For the papyri this view has been thoroughly discredited.[28]

---

[25] R.P. Saller, "Men's Age at Marriage and its Consequences in the Roman Family," *Classical Philology* 82 (1987) 21–34 at 32–3.

[26] E. Westermarck, *History of Human Marriage* 5th ed. (London 1921) I, 135–6.

[27] E. Revillout, "Les Contrats de mariage Égyptiens," *Journal Asiatique* 7th Ser., 10 (1877) 261–84 at 276–80.

[28] L. Mitteis, *Grundzüge und Chrestomathie der Papyruskunde. Juristische Halfte, Grundzüge* (Leipzig 1912) 200.

We do not have the leisure in this forum to examine the Talmudic passages Ilan cites, and all I can reasonably do here is to indicate the main lines of the argument for the assertion that her reading of the passages is unsustainable. First, her reading begins with the apparent assumption that the Hebrew word for "being alone together," מתייחד, is a euphemism for sexual intercourse. Now indeed rabbinic literature is famous for euphemizing discourse about sex, but this word is not one of the euphemisms. The word bears most strikingly the sense of "being alone together and *not* having sexual contact" in M. Kidushin 4.12: לא יתיחד אדם עם שתי נשים אבל אשה אחת מתיחדת עם שני אנשים. רבי שמעון אומר אף איש אחד מתייחד עם שתי נשים בזמן שאשתו עמו וישן עמהם בפונדקי מפני שאשתו משמרתו. מתייחד אדם עם אמו ועם בתו וישן עמהם בקרוב בשר ואם הגדילו זו ישנה בכסותה וזה ישן בכסותו. "A man may not מתייחד with two women, but one woman may מתייחד with two men. . . . A man may מתייחד with his mother and daughter. . . ." Second, in the text which Ilan considers most closely associated with our papyrus, M. Ketubot 1.5 האוכל אצל חמיו ביהודה שלא בעדים אינו יכול לטעון טענת בתולים מפני שמתייחד עמה "In Judaea a man who eats in the home of his father-in-law without witnesses cannot then claim *ta'anat b'tulim* [that contrary to his expectation his wife is not a virgin], because he is alone (מתייחד) with her," taking the term מתייחד to mean pre-marital cohabitation as trial marriage renders the *ta'anat b'tulim* senseless.[29]

The more serious challenge to Lewis' and my interpretation comes from Hannah Cotton. She presents as a definitive objection that she can prove, she says, that Salome could not have been a minor when our papyrus was written, because in P.Hever 63, written, as we said, in 127 CE, there is a reference to another man, Sammouos son of Shim'on, as the husband of our Salome.[30] There are two things wrong with Cotton's objection. First, Lewis and I did not say Salome was a minor at the time P.Yadin 37 was written. On the contrary, we suggested she was a minor when her provisional marriage *began*, and that this document was written sometime after she attained legal majority and her marriage was rendered permanent. Second, P.Hever 63 may indeed show she was *married* in 127, but not that she was an adult in 127, because adulthood of the wife was not a precondition of Jewish marriage then.

---

[29] So too in the associated *beraita*, T.Ketubot 1.4 and B.Ketubot 12a.
[30] Cotton (supra note 3) page 227.

Cotton proposes instead

a) that the living together before this document was written, is the "institution" of *gamos agraphos* followed by *gamos engraphos* of the Egyptian/Greek papyri (the "written" and "unwritten" marriages referred to above),

b) that this cannot be squared at all with Jewish tradition, which, she says, requires a ketuba, marriage document, for the validity of a marriage, citing as authority the ruling of Rabbi Meir that "a man may not keep his wife even one hour without a ketuba,"[31]

c) that this document "is not the ketubbah that would turn pre-marital cohabitation into a proper Jewish wedlock,"[32]

d) and that these Jews, which she also claims are typical of Judaea, are thoroughly assimilated to the Hellenistic culture known from Egypt, and completely removed from the traditions of rabbinic literature, a position she has taken in many studies over the last few years.[33]

However,

a) There was no "institution" of *gamos agraphos*, unwritten marriage, in Graeco-Roman Egypt. Indeed the term is modern. Rather, in the society reflected in the papyri from Roman Egypt there was a single institution of marriage which was often, but not necessarily, accompanied by writing.[34]

b) The view cited above that a ketuba is a requirement of marriage, and the associated ruling that cohabitation without the obligation of the husband to a ketuba payment of 200 zuz for a virgin or 100 for a second marriage is considered a promiscuous union,[35] are those of R. Meir. However, his rulings refer to the obligations, not to the writing of them.[36] It is not that

---

[31] B. Bava Kama 89a, quoted by Cotton at second hand (supra note 3) 228. אסור לו לאדם שישהא את אשתו אפילו שעה אחת בלא כתובה.

[32] Cotton (supra note 3) page 228–9.

[33] E.g., H. Cotton, "A Cancelled Marriage Contract from the Judaean Desert," *Journal of Roman Studies* 84 (1994) 64–86; "The Rabbis and the Documents," in M. Goodman, ed., *Jews in a Graeco-Roman World* (Oxford 1998) 167–79.

[34] H.J. Wolff, *Written and Unwritten Marriages in Hellenistic and Post-Classical Roman Law* (Haverford, Pa., 1939) 66–9. Cotton quotes Wolff correctly on page 229, but seems not to be aware of the effect on her argument.

[35] M.Ketubot 5.1 רבי מאיר אומר כל הפוחת לבתולה ממאתים ולאלמנה ממנה הרי זו בעילת זנות.

[36] M.A. Friedman (supra note 18) 240 note 5 observes that in the Mishna the term *ketuba* appears only once (M.Ketubot 9.9) in the sense of the marriage document. Elsewhere it means the sum(s) due the wife.

the obligations validate the marriage, but that the marriage creates the obligations. The Mishna is explicit: M.Ketubot 4.7 לא כתב לה כתובה בתולה גובה מאתים ואלמנה מנה מפני שהוא תנאי בית דין "If [the husband] did not write a ketuba, a [woman who married as a] virgin will collect 200, a [woman who married as a] widow will collect 100, because it (sc. the obligation) is statutory." Both Talmudim identify this as the view of R. Meir. More important, whereas later halacha did adopt the view of R. Meir,[37] his was not a unanimous view in his day. "This is the opinion of R. Meir; but sages say a man may leave his wife for two or three years without a ketuba."[38] Among these sages are identified R. Yossi and R. Judah.[39] All three figures were prominent disciples of R. Akiba, hence contemporary with the document under discussion. Lines of continuity with R. Judah are of particular interest, for they are found in connection with other Judaean Desert documents as well. It is R. Judah who, in opposition to others, says that a gift in contemplation of death is to be phrased as "from now and after death" (M.Bava Batra 8.7; compare P.Yadin 19.21–23); that a debtor may require surrender to himself of the obligatory document in return for payment (M.Bava Batra 10.6; compare P.Hever 8.7, P.Hever 69, P.Yadin 18.57, and other documents listed by Yardeni);[40] that in the financial aspects of a marriage variance from the standard usage is acceptable (בדבר שבממון תנאו קיים, B.Ketubot 56a, and parallels; compare P.Yadin 18.59, where on one inter-pretation the wife seems to be given the right to receive her dowry on demand, unconditioned on divorce or death of the husband).

c) The notion that any deviation from a fixed formulary of the ketuba is halachically unacceptable did become a staple of orthodox anti-reformist rhetoric in the nineteenth and twentieth centuries and occasionally in medieval sources. However, it was certainly not present in the talmudic period.[41] What R. Meir

---

[37] Shulchan Aruch, Even Ha'ezer 66. It was not accepted to the point of inval-idating a marriage in the absence of a written ketuba. See the references in B. Adler, *Hanisu'in Kehilchatam²* (Jerusalem 1985) 278 note 5 (Hebrew).

[38] B.Ketubot 57a.

[39] B.Ketubot 56b.

[40] (supra note 3) p. 17 note 22.

[41] Friedman (supra note 18) 3–7.

had in mind as the *sine qua non* is neither language nor diplo-
matics, nor even writing, but the obligation of no less than 200
zuz to the wife (M.Ketubot 5.1). R. Meir, then, would have
found fault with the *amount* to which the husband is committed
in P.Hever 65, 96 dinars, if that indeed represented his total
commitment, but not with the Greek "ethos."

d) To judge from rabbinic literature, Jews in the Talmudic period
   varied in their practices on writing a ketuba. People either did
   write a marriage contract or did not write, and the marriage
   was equally valid and acceptable. In fact, both talmudim interpret a series of mishnayot in Tractate Ketubot as referring to
   מקום שלא נהגו לכתב—place where writing the ketuba was *not*
   customary—as being the default situation.[42] If a ketuba was
   written, it could be at various times, with the betrothal and
   the marriage being typical occasions.[43] Now this is exactly what
   Hans Julius Wolff said about written and unwritten marriages
   in Hellenistic Egypt. For that matter that is also the case for
   Rome. In Roman law, in Hellenistic law, and in Jewish law,
   writing often, but not necessarily, accompanied marriage. That
   is a very low common denominator.

However, the most important contribution which Cotton made to
this papyrus is her restoration of line 4. She argues at considerable
length that it should be restored, let me state it more conservatively,
it can equally be restored, not *elephenai*, but *pros*. "Iesous agreed with,
or declared to, Salome that he received as dowry and so on."

Well! That puts a whole different light on things. This is not a
marriage contract, but a dowry receipt! The couple has been married for a while just as it says in lines 5 and 6, and now some dowry
is being given. Indeed, nowhere in the document does it say that
they were previously living *agraphos*, without a marriage contract.
Why is a dowry being given now? We do not know. Perhaps the
wife's family came into some money, and is now delivering some of
a previously promised dowry. Perhaps there was some trouble in the
marriage and the family tried to throw money at it. It happens in
the best of families. The young couple gets over the hump and lives

---

[42] E.g. B.Ketubot 16b, B.Ketubot 89a, Y.Ketubot 1.2.28b, Y.Ketubot 9.9 33c.
[43] H. Albeck, "Ha'erusin v'shitroteihem," in *Kovets mada'i l'zekher Moshe Shor* (Moshe
Schorr Memorial Volume) (New York 1944).

happily ever after. The promise of the husband to continue living with his wife may point in that direction.

Sorry, folks. No smoking gun. No premarital co-habitation, no trial marriage, no far-reaching assimilation, maybe no minor orphan bride. Just one more dull uninteresting papyrus.

P.YADIN 21–22: SALE OR LEASE?

Amihai Radzyner

Introduction

The central question posed in connection with P.Yadin 21 and 22 may be stated as follows. Do they document a sale, as Prof. Lewis titled them: "21: purchase of a date crop, 22: sale of a date crop;"[1] or do they constitute a labor contract whereby Simon leases the plantation of Babatha to harvest its fruit, in return for a share of these fruits? I propose that at the very least the documents exhibit elements of a labor-lease agreement, even if their overall formulation is that of a deed of sale.

I will conduct my analysis through two avenues of comparison. The first is to examine these documents in light of Greco-Roman documents that have been found in Egypt. The second is to probe the precise formulation found in these documents in light of the bill of share-cropping found in Tannaitic literature.

The question regarding these bills was raised by B. Isaac:[2]

> Documents 21 and 22: Is this the sale of the date crop (thus Lewis), or rather a lease of the right of working the orchard in exchange for a share in the produce? Babatha is to receive dates or money. Who would sell a crop of dates in exchange for dates? [note 46: Cf. Broshi].[3]

Lewis, defending his contention that P.Yadin 21 is for the "purchase of a date crop," while P.Yadin 22 represents the "sale of a date crop," responded:[4]

---

[1] N. Lewis, Y. Yadin and J.C. Greenfield, *The Documents from the Bar Kokhba Period in the Cave of Letters, Greek Papyri* (Jerusalem 1989) 94–101.

I would like to thank Prof. Ranon Katzoff, Uri Yiftach, and the anonymous referee. Responsibility for the claims made herein, of course, is mine alone. Except where noted otherwise, translations of Mishna, Tosefta, and Yerushalmi are those of J. Neusner.

[2] B. Isaac, "The Babatha Archive: A Review Article," *IEJ* 42 (1992) 62–75 at 75.

[3] M. Broshi, "Agriculture and Economy in Roman Palestine According to Babatha's Papyri," *Zion* 55 (1990) 269–81 at 274 (Hebrew).

[4] N. Lewis, "The Babatha Archive: A Response," *IEJ* 44 (1994) 243–6 at 246.

This question misunderstands the nature of the transaction. These documents are not leases: ὁμολογῶ ἠγορακέναι (21) and ὁμολογῶ πεπρακέναι (22) leave no doubt that the parties were engaging in a sale and purchase—what the Romans called *emptio venditio*. As pointed out in the introduction to Documents Nos. 21–22, what is being sold here is a crop of dates just beginning to ripen; there is no question of "working the orchard," but merely of starting in a few days to pick the ripe dates. The buyer would harvest and own the crop, and would pay Babatha a stated return in kind or, failing that, in money. Such sales of "standing crops" are numerous in Greek papyri and are still common practice today. [note 8: Cf. Broshi,[5] where he cites ancient and modern parallels, and adds: "indeed, no other crop in this part of the world lends itself to sharecropping as well as dates."]

Lewis' position is subject to criticism on two accounts:

1. An examination of Greek documents from Egypt dealing with the sale of crops prior to harvest shows that they do indeed contain elements of lease.

2. The reliance on Broshi as a central support raises a difficulty. A careful reading of Broshi reveals that he adopts assumptions contrary to those maintained by Lewis. Indeed Broshi writes in his English version:[6]

> From P.Yadin 21–22 we learn that Babatha sold the yield of her palm groves in a sort of share-cropping arrangement, in which the sharecropper pays a certain amount of the yield...

However, in his Hebrew version[7] which was used by Prof. Isaac, he defines Simon as a lessee, and uses the root הכר,[8] to lease, four times in the passage that discusses P.Yadin 21–22. This discrepancy highlights the difficulty of pinning down definitions within this legal system.

---

[5] M. Broshi, "Agriculture and Economy in Roman Palestine: Seven Notes on the Babatha Archive," *IEJ* 42 (1992) 230–40 at 233–4.

[6] Broshi (supra note 5) 233.

[7] Broshi (supra note 3) 274.

[8] "From bills 21–22, we learn of the existence of the institution of leasing..." It should be noted that in Mishnaic Hebrew there is great significance in the use of the term הכירה (leasing) and its conjugate forms, as opposed to the terms שכירות (rent) and אריסות (tenancy or sharecropping), as these terms are already delineated and distinguished within the Mishnaic lexicon. We find within Tannaitic literature three arrangements whereby a laborer receives a field to work and receives a share of the produce in lieu of payment: הוכר, שכיר, אריס. It would seem that the difference between them is to be found in the form of the payment. In the first chapter of M.Bikurim we find the אריס and the הוכר as distinct classifications in two places. The second mishnah states that האריסין והחכורות do not bring bikurim because they

Second, Broshi also maintains what is known from the literature that deals with the cultivation of the palm tree, that the labor intensive aspect of palm grove cultivation is the harvesting of the fruit, which constitutes about half of the annual labor investment in the plantation.[9] This renders problematic Lewis' assertion that, "there is no question of working the orchard."

The Egyptian καρπωνεία contracts

Indeed, contracts integrating the sale of fruit and lease are familiar from Hellenistic law. This subject has been broadly surveyed by Pringsheim[10] and Hermann,[11] the former in the broader context of the law of sale, the latter in that of hire. We will concentrate here on documents of καρπωνεία, that is to say, the sale of fruit on the tree for harvest.

---

are incapable of reading 'ראשית ביכורי אדמתך: "... Lessees, tenant farmers ... do not bring firstfruits ... because it is written, 'the first of the firstfruits of your land.'" (J. Neusner, *The Mishna—A New Translation* [New-Haven and London 1988], 167, uses the term 'sharecroppers' for חוכר, but I prefer 'lessee.') An opposing view, that of R. Judah, is found in mishnah 11, to the effect that they do bear some degree of ownership over the property, and therefore do bring bikkurim: רבי יהודה אומר אף בעלי אריסות והכורות מביאין וקורין. "R. Judah says, Even the lessees and tenant farmers bring and recite." It is unclear from this mishnah what distinguishes the חוכר from the אריס, although it is clear that they are not identical. The distinction between the שוכר and the חוכר is delineated in T.Demai 6.2: "מה בין שוכר לחוכר? שוכר במעות חוכר בפירות": "What is the difference between one who rents and one who leases? One who rents [pays the owner] in coin; one who leases [pays the owner] in kind." Since many sources imply that a sharecropper also pays in kind, we may adopt the distinction made by many of the Rishonim, found already in the Y.Demai 6.1 25a: "החוכר בפירות, השוכר במעות, מקבל למחצה לשליש ולרביע": "One who leases [a field from its owner pays back the owner] in kind; one who rents [a field from its owner pays back the owner] in coin. One who sharecrops [a field for its owner receives for his work a fixed, agreed upon percentage of the total yield, for example,] for half, [or] for a third, [or] for a quarter [of the total yield]." (tr. R.S. Sarason, *The Talmud of the Land of Israel* [Chicago 1993] 194). Despite these distinctions, there is still a lack of clarity concerning these terms. For example, the term קבלן represents אריס in the quoted passage from the Jerusalem Talmud. Yet in M.Bava Batra 10.4, for example, it appears to represent חוכר (see the commentary of Maimonides to M.Bava Metziah 9.2). This lack of clarity in the Tannaitic lexicon may indicate that the laws mentioned concerning the אריס apply to the חוכר or קבלן as well, or the opposite. The Murabbaʿat documents as well as P.Yadin 42–46 employ the verb הכר for the contract of the recipient of land who pays a fixed sum of cash in advance.

[9] Supra note 5.

[10] F. Pringsheim, *The Greek Law of Sale* (Weimar 1950) 295–310.

[11] J. Herrmann, *Studien zur Bodenpacht im Recht der graeco-aegyptischen Papyri* (Munich 1958) 222–9.

Pringsheim puts on display an array of contracts. At one end of the spectrum he identifies pure deeds of sale, and at the other end pure deeds of lease. Between them he finds contracts that combine elements of both lease and sale. As he puts it, there is a possibility that a contract of lease will appear in the guise of a deed of sale, or that a deed of sale will contain elements of a lease. These hybrid formulations are particularly common when the object of the contract is the fruit and not the land, the time of the contract is close to the time of the harvest, and the contract deals with a crop which is not labor intensive, such as dates.

The circumstances of the transactions recorded in P.Yadin 21 and 22 have all three characteristics. Indeed, the only labor mentioned is the harvesting of the fruits, and the contract was dated just before harvest time, usually around September-October-November. As Pringsheim observes, it is clear that it is in the interest of the buyer/lessee that the contract be drafted as a bill of sale, while it is in the interest of the seller/lessor that the deed reflect a deed of lease. It is no surprise, then, that the documents before us reflect a primary formulation as a deed of sale, integrated with a secondary element of lease. We should remember that in our case, Simon proposes to Babatha that he harvest her fruit in return for a share of the fruit. There is no doubt that his main interest lies in the purchase of the fruit, while the labor required of him consists of the harvesting and drying alone. These constitute unusually lenient demands of a lessee, who usually performs all the tasks of the field. Because of that, Simon draws up his bill (no. 21), which was demonstrated by Prof. Lewis to be the first of the two,[12] as a deed of sale, although he does not ignore the element of work/lease, as will be demonstrated shortly.

The contractual model that begins as sale and continues as a lease is found in P.Col.Zen. 85 and in P.Tebt. III 815. There are also examples of contracts which contain the reverse arrangement.

The paradigmatic καρπωνεία contract is P.Oxy. IV 728 of 142 CE. On this, Taubenschlag writes:[13]

---

[12] *P.Yadin*, page 94.
[13] R. Taubenschlag, *The Law of Greco-Roman Egypt in the Light of the Papyri.* 2nd ed. (Warsaw 1955) 340.
See also Pringsheim (supra note 10) 306–7.

καρπωνεία is a mixture of sale and lease. On one hand the buyer has to pay the price of the crop and on the other he has—like the lessee—to gather it himself. Like the lessee, too, he acquires the ownership by the act of cutting and carrying it, i.e. by self-help. The contract is called a purchase of fruit (καρπωνεία). Consequently the buyer does not have to cultivate the land which is put at his disposal for gathering the crop only. In the Ptolemaic period the sale of fruit and lease were combined in a rather primitive manner, so that only step by step there developed the new and coherent καρπωνεία of the Roman period.

P.Yadin 21–22 may be seen, then, as a καρπωνεία contract. Although among all of the καρπωνεία documents noted by the three scholars cited above, and other documents as well, there is not one that is fully identical with our bills, καρπωνεία is nonetheless the closest model, from a juristic standpoint, to our bills. However, differences should be noted. First, in all known καρπονεία contracts the sale of crop is in exchange for money. P.Yadin 21–22, on the other hand, refer to the bestowal of a share of the crop, corroborating the presence of an element of lease. There are also differences in the category of produce (mostly hay or animal fodder), in the form of payment (generally money), in various assurances not found in our bills, in attention to taxation and other obligations, and more. Yet it would seem that the most significant difference was in the formulation. Generally, the sharecropper/buyer would declare his purchase, with no additional deed. In our case there are two distinct deeds, one for the buyer and one for the seller.[14]

To summarize thus far, P.Yadin 21 and 22 integrate elements of sale and lease. Simon pays a fixed amount of fruit and undertakes to harvest them and give them to Babatha, and in this regard, the deed resembles a deed of lease. Similarly, he also declares that the fruits he will receive are in exchange for his work. On the other hand, it is clear that his interest lies in the receipt of the fruit from

---

[14] The deed which is closest is P.Tebt. II 379, of nearly the same period—128 CE. It is formulated as the declaration of a woman and her guardian and her brother concerning the sale of produce, it would seem, from a field that had been bequeathed to them by their father. Formulated in the first person plural, it states that part of the produce is sold to him for him to harvest and dry, and that they have paid him (or perhaps they paid the previous sharecroppers mentioned, so that there would be no claims), but with no indication of the sum. It is plausible to assume that the payment would be by part of the produce, as they assume responsibility for it in the event of its disappearance for whatever reason. In our case, responsibility is assumed only for claims concerning the field. See Pringsheim (supra n. 10) 303, and Herrmann (supra n. 11) 229.

the plantation, and that he is obliged to perform the tasks of harvesting and drying alone. That is to say, Babatha's interest is in Simon's labor (which will let her enjoy the fruit), and Simon's is in the fruit. The object of the deed is really the fruit and not the labor, as Pringsheim maintained, namely, that when the sole task performed by the lessee is the harvesting, the form of the contract will likely be that of a deed of sale.[15]

> ἀντὶ τῶν ἐμῶν/σῶν κόπων καὶ ἀναλωμάτων—*in return for my/your labors and expenses*

Further support for seeing the element of labor-leasing as essential in these documents, and as having very interesting implications for our understanding of bills of lease in Eretz-Israel in the second century CE, comes from the expression ἀντὶ τῶν ἐμῶν/σῶν κόπων καὶ ἀναλωμάτων, "in return for my/your labors and expenses," which appears in P.Yadin 21.20–21 and P.Yadin 22.24 and 28. The triple invocation of this term seems a consistent formula, bearing most emphatically the element of labor in the bills. It obviously corroborates the evidence that these bills represent an agreement of leasing alongside an agreement of sale. What is the nature of the labor that appears in this term? While the purported labor is not explicitly mentioned, it is implicitly understood to consist of harvesting and perhaps also drying. This is borne out in the statements of the parties and from the documents' date. The obligation to dry is not as obvious as the obligation to harvest, but it is stated that the dates will be brought to Babatha in the season of the drying.[16]

---

[15] A fragmentary Aramaic papyrus document discovered by Prof. H. Eshel in the Abior cave near Jericho and now published as P.Jericho 7, *DJD* XXXVIII (Oxford 2000) pp. 57–8, may also represent such a transaction, a lease/work contract styled as a sale of the crop. The main verb in the operative section is זבן (lower part, line 2; see also lines 4, 5, 8). The same verb is used in the subscriptions of P.Yadin 21.28 (Aramaic) and 22.31 (Nabatean).

[16] See also T. Bava Metzia (Lieberman ed.) 9.19–20: יט: המקבל כרם מחבירו חייב ליטפל בו עד שיעשנו יין זתים עד שיעשם ציבור פשתן עד שיעשנו קירצין חולק ונותן לו זה מכניס חלקו וזה מכניס חלקו זה מכניס חלקו לעיר וזה מכניס חלקו לעיר. כ: המקבל שדה האנים מחבירו מקום שנוהגו לעשותן קציעות עושה אותן קציעו' נרונרות עושה אותן נרונרות דבילה עושה אותן דבילה ואין משנין ממנהג המדינה. "19: He who leases a vineyard from his field is liable to tend it until he produces wine; olives—until he makes a pile of them; flax—until he makes them into fibers. He then splits up the crop and pays off [the landlord]. This party takes his share, and that party takes his share. This party brings his share to market in the city, and that party brings his share to

The notion that we have here a term that was mutually understood and intended, whereby the element of Simon's work is an integral and central part of the contract, is further buttressed when we
examine the monetary compensation of the parties in the guarantee
clauses (22.17–20, 22–25). A simple calculation shows that the sum
that Babatha is to receive if Simon fails to deliver the fruit is far
higher than the sum she would pay if she fails to clear the title for
Simon. For the "splits" alone she is to receive eighty-four denarii.
The value of the "black" that would be paid for the "Syrian" and
"Naarian" is problematic, but it is well within reason to estimate
that the total sum to which Simon would be obligated is at least
seven or eight times higher[17] than the sum that Babatha would be
obligated to give him, namely, twenty denarii. We do not know how
much fruit Simon was supposed to receive, which fruit, as the deed
states (21.18–21; 22.25–28), he is to take from the remainder after
giving Babatha her share. However, if we assume with Broshi[18] that
the lessee receives between a third and a half of the crop, and take
into consideration the rabbinic leasing bill, which speaks of פלגא, "a
half," we can see that the difference between the compensation Simon
agreed to receive and what he was obligated to pay was very large.[19]

---

market in the city. 20: He who leases a field of figs from his fellow—in a place in
which they are accustomed to pack [the figs], [the tenant is expected to] pack them.
[If they are accustomed to turn them into] dried figs, he makes them into dried
figs. [If they are accustomed to make them into] pressed figs, he makes them into
pressed figs. And they do not vary from the accepted practice of the province."
That these are the conventional practices concerning sharecroppers in Eretz Israel
is indicated by the reference to "the accepted practice of the province."

[17] See H.M. Cotton and A. Yardeni, *P.Hever*, p. 185: "Failure to fulfill the terms
of the contract will result in a fine of two *denarii* for each talent of 'splits,' i.e. 84
denarii, and one 'black' for each *se'ah* (?) of Syrian and naaran dates, i.e. 65 'blacks'."

[18] Supra note 3.

[19] The subject of tax is not mentioned at all. Even if Babatha was supposed to
pay the tax from her share, and even if the rate of the tax is fifty percent, as Broshi
claims (ibid. 274–9), her share of the profit is still far greater than Simon's. In any
event, even if there is a tax, it is not necessarily the case that Babatha is to pay
all of it. See A. Gulak, *Lecheker Toldot HaMishpat HaIvri Bitkufat HaTalmud, Part I:
Dinei Karkaot* (Jerusalem 1929) 110–3 (Hebrew), concerning the proportion paid by
the sharecropper and the lessee, and his assumption that generally speaking the
owner of the property would pay the tax. Yet even on the assumption that Babatha
is to pay from her share 50% of the tax, the difference is still great, especially when
considering that the payment was to be made in cash, while the tax was generally
paid in produce. See P.Yadin 16. Even if we suppose that Simon's contains an element of fine and Babatha's does not, a circumstance which in itself would require
explanation, nonetheless the difference is great.

In my opinion, that proportion suggests that Babatha is to receive money for the dates while paying for Simon's work and expenses. In other words, the reparation to be paid in the event that the "purchase" of Simon is not put into effect, is only for his labor and the expenses, and not for the fruit he could have received. The value of the fruit, of course, is far greater than the value of the harvesting work alone. This suggests that the labor element is not marginal at all. Property rights to the fruit belong only to Babatha, and not to Simon. This is rather similar to the Egyptian Greek leasing bills, in which the fruit belongs to the owner of the plantation until he receives his share from his lessee. There is no assurance to Simon that he will receive the value of the fruit in case of a third party's claim.[20] Once again we see here payment for labor and a transaction in which labor is the essential element.

These documents in light of Tannaitic literature

To the best of my knowledge, the expression κόπων καὶ ἀναλωμάτων has not been found in any other Greek papyrus, save one Byzantine document of 551 CE, P.Cair.Masp. I 67032 .50 = *Jur. Pap.* 52. Clauses with different wording to the effect that the lessee receives his part of the crop in exchange for his labor and expenses do appear occasionally in lease documents, but only in those of the late Roman and Byzantine periods.[21] On the other hand, a precise parallel is the formula of the leasing contract that appears in the Tosefta, yet again strengthening the probability that our documents contain a partial

---

[20] Physical damage to the fruit is not mentioned at all. This may be due to the fact that the bills were written just before harvesting, so that the risk of such damages was deemed minor.

[21] P.Oxy. VI 913 (442 CE), P.Oxy. XLV 3255 (315 CE), P.Oxy. XLV 3256 (317/18 CE), P.Oxy. I 103 (316 CE). The phrasing in P.Oxy. II 277 (19 CE), "the field is hereby given to the lessor so that he may sow it . . . in exchange for half of the harvest," differs from those listed above in that in those deeds labor is given for fruit, and not fruit in exchange for the labor. See also G. Eißer in *ZSav.* 49 (1929) 552, highly critical of F. Kobler, *Der Teilbau im römischen und geltenden italienischen Recht* (Marburg 1928). Inter alia, he criticizes the lack of attention to the pre-Hellenistic Oriental and Egyptian law. Particularly germane to our discussion are his comments on p. 553, and note 1, to the effect that the author should have been mindful of late Roman and Byzantine sources, since the material from these periods contains many bills of lease in exchange for a portion of the harvest. In the note he lists sources beginning from the year 332 CE through the 7th century CE. Concerning late bills of lease generally, see: A. Jördens, *Vertragliche Regelungen von Arbeiten im späten griechischsprachigen Ägypten* (Heidelberg 1990), especially ch. 5.

element of leasing. I suggest that the bills contain a formula which is unfamiliar to Hellenistic law but reflects the local law in Eretz-Israel, whose sources are probably oriental, as we shall shortly see.[22]

At the outset of my discussion of the Tannaitic halakha concerning leasing, I wish to clarify that I do not claim that the halakha influenced the form or formulation of our documents. Rather, it would seem that the Tannaitic leasing bills and their conditions reflect local leasing formulae and customs in Eretz-Israel, and were not necessarily created by the dictates of the Sages. As we shall see, the Halakha adopted elements of local customs in the institution of leasing. Comparisons here with the Tannaitic sources are made in order to draw historical information from them,[23] and not in order to claim that the halakha contributed to the formulation of our bills. In our case, I can accept what Prof. Cotton writes about the absorption of local juridical customs and formulae into the Tannaitic halakha.[24] As we shall see, the Tannaitic sources themselves say that the origin of the formulae of their leasing contracts is non-Jewish, or, at least, was not originated by the Sages. It is worth noting that there is no other field in the entire corpus of rabbinic law in which the influence of local custom is so pervasive as in labor laws in general, and laws of land tenancy and leasing in particular. The term מנהג המדינה "the custom prevailing in the province" is found five times in chapter nine of Tosefta Bava Metsia, a greater concentration than found anywhere else in Tannaitic literature.[25]

---

[22] For a discussion of the phenomenon that Jewish or Oriental formulations, extant in Eretz-Israel, begin to appear in Greek in Byzantine documents in Egypt, see R. Yaron, "The Murabba'at Documents," *JJS* 11 (1960) 157–71 at 169 and n. 36.

[23] It is important to underscore that we do not have at our disposal much material pertaining to leasing in Eretz-Israel, beyond what we can glean from rabbinic sources, concerning the lessee and the sharecropper, and the bills that were found at Wadi Murabba'at. Some attempts have been made to "recreate" the laws of sharecropping in Eretz-Israel in the first century, through the parable of the sharecropper that appears in three of the synoptic gospels, and in comparison with Egyptian papyri. See: J.D.M. Derrett, "Fresh Light on the Parable of the Wicked Vinedressers," *RIDA* 3 ser. 10 (1963) 11–41; C.A. Evans, "Jesus' Parable of the Tenant Farmers in Light of Lease Agreements in Antiquity," *JSP* 14 (1996) 65–83. Criticism of this approach, and an attempt to summarize the status of sharecropping and leasing in the first centuries of the common era in Eretz-Israel is found in D.A. Fiensy, *The Social History of Palestine in the Herodian Period* (Lewiston 1991) 80–5.

[24] Cotton (supra n. 17) 154–5.

[25] See also M.Bava Metzia 9.1; T.Bava Metzia 9.11, 14, 18, 20, 21. In the entire Tosefta this phrase appears 12 times. Add to this the appearance of the term מקום שנהגו, that is, the law is according to the local custom. This phrase appears seven

If we turn to the formulation of the leasing contract known to the Sages, it is clear that the sides had to prepare a written document in a case of land tenancy or leasing. The bill of lease is mentioned in the tenth chapter of the Mishnah Bava Batra, which, treating the various types of documents, says that a leasing bill is written and given to both sides.[26]

What was the content of this bill? Though rabbinic literature does not provide us with the bill's precise formulation, Tannaitic literature does preserve two clauses from tenancy and leasing contracts. Both are written in Aramaic, like other bills in those sources, a feature which points to the age of the formulae and also to their Oriental source. Both clauses appear in the Tosefta,[27] and the first clause (T.Bava Metzia 9.12 end) is also found in the Mishnah.[28]

---

times in the aforementioned chapter of the Tosefta. If we add to this the other areas of labor law in the Tosefta that were influenced by custom (a worker— T.Bava Kamma 11.18, rental payments, and more), we find that the laws of labor and their conditions are the area of law most influenced by local custom. Therefore, one can assume that the bills of leasing are the source from which we learn the laws of leasing, and reflected through them are the local customs. According to the opinion of R. Simon b. Gamliel, M.Bava Batra 10.1, all contract law is influenced by local custom in Eretz-Israel.

[26] M.Bava Batra 10.4: הכירה=] "אין כוחבין שטרי אריסות וקבלנות משנה, בבא-בתרא י' ד': אלא מדעת שניהם'." קבלות: ברוב כתבי-היד: "They write documents of tenancy and leasing only with the knowledge and consent of both parties." This is in contrast to what is said there concerning a bill of sale (10.3): "They write a writ of sale to the seller, even though the buyer is not with him. But they do not write a writ of sale for the purchaser, unless the seller is with him." On the question concerning the party in whose name the bill is written, see Gulak (supra note 19) 116 and note 3. On the "doubling" of the documents P.Yadin 21 and 22, see Appendix.

[27] T.Bava Metzia 9:12–13: יב: המקבל שדה מחבירו משזכה בה הבירה שמן אותה כמה היתה ראויה לעשות ונותן לו ואין שמין אותה כנגד שדות שבצדה שמא זו נירה וזו אינה נירה זו מזובלת וזו אינה מזובלת זו מטייבת וזו אינה מטייבת אלא שמין אותה כמה היא ראויה לעשות ונותן לו שכותב לו אם אביר ולא אעביד אשלם במיטבא. יג: המקבל שדה מחבירו ולא עשה אם יש בה כדי לעמוד כרי חייב ליטפל בה שכך הוא כותב לו אנא אניר ואזיע ואכיש ואחצוד ואוקים כריא ואת תיתי ותיסב פלנא בעיבורא ובתיבנא ואנא בעמלי ובנפקות ידי פלנא וכשם ששדה הזרע אם יש בה כדי להעמיד כרי מיטפל בה שדה בית האילן אם יש בה כדי להעמיד יציאותיו מיטפל בה ואם לא אין מיטפל בה. "12. He who leases a field from his fellow, [and] after he had taken possession of it, he let it lie fallow, they make an estimate of how much [the field] is suitable to produce, [and the tenant] pays [that amount] to [the landlord]. And they do not make an estimate relative to fields which are round about it, for this one is ploughed and that one is not ploughed, this one is fertilized and that one is not fertilized, this one has been worked, and that one has not been worked. But they make an estimate of how much [the field] is suitable to produce, [and the tenant] pays [that amount] to [the landlord]. For thus does he write to him [in the lease], 'If I let the field lie fallow and do not work it, I shall pay you back at the rate of its highest yield.' 13. He who leases a field from his fellow, and it did not produce [a crop], if there was in it [nonetheless, sufficient growth] to produce a heap [of grain]. he is liable to tend it. For thus

Now, it is evident that the formula in T.Bava Metzia 9.13: "and for my work and expenses I shall take half," seems an exact Aramaic counterpart of ἐμαυτὸν ἀντὶ τῶν ἐμῶν κόπων καὶ ἀναλωμάτων. I think that the Greek formula is a translation of the Aramaic one, which was a part of the leasing bill in Eretz-Israel at that time.

In the Tosefta, the two formulae are juxtaposed, as they are in later halakhic land lease contracts.[29] We may assume that those two formulae came from the same source. What might that source be? In my opinion the roots of the leasing bill formulae are very ancient and find their source in the laws and documents of the First Babylonian Period. Similar formulae are found also in Neo-Babylonian documents (sixth century BCE). It is generally accepted that in the Persian Period the Babylonian formulae were prevalent all over the Near

---

he writes in the lease: 'I shall plough, sow, weed, cut, and make a pile [of grain] before you, and you will then come and take half of the grain and straw. And for my work and expenses I shall take half.' And just as in the case of a field which is planted with seed, if there was in it sufficient growth to produce a heap of grain, one is liable to tend it, and if not, he is not liable to tend it, so in the case of an orchard-field, if there was in it sufficient produce to cover his expenses, he is liable to tend it, and if not, he is not liable to tend it."

It should be noted that the Tosefta is a compilation of material from the Tannaitic period, of which a large part is not recorded in the Mishnah. Though it is generally held that it was redacted after the Mishnah, recent research has shown that in many cases the Tosefta contains material earlier than the Mishna, which would have been the basis upon which Rabbi Yehudah Hanasi redacted the Mishnah as a codification of the Tannaitic Halakha. The Tosefta, then, provides us with sources from a period of close proximity to the time of P.Yadin.

[28] M.Bava Metzia 9.3: המקבל שדה מחברו והוביר‎ה שמין אותה כמה ראויה לעשות ונותן‎ לו, שכך כותב לו: אם אוביר ולא אעביד אשלם במיטבא.‎ "He who [as a sharecropper] leases a field from his fellow and then let it lie fallow—they make an estimate of how much [the field] is suitable to produce, [and the tenant] pays [that amount] to [the landlord]. For thus does he write to him [in the writ of occupancy or lease], 'If I let the field lie fallow and do not work it, I shall make it up to you at its highest rate of yield.'" The commonly printed text, as given, is supported by the Kaufmann manuscript and in the Yemenite manuscripts of the Mishnah. In the Lowe and Paris manuscripts, the reading here is שכך אמר לו. In all textual witnesses of the Tosefta the reading is כותב.

[29] As seen in the example of the leasing bill in the anthology of bills of R.Yehuda of Barcelona (ed. S.Z.H. Halberstam, Berlin 1898) 99: ...‎ ותיתי את ותשקול באריעך פלנא‎ ואנא בעמלאי ובלאותי ובנפקת ידי פלנא. ואם אוביר ולא אעבוד אשלם במיטבא.‎ "You will then come and take half from your field's yield. And for my work and expenses I shall take half. And If I let the field lie fallow and do not work it, I shall make it up to you at its highest rate of yield." See also J. Rivlin, *Bills and Contracts from Lucena* (Ramat-Gan 1994) 104 and 110 line 6 (Hebrew); B.Z. Dinur, *Israel in the Diaspora* 2:2 (Tel-Aviv and Jerusalem 1966) 209–10 (Hebrew); A. Gulak, *Otzar Ha-shtarot Ha-nehugim B'Israel* (Jerusalem 1926) 256–7 (Hebrew).

East, and, in their Aramaic form, influenced practice in Eretz-Israel
and in Egypt.[30]

The Tosefta in the fourth chapter of Ketubot[31] addresses five cases
in which the Tannaim used legal documents, which were not written according to the Sages, in order to learn new laws. In Hebrew
the term is דרשת לשון הדיוט "to make an exegesis of a layman's formula." One of the cases is the first formula of the leasing document,
4:10.[32] I suggest that if this formula represents a "layman's formula,"
so does the other: "for my work and expenses". While the term
לשון הדיוט, "layman's formulary," has been much discussed,[33] there

---

[30] With specific reference to the condition of leasing, see Gulak (supra n. 19)
113–4. With general reference to the trend, see Y. Muffs, *Studies in Aramaic Legal
Papyri from Elephantine* (Leiden 1969) ch. 7; J.C. Greenfield, "The Aramaic Legal
Texts of the Achaemenian Period," *Transeuphratène* 3 (1990) 85–92. The first condition, "... אם אוביר ולא אעביד" is seen in the codes of Hammurabi, par. 43, and
thereafter in many bills. See L.N. Dembitz, "Babylon in Jewish Law," *JQR* (1907)
109–26 at 114; Y. Rosenthal, "The Laws of Amerphel (= Hammurabi) the King
of Shin'ar," *Ha-mishpat Ha-ivri* I (Moscow 1918) 133–61 at 142 (Hebrew); Gulak,
ibid.; S. Greengus, "Filling Gaps: Laws Found in Babylonia and in the Mishnah
but Absent in the Hebrew Bible," *Maarav* 7 (1991) 149–71 at 156.

[31] T. Ketubot 4.10 דרש ר' מאיר המקבל שדה מחבירו ומשוכה בה הבירה, שמין אותה
כמה היא ראויה לעשות ונותן לו, שכך כותב לו אם אוביר ולא אעביד אשלם במיטבא.
R. Meir expounded, "He who receives a field [as a sharecropper] from his friend,
and once he had acquired position of it, he neglected it—they make an estimate
of how much it is suitable to produce and he pays the sum to him. For thus does he
write him, 'If I neglect and I do not work it, I shall pay you from the best produce.'"

[32] The Babylonian Talmud (B. Bava Metzia 104a) says explicitly: רבי מאיר היה
דורש לשון הדיוט; דתניא, רבי מאיר אומר : אם אוביר ולא אעביד אשלם במיטבא. "R. Meir
made an exegesis of ordinary language. . . ." The exegesis apparently consists of an
appraisal of how much the field should yield. In other words, the payment of the
sharecropper is the equivalent of the fruits that he committed to give, and not the
equivalent of the damage done to the property, in distinction from the modes of
appraisal executed in ancient Oriental law. See also S. Lieberman, *Tosefta Ki-fshutah*,
VI (New York 1967) 247 (Hebrew), concerning the position of the Rishonim as to
what the exegesis of R. Meir was for. It is worth noting that while Hillel, in T.
Ketubot 4.9, explicated a lay formula specifically to save people from being considered *mamzerim*, R. Meir did so for the purpose of establishing normative halakha.
In any event, this testifies to the fact that it was customary to write this in a bill,
a custom of laymen not resulting from the dictates of the Sages, though the Sages
were prepared to legitimize it. Thus it appears in the Mishnah and the Tosefta of
Bava Metsia as part and parcel of the bill itself. In our bills, P.Yadin 21–22, it
would be irrelevant to mention what the yield of the field would have been, for
the fruits exist. However, without the labor of harvesting, Babatha would not have
had them, thus Simon pays her in the event that he does not deliver the amount
to which he committed himself.

[33] See Lieberman (supra note 32) 246; E.E. Urbach, *The Halakha* (Giv'ataim 1984)
74 (Hebrew); Z. Frankel, *Introduction to the Mishna* (Warsaw 1923) 96–7 n. 9 (Hebrew);
M. Elon, *Jewish Law—History, Sources, Principles* (Philadelphia and Jerusalem 1994)

is no doubt in my mind that it represents the willingness of the Sages to adopt foreign formulae into their halakha.

On this note, I would like to cite one passage from last chapter of Prof. Muffs' book.[34] In his discussion of what he terms "the Aramaic common law," which influenced the whole Near East in the Persian period, he writes:

> ... Furthermore, the fragments of deeds preserved in the Talmud are also part of the Aramaic common-law tradition. In calling these deeds *leshon hedyot* or "layman's formulary", the rabbis tacitly admitted the non-rabbinic provenience of the documents. Furthermore, many of the stipulations used in the deeds, being reflexes of non-Jewish traditions, were not always in accord with formal rabbinical jurisprudence. Nevertheless, aided by a realistic use of legal fiction, the rabbis often accepted such conditions as valid ...

I maintain that R. Meir and his circle did see a leasing bill,[35] of the type used in their time in Eretz-Israel. One of its formulae is found also in Babatha's archive. We have identified, then, the element of a lease in our papyri, and have also found another non-Greek influence in Babatha's archive in addition to those with which we are already familiar.[36]

Why did the Tannaim have to resort to layman's formulae? It seems to me that an answer to this question will buttress the claim

---

422–32, esp. 428–9 and n. 26; M.A. Friedman, *Jewish Marriage in Palestine* I (Tel-Aviv and New-York 1980) 2–3 and note 6, and 15. Concerning the exegesis of lay formulary conducted by Hillel by way of comparison with Egyptian marriage contracts, see: R. Katzoff, "Philo and Hillel on Violation of Betrothal in Alexandria," in I.M. Gafni et al., eds., *Jews in the Hellenistic-Roman World—Studies in Memory of Menachem Stern* (Jerusalem 1996) 39*–57*.

[34] Supra note 30, 193.

[35] Compare the language of the Y. Ketubot 4:8 29a [= Y. Yebamot 15:3 14d] רבי מאיר עבד כתובה מדרש רבי מאיר המקבל שדה מחבירו משזכה בה חבירו שמין אותה כמה היא ראויה לעשות ונתן לו שהוא כותב לו אם אוביר ולא אעביד אישלם במיטבא "R. Meir expounded the language of a contract: He who receives a field as a sharecropper from his friend, and, once he had acquired possession of it, he neglected it (reading הוביד for the meaningless חבירו)—they make an estimate of how much it is suitable to produce and he pays that sum to him. For thus does he write him, 'If I neglect and I do not work it, I shall pay you from the best produce.'" *Ketubah* here means 'bill', hence it seems that R. Meir actually beheld a bill before him which reflected the local custom concerning the sharecropper in Eretz-Israel.

[36] On P.Yadin 18 see N. Lewis, R. Katzoff and J.C. Greenfield, "Papyrus Yadin 18," *IEJ* 37 (1987) 229–50; R. Katzoff, "Papyrus Yadin 18 Again: A Rejoinder," *JQR* 82 (1991) 171–6. On P.Yadin 19 see R. Katzoff, "An Interpretation of P.Yadin 19: A Jewish Gift after Death," in A. Bülow-Jacobson, ed., *Proceedings of the 20th International Congress of Papyrologists* (Copenhagen 1994) 562–5.

that the Tannaitic leasing laws in general, and the formulation of
their bills in particular, are rooted in local custom, and not necessarily in pre-existing halakhic sources.[37] These customs and formulae were taken from the Oriental law. I suspect that R. Meir turned
to non-halakhic documents to address the case of a lessee who had
abandoned the field because the "halakhic" bills could not help him
with that case.

In addition to the documents of Babatha, we have Hebrew and
Aramaic leasing bills from almost the same period and locale. These
are P.Yadin 42–46[38] and the fragments of P.Mur. 24.[39] An examination of the bills of P.Mur. shows how "primitive" they are. The
element of payment is indeed very similar to the parallel element in
the bills of Babatha. In both, the payment is stated as a quantity of
produce which is to be measured and weighed in the presence of
the owners according to a standard weight mentioned in the bill.
However, the P.Mur. fragments lack any element of warranty or
surety, either of the lessee or of the lessor, and also lack specification
of the labors to be obligated. It seems that these bills were indeed
drafted according to the halakha of the Sages in the period of the
Bar-Kokhba revolt. These bills clearly were written by Jews for whom
halakha played a central role. This is evidenced in the term of the
lease, which ends in all these bills just before the onset of "shmita,"
the sabbatical year, and in the obligation which the lessee accepts
to tithe the crop before its division,[40] which shows a deep recogni-

---

[37] It is noteworthy that leasing laws are entirely absent from the Torah, especially when seen in contrast with the highly developed body of law in this regard
found within Oriental law. See S.E. Loewenstamm, "The Law," in B. Mazar, ed.,
The History of the People of Israel III (Jerusalem 1967) 132 and note 29 (Hebrew).

[38] On them, see Y. Yadin "Expedition D—The Cave of The Letters," *IEJ* 12
(1962) 227–57, 248–57; K. Beyer, *Die aramäischen Texte vom Toten Meer*, vol. 2 (Göttingen
1994) 184–5; G.W. Nebe, "Die Hebräische Sprache der Nahal Hever Dokumente
5/6 Hev 44–46," in T. Muraoka and J.F. Elwolde, eds., *The Hebrew of The Dead
Sea Scrolls and Ben-Sira* (Leiden 1997) 150–7. These bills deal with the leasing of
land in exchange for money, and are thus of less interest in the present study.

[39] P. Benoit, J.T. Milik and R. de Vaux, *Les grottes de Murabba'at, (DJD II)* (Oxford
1961) 122–34. See also: B.Z. Wacholder "The Calendar of Sabbatical Cycles During
the Second Temple and the Early Rabbinic Period," *HUCA* 44 (1973) 153–96 at
176–9.

[40] This is the obligation of the lessee to pay tax to the king, according to T.Demai
6.3. In the aforementioned bills, the lessor is Hillel ben Garis, who leased from
"the king"—Bar-Kochba—and in all likelihood has the standing of a courtier of
"the king," and also receives his share after tithing.

tion of the halakha.[41] If we see the formulation in these documents as representative of rabbinic formulation, we can understand why R. Meir had to make exegesis of a "layman's formula" to create the halakha of the lessee's guarantee to pay.

There is yet additional information that can be derived from the Tannaitic sources. Among the various models of leases that can be found in the Mishna and Tosefta Bava Metsia Chapter Nine and in other places there is also one similar to the agreement of Babatha and Simon, namely, where a lessee's only duty is to reap or harvest.[42]

Were the Tannaim also familiar with a practice of selling produce before the harvest without mentioning the duty to harvest them, as in the καρπωνεία? The answer is that the Tannaim did not mention the sale or purchase of produce without the accompanying trees or land. The halakhic term קנין פירות "ownership of the fruit alone," which is found almost forty times in the Babylonian Talmud, is found neither in the Tannaitic sources nor in the Palestinian Talmud.[43]

---

[41] Concerning the entire matter, and further attempts to correspond between P.Mur. 24 and the halakha, see M.R. Lehmann, "Studies in the Murabbaʿat and Nahal Hever Documents," *Revue de Qumran* 4 (1963) 53–81, 72–81.

[42] T.Peah 3.1: המקבל שדה לקצור, לא ילקט בנו אחריו. ר' יוסי או' יוסי בנו אחריו. אבל העריסין (והעכורות) וההחכורות והמוכר קמתו לחברו לקצור, ילקט בנו אחריו. "He who receives [as part owner] a field to harvest—his son may not collect gleanings behind him . . . But [with regard to] (1) sharecroppers, (2) [those who] lease fields, (3) or one who sells his standing [crop] to his neighbor to harvest, his son may collect gleanings behind him."

T.Demai 6.6: ישראל שקיבל מחבירו שדהו לקצור כשהוא שבלין, כרמו לבצור בענבים, זיתיו למסוק בזיתים . . . "An Israelite [sharecropper] who received from his fellow his field to harvest when [the crop] was in the status of sheaves [emend to follow the pattern below: 'in return for (a rental payment in) sheaves'], [or] (2) his vineyard to cut in return for [a rental payment in] grapes, [or] (3) his olive grove to harvest in return for [a rental payment in] olives. . . ."

T.Bava Metzia 9.30: החוכר שדה מחבירו לשחת, ונוזזה, כל פירות שעושה הרי אילו שלו, חכרה לזרע, ונוזזה לשחת, לא יאמר הריני ממתין עד שיכלה אותו המין מתוכה, אלא כל הפירות שעושה הרי אילו שלו. "He who sharecropped a field of his friend for fodder, and he took the gleanings—all the produce which it yields, lo, these are his."

[43] See also I. Herzog, *The Main Institutions of Jewish Law* (London and New York 1965) I, 319. Indeed, a study of the issue of the sale of the fruit of the palm (B.Yevamot 93a, and elsewhere) reveals that the issue is disputed by sages of the second and third generations of Babylonian Amoraim as a new question, and it seems from the pericope that they (or the Talmud) are aware of the fact that there are no early sources for halakha in this regard. The Jerusalem Talmud has no discussion of this topic. The dispute between Resh Lakish and R. Yochanan in B.Bava Metzia 96a and elsewhere deals with "one who sells his field to his neighbor for eating its fruits," a form of acquiring the yield through the acquisition of the land. In my opinion, this is irrelevant to our discussion. Generally, the fruits of a field are considered part of it. See M.Bava Batra 4:8.

Indeed, one finds a number of halakhot that relate to a property right in unharvested fruit, such as the privilege of the husband to the fruit of his wife's assets, or similar privileges in the laws of succession, but these cases are the exceptions that demonstrate the rule.[44]

I would suggest that from this fact we can deduce that it was not prevalent at this time in Eretz-Israel to sell unharvested fruit separately, while leasing only for harvest or picking was, in all likelihood, a prevalent institution. In other words, because they were not accustomed to sell unharvested fruit for money, they sold it in exchange for labor, that is to say, through a leasing agreement.[45] If so, it may be that Simon and Babatha drew up their contract as a fruit-selling agreement, in accordance with the Egyptian practice. Yet, because local practice did not recognize a sale of this sort, a small element of leasing was added.

Conclusions

To summarize, our bills contain two transactions: Babatha sells a share of the fruit in exchange for a share of the fruit, while Simon sells his labor and expenses in exchange for the share that Babatha sells. Indeed, the formulation of the declarations in the beginning of the deeds show that Lewis is right when he says that we have here "a purchase of a date crop." However, we cannot ignore the fact that there is also an employment agreement. Simon, as we know, was obliged to give his work (and expenses) for the fruit he received, a fact which is reminiscent to us of a leasing contract, wherein the lessee is (besides his work) obliged to pay a fixed and agreed amount of crop to the owner of the field or plant, in exchange for the rest of the crop. It can be assumed that the real profit of the plant's owner is not the part of the crop that he receives, because origi-

---

[44] Gulak (supra note 19) 143–5. Indeed, it would seem that in the case of the Babylonian Amoraim that the issue did arise, but through negotiation. Yet we cannot ascertain from here anything concerning the state of affairs in Eretz-Israel during the Tannaitic period, and perhaps can see from here evidence to the contrary, as I said earlier, supra n. 43. Concerning the entire matter see: B. Cohen, "Usufructus in Jewish and Roman Law," *Jewish and Roman Law* (New York 1966) 557–77; S. Shilo, "Split Ownership Rights in Property in Talmudic Law," *Diné Israel* 12 (1984–1985) 173–95 (Hebrew).

[45] Cohen (supra note 44) 573.

nally all the crop belongs to him, but the work, and in our case the picking and drying. Without them Babatha could not enjoy her crop at all. That is why it is reasonable for her to "sell a crop of dates in exchange for dates."

From a juristic aspect, the most similar deed to ours is the Egyptian καρπωνεία which combines leasing and selling transactions. It was mentioned that the interest of the lessee/buyer is that the deed be formulated as a bill of sale, which affords him better protection. In our case Simon is the initiator of the deal and he writes the first bill. We can suppose that he wanted to formulate it as bill of a crop sale anyway, even if it looks like the fruits do not pass to his possession, and he will receive them only in return for his "work and expenses," like an ordinary lessee.

We also showed that the Tannaitic halakha recognizes a kind of lessee, whose only duty is to reap or to harvest, and who is treated as a buyer, in terms of sale and purchase. That is to say, in Eretz-Israel also we find a relation to that certain kind of lessee for harvest as a kind of buyer, whose level of ownership in the crop is higher than that of other kinds of lessee. The most similar model to that sort of deal in the Jewish sources is a lease contract, to which P.Yadin 21–22 is comparable. The Tannaitic leasing bill reflects Palestinian local practices, not necessarily Jewish. Indeed, the bill which is found in Tannaitic sources does not contain the terminology of 'sale' or 'purchase.' However, the Tannaitic lease contract is the only source which contains an exact parallel to the formulation by which the fruit which Simon received is a compensation for his labor and expenses. Hence in both the linguistic and the juristic aspects there is a similarity between P.Yadin 21–22 and a deal of leasing.

Appendix

One may speculate as to why we have two deeds, P.Yadin 21 and 22. Lewis states categorically that bill 22 was written after bill 21, but very soon after, and by the same scribe. The sole significant difference between the two is the condition of security that Babatha offers him in the event that the field is taken by a third party. (One notes that no security is offered for damage to the fruits due to wind, or locusts, etc., as provided for in Tannaitic contracts and in Oriental deeds. It stands to reason that the fear of damage to the fruit is reduced in a bill such as this, which speaks of fruit just before harvesting).

Lewis has already demonstrated that the custom in Egypt was to write one bill, and to copy it if necessary for both parties. In rabbinic literature, too, one thinks of a single deed, with the consent of both sides, both with regard to leasing and with regard to sale. We should note, however, that no discoveries have been made of other deeds in Eretz-Israel that bear a declaration of the purchaser. It would appear that it was not customary to compose such deeds. It is plausible that Simon composed his bill because he was also 'selling' something, namely, his labor, a clear element of leasing.

A more speculative suggestion would be that Simon's bill was meant to serve as the primary bill, perhaps even the sole bill, in accordance with the statute that a bill of leasing is written for the possession of the lessee (see the previous note), yet Simon demanded an additional bill for the following reason. The sole difference between the two documents, as I have said, is the condition of security that Babatha offers Simon. It may be that Simon demanded this clause, which entailed the drawing up of a bill that included this stipulation as well as all the details that appeared in the bill that Simon had written, because he knew that there were problems concerning the rightful ownership of Babatha's groves, and by extension, of their fruits. This fear is evident in Simon's formulation: 21.11: ἃ κατέχις, ὡς λέγις, properties you distrain, *as you say*, in lieu of your dowry . . . Compare this with the more confident formulation offered by Babatha: (22.9–10): κατέχω αὐτὰ ἀντὶ τῆς . . ., I distrain in lieu of my dowry. . . . As Lewis states in his note to lines 22:20–25: ". . . Babatha here undertakes to protect the buyer of the crop against possible counter-claims to the ownership of the orchards. Such a counterclaim in the name of Jesus' orphans had presumably—like the claim that was withdrawn in 20—already been asserted, and its sequelae appear in 23 and 24, dated some two months after 21–22." In all likelihood, the suspicion was realized, and the deal was never carried through, and this is why both of the bills were in Babatha's possession. In other words, the deal never started, and Simon never began his work, and hence there was no reason to remunerate him. As stated, the remuneration was only for labor and expenses, not for the loss of the sale, and hence there was no remuneration as there was no sale.

Whether the groves referred to in 23–24 are the same groves referred to in 21–22 is debated. See Lewis (supra note 1)—negative; H.M. Cotton and J.C. Greenfield, 'Babatha's Property and the Law of Succession,' *ZPE* 104 (1994) 211–224 at 213—positive.

GIFT AND INHERITANCE LAW IN THE JUDAEAN DESERT DOCUMENTS

Yosef Rivlin

1. *Introduction*

I would like to address three issues concerning gift law and inheritance law as found in the Judaean Desert documents: First, an exposition—what are the laws exhibited by these documents? Second, I would like to examine the corresponding body of law within Jewish Law; and lastly, I would like to entertain the question: Do the two systems arrive at common conclusions in these cases?

2. *P.Yadin 7*

The first issue: what can we learn about gift law and inheritance law from these documents? I would like to limit my focus to those documents that have already received scholarly attention. The first is the Aramaic deed of gift found at Nahal Hever, P.Yadin 7.[1] The deed is dated 13 July 120 CE. In it Shimon son of Menahem, the father of Babatha, grants all of his possessions to his wife, Miriam daughter of Yosef in an immediate gift. Cotton categorizes this gift as a "gift after death,"[2] but more likely is the definition advanced by Yaron, who terms this gift as the "gift of one in good health."[3] This designation more closely approximates the formulation of the

---

[1] First published by Y. Yadin, J.C. Greenfield, and A. Yardeni, "A Deed of Gift in Aramaic Found in Nahal Hever: Papyrus Yadin 7," *ErIsr* 25 (1996) 383–403 (Hebrew) with summary in English at 103*. Republished in Yigael Yadin, Jonas C. Greenfield, Ada Yardeni, Baruch Levine, eds., *The Documents from the Bar Kokhba Period in the Cave of Letters. Hebrew, Aramaic and Nabatean-Aramaic Papyri*. (Jerusalem 2002).

[2] H.M. Cotton, "Deeds of Gift and the Law of Succession in the Papyri from the Judaean Desert," *ErIsr* 25 (1996) 410–5 at 410 (Hebrew) with summary in English in *103–*104; For the English version see: "Deeds of Gift and the Law of Succession in the Documents from the Judaean Desert," in B. Kramer et al., eds., *Akten des 21. Internationalen Papyrologenkongress Berlin, 13.–19.8.1995* (*ArchPF* Beiheft 3, Berlin 1997) 179–88 at 179.

[3] R. Yaron, "Acts of Last Will in Jewish Law," *Recueils de la Société Jean Bodin pour l'Histoire Comparative des Institutions* 59 (1992) 29–45.

deed, מן כען יהבת לכי מתנת עולם, "From this moment I am giving you a gift forever."[4] Several salient points emerge from the record of this gift. First, the gift is an irrevocable one, as demonstrated by the wording, מתנת עלם די לא תעדה, "a gift forever that I shall not revoke."[5] Second, this gift includes all of the possessions currently belonging to Shimon, as well as עם כל די אקנא, "all that I will acquire in the future."[6] Third, Shimon the donor, retains the usufruct until his death, as the deed states, "on the condition that I have rights of sustenance and to pay off debts."[7] Fourth, he retains the right to sell these possessions or any part of them for the sake of personal sustenance. This is derived from the wording: במה די אשבוק מנהון ודי לא אשתרהן ולא אחזבן לפרנוס נפשי מן באתר דנה, "what I shall have left to them which was not given as a pledge or sold for my sustenance."[8] In other words, the broad rights of usage nonetheless remain in the hands of the giver until his death. Following his death, all that remains of his possessions is ceded for the use of the beneficiary.

In his critique, Yaron highlights two points that distinguish between the norms depicted in the Judaean Desert documents and those found in Talmudic law: First, this Judaean Desert document permits a donor to cede ownership of goods that have yet to be acquired; second, the global gift here of *all* possessions allows for an escape clause, namely, the giver retains the right to sell off possessions for the sake of his personal sustenance. Yaron claims that the Talmudic jurists were aware of these procedural possibilities and expresses surprise that these were not incorporated into the Talmudic system for gift giving.[9] Further on I will try to offer an approach to resolve Yaron's problem here.

3. *P.Yadin 19*

The second document I would like to examine is the Judaean Desert deed of gift, P.Yadin 19.[10] Here we read that Judah son of Eleazar

---

[4] Lines 5/35–36.
[5] Line 2/32.
[6] Line 4–5/35.
[7] Lines 14–15/52.
[8] Lines 15–17/53–55.
[9] Yaron (supra note 3) 45.
[10] Published in N. Lewis, *The Documents from the Bar Kokhba Period in the Cave of Letters. Greek Papyri* (Jerusalem 1989).

Khthousion makes a gift of his residence in Ein Gedi to his daughter Shelamzion, whereby half of the residence is to be ceded immediately, and half upon his death. The relevant passage reads as follows: "Judah son of Eleazar Khthousion of Ein Gedi who resides in Mahoza bequeaths to Shelamzion his daughter all of his property in Ein Gedi, consisting of half of the courtyard... half of the structures, and their lofts, with the exception of the small adjoining courtyard, while the other half of the courtyard and its structures Judah bequeaths to that same Shelamzion upon his death... in a binding and permanent manner."[11]

The document reveals three points of interest: First, it allows for a two-stage gift: half is ceded from today, and half only after death. Second, we see the gift executed here through the use of the Greek verb for 'bequeath.' Finally, we see that the deed concludes with the stipulation that this gift is being executed "in a binding and permanent manner," a phrase that requires further elucidation. Katzoff has suggested that the gift described here should be categorized as מהיום ולאחר מיתה, "from today and after death," and constitutes an irrevocable gift. In his study, he addresses two problematic aspects here: First, the use of the language "to bequeath" instead of "to bestow." Second, the deed proposes a split, but not the standard split between the substance and usufruct but between one act of cession to take effect at present and a second act of cession to take effect on the remainder following death.[12] I submit that Katzoff's approach leaves several issues unresolved, and I will attempt further on to propose an alternative interpretation.

4. Deed of Gift

The third deed I would like to examine is the deed of gift from the archive of Salome daughter of Levi, P.Hever 64.[13] In the year 129,

---

[11] See: R. Katzoff, "P.Yadin 19: A Gift After Death from the Judean Desert," in D. Assaf, ed., *Proceedings of the Tenth World Congress of Jewish Studies, Jerusalem 1989* Div. C. Vol. 1. (Jerusalem 1990) 1–8 (Hebrew) (henceforth: Katzoff, 1990) 1–2. see also: R. Katzoff, "An Interpretation of P.Yadin 19: A Jewish Gift after Death," in A. Bülow-Jacobson, ed., *Proceedings of the 20th International Congress of Papyrologists* (Copenhagen 1994) 562–5 (henceforth: Katzoff, 1994).

[12] Katzoff (1990) (supra note 11) 7.

[13] First published, H.M. Cotton, "The Archive of Salome Komaise Daughter of Levi—Another Archive from the 'Cave of Letters,'" *ZPE* 105 (1995) 171–208 at 183–203; Cotton (1996) (supra note 2) 411 ff.

Salome Gropte bestowed a gift upon her daughter, Salome Komaise, consisting of a grove of date palms and half a courtyard. The gift is bestowed employing the language "from this day and forever," implying an immediate cession in a binding and permanent manner.[14]

Cotton reached several conclusions from this papyrus and the two mentioned before. In my opinion, these findings were based on assumptions that are difficult to prove in a conclusive fashion. In a new article she reverses her opinion concerning several of her earlier conclusions.[15] I concur with the conclusions she reaches in this most recent publication. In it, she concludes that the norms reflected in the Judaean Desert documents do not necessarily conflict with those set out in Jewish law,[16] and this is the thesis I wish to show in this article.

5. An Immediate Gift

Within Jewish law, there is the starkest contrast between the laws of inheritance for a widow on the one hand, and the law for a daughter on the other. A widow does not have any standing in the line of succession, while a daughter has a normative place of standing in the line of succession, when there are no sons alongside her. This biblical ruling remains unchallenged throughout the entire corpus of halachic literature.[17] When we discover that a father bestows a gift to his daughter we should not assume that this automatically stands in contradiction to Jewish law. As Cotton rightly hypothesizes, a father may bestow a gift upon his daughter in anticipation of the eventuality that a son may later be born, thus removing the daughter from the process of succession.[18] By means of a gift he can "head off" this problem by circumventing the laws of succession.

Moreover, it seems to me that we can draw no conclusions whatever concerning the rights of inheritance of the daughter from this papyrus, which speaks solely of an immediate gift, with no component reserved until after death. By way of analogy: if a father bestows

---

[14] Cotton (1995) (supra note 13); Cotton (1996) (supra note 2).
[15] H.M. Cotton, "The Law of Succession in the Documents from the Judean Desert Again," SCI 17 (1998) 115–23.
[16] Ibid. 122.
[17] Numbers 27:8–11; M.Bava Batra 8.1; Maimomides, Nachaloth, 1, 1, 8.
[18] Cotton (supra note 15) 116.

an immediate gift upon a son, does that necessarily imply that the son is not eligible to inherit from his father? Clearly this is not the case. An immediate gift is designed to grant the donee immediate rights to the property, without having to wait until the death of the donor, at which time the donee would receive ownership of the property through inheritance.

The very fact that a man bestows a gift upon his daughter does not automatically imply that barring the gift she would have no standing in the order of succession. As Cotton herself surmises, there was an ever-present concern that a son would later be born, thereby denying the daughter rights of succession. And, as I pointed out, the discussion of the rights of succession of the daughter is a discussion entirely unrelated to the other documents we examined in which the gift was an immediate gift, and not a gift after death. A person who bestows a gift—to his son, his daughter, or to any one else for that matter—does so with the intention that the donee should immediately derive the full rights. Such a gift is executed regardless of the rights that such a beneficiary would potentially enjoy following the death of the donor. I therefore suggest that we refrain from arriving at any conclusions from a deed such as this, which speaks only of an immediate gift.

Cotton sees several aspects common to all three of these documents: First, all three were drafted on behalf of women; second, none of the documents makes any mention of existing sons; third, it would appear from these records that a married woman can exercise ownership over her own property without interference from her husband.[19]

6. *P.Yadin 20, 23–24*

In P.Yadin 20, dated 19 June 130, the guardians of the nephews of Judah son of Eleazar Khthousion cede a courtyard to Shelamzion, Judah's daughter. Cotton asserts that from this we may conclude that nephews were of higher standing in the order of succession than were daughters. Ultimately, however, she questions this view, and suggests that the guardians' challenge concerned the very rights that

---

[19] Cotton (1996) (supra note 2) 411; Cotton, *Akten* (supra note 2) 182.

Judah had over the property, and that therefore, this document supplies no proof concerning the order of succession.

Cotton finds basis for the preferred status of nephews over daughters within the order of succession from other documents, namely
P.Yadin 23 and 24. Here, Besas son of Judah, guardian of the orphan
nephews, challenges Babatha's claim to the date palm grove that her
husband had assigned to her. Cotton assumes here that Shelamzion,
Judah's daughter, was alive at the time, and yet is not mentioned
as a party to the claim, thereby demonstrating that the claim of the
nephews is stronger than the claim of his daughter.[20]

Yet, it seems that here as well, Cotton should have exercised the
caution that she did in her interpretation of P.Yadin 20. In other
words, to realize that the claim of the guardian against Babatha "to
demonstrate what document grants you ownership of the date palm
grove" may reflect a challenge of her husband's very ownership of
the grove in the first place. According to the guardian, the grove
never rightfully belonged to Judah, and hence he had no right to
cede it to Babatha. Because the basis of the claim in these cases is
unclear, I maintain that we cannot categorically conclude that these
documents demonstrate a legal norm that stands in contradiction to
the laws of succession of Jewish law. Biblical law clearly delineates
the order of succession: first the son and daughter, and only after-
ward the brothers and their offspring.[21]

7. The Widow's Rights

Furthermore, Cotton's assertion that Judah registered these properties in the name of Babatha in lieu of the marriage contract payment—an action contrary to the norm within Jewish law—is equally
lacking in basis. All of the Judaean Desert documents pertaining to
marriage relate that all of the husband's belongings are to be assigned
for the redemption and payment of the marriage contract,[22] in a
fashion identical to the obligations of a debtor to a creditor. Nowhere
in these documents is it stated that a particular property was regis-

---

[20] Cotton (1996) (supra note 2) 412; Cotton, *Akten* (supra note 2) 183–4.
[21] Numbers, ibid.
[22] P.Yadin 18, 37.

tered in the name of a creditor. Thus, in the Mishnah for example, we find that if a husband registers a certain property for his wife in lieu of the marriage contract payment, the move has no legal standing; when the obligation devolves upon him or his inheritors to pay her the marriage contract, the property is assessed anew, and full payment must be made according to the terms stipulated by the marriage contract.[23] The record in P.Yadin 21 and 22 to the effect that Babatha took ownership of three date palm groves that had belonged to her husband, "in lieu of the marriage contract payment and the debt" does not undermine my contention. What emerges in these documents is that in marriage, Babatha had no formal relationship whatever to these groves. They were simply the form of payment chosen by Judah's successors to pay off her marriage contract following his death.

8. *The Woman's Right of Possession*

The autonomous and full ownership enjoyed by a woman over her own possessions is likewise recognized within Jewish law. As we know, a woman may opt to offer her belongings as a dowry whose value is registered in the marriage contract, which value is ultimately to be paid out to her together with the other components of the marriage contract. Here, these possessions are categorized as נכסי צאן ברזל, "possessions whose value is estimated." Alternatively, these goods could remain in her ownership. The Mishnah, moreover, stipulates that a husband and wife may arrange an agreement whereby he entirely cedes his rights to her possessions, stating, דין ודברים אין לי בנכסייך, "I have no claim whatever to your possessions."[24] In such a case, the husband derives no use or benefit from the usufruct of those possessions, and they remain entirely within the control of the wife. Our interim conclusion, therefore, is that the evidence from these documents does not point in a categorical fashion to divergence between the two legal systems.

---

[23] M.Ketubot 4.7.
[24] M.Ketubot 9.1.

9. *The Last Will in Jewish Law*

I would like now to address the questions raised by Yaron concerning P.Yadin 7, and the interpretation offered by Katzoff of P.Yadin 19. I begin by offering an accurate account, in my view, of the development and evolution of the last will and testament in Jewish law. This overview, I believe, can help us resolve many of the outstanding questions and issues raised by these sources.

I concur with the school that maintains that the notion of a will was a feature of Israelite law from an early stage.[25] Its use, however, was highly limited, as the prevailing theology dictated that since the universe is the property of the Almighty, the mortal owner of a parcel of land had no business changing the divinely sanctioned order of succession. Hence, we find no trace, mention or remnant of the institution of a will in ancient Israel. Nonetheless, we do see several instances where possessions are disposed of after death. Even when a person desired to dispose of his possessions not in accordance with the norms of succession, he would still do so only within the framework of those eligible for succession, by favoring one successor while diminishing the portion of another. Nonetheless, we do find instances where possessions are disposed of to strangers—those who stand entirely outside the normative order of succession. In all likelihood these were oral arrangements, and only in rare instances relegated to a written document. Because the use of this institution was rare, it received no juridical structure or definition, to the point that some scholars maintain that the written will made its first appearance in Israel in the Tannaitic period.[26]

Near the close of the second commonwealth, the *diatheke* bill began to be incorporated into the Jewish legal system. Its essence was to allow the disposition of possessions after death. Its formulation read, "דא תהא לי לעמוד ולהיות, אם מתי יינתנו נכסי לפלוני," that is, "let this gift remain in force, even should I die."[27] This formula could be

---

[25] A. Gulak, *Legal Documents in the Talmud*. Edited and supplemented by R. Katzoff (Jerusalem 1994) 155; Z.W. Falk, "Testate Succession in Jewish Law," *JJS* 12 (1961) 67–77 at 73; idem, *Introduction to Jewish Law in the Second Commonwealth* II (Tel Aviv 1971) 319 (Hebrew).

[26] I.F. Baer, "The Historical Foundations of the Halakha," *Zion* 27 (1962) 117–55 at 132 (Hebrew).

[27] T.Bava Batra. 8.10; Y.Peah 3.9 17d; B.Bava Metzia. 19a.

adopted either by a person in good health or by a person on his deathbed. Its formulation remained uniform no matter what the physical condition of the individual invoking its powers. In order to demonstrate the full resolve of the donor to dispose of the possession, the donee was required to receive a deed from the donor. Delivery of the deed itself did not constitute cession of the possession, but rather final intent to bequeath the possession.[28] Since the bequest would only take effect after death, the donor could retract it at any time.[29] The retraction could be formalized either by retrieving the original *diatheke* from the donee, or by drafting a second *diatheke* nullifying the first one. There is no textual source for the division proposed by Katzoff whereby there were two modes of disposition in Israel: one, the *diatheke* which was revocable, and a second, the "gift from after death" which was irrevocable.[30] The Tosefta differentiates between the two as follows: "He who writes a will (a *diatheke*) can retract. He who writes a deed of gift cannot retract. What is a will (a *diatheke*)? "Let this be confirmed: If I die, let my estate be given to so-and so." And what is a deed of gift? "As of this date let my property be given to so-and-so."[31]

This halakhah does not refer to a gift after death, but to an immediate gift. The phrase, "as of this date let my property be given to so-and-so," allows no other interpretation. Lieberman posits that the two statements of the Tosefta both refer to the gift of a person on his deathbed. In the first statement, the Tosefta relates that a person on his deathbed may dispose of his possessions by a *diatheke*, in which event he retains all the advantages of someone who disposes of his possessions in contemplation of death, a disposition that may be retracted. In the second statement, the Tosefta rules that if a person on his deathbed bestows a regular gift using the formula "from today I bestow my possessions," the gift takes immediate effect, and is irrevocable.[32] In my opinion, however, the second statement, which speaks only of מתנה, a gift, need not be equated with the gift by a person on his deathbed. Rather, the Tosefta could be proposing the

---

[28] T.Bava Batra. 8.9. See also ibid., 8.6; 8.11.
[29] *Ibid.* 8.10.
[30] Katzoff (1990) (supra note 11) 5.
[31] T.Bava Batra 8.10.
[32] S. Lieberman, *Tosefta ki-Fshuta, A Comprehensive Commentary on the Tosefta* (New York 1955–1988) Bava Batra 428.

following distinction: the second statement, which speaks of מתנה, a gift, is referring to an immediate gift by a person in good health, which takes effect immediately. The first statement, on the other hand, refers to a *diatheke*, which takes effect only after death. This, in fact, is how the Tosefta was interpreted by the Palestinian Talmud: "What sort [of declaration is involved in a deathbed] gift? All of my possessions hereby are given to so-and-so as a gift from this very moment."[33] The Babylonian Talmud, however, understood the Tosefta differently, as we shall see shortly.

This being the case, what emerges is a single method of disposition in Israel, but one which evolves over time. It seems to me that the principal evolution occurred sometime during the Tannaitic period. It was then that a number of rulings were adopted that curtailed and restricted the manners in which a person could dispose of possessions and bequeath them upon death. The driving factor behind this evolution, I believe, is rooted in the adoption of two positions: the first is that אין שטר לאחר מיתה, "a deed has no validity after death," that is, a deed that prescribes that cession will take effect only after the death of the donor is an invalid deed. The second, is that אין קנין לאחר מיתה, "there is no transfer of title after death," meaning, that a person may not initiate a process today to cede ownership only after death. The rules stated in this language are cited in the name of Shmuel, one of the early Babylonian Amora'im. Later talmudic scholars extended this ruling to all deeds.[34] Yet, out of a desire to accommodate a person on his deathbed, or a person who was contemplating death, they ruled that these restrictions would be lifted, and that the deed of disposition would take force. Yet once the sages resolved that adaptations needed to be implemented in the *diatheke*, a complex process began, and here Talmudic sources help us trace the evolution of this area of law.

The incorporation of the twin principles, "a deed has no validity after death," and "there is no transfer of title after death," were to leave a permanent impression on the laws of disposition in Israel. In the first stage it was determined that a person in good health could not dispose of possessions through the agency of a *diatheke*. Disposition through this vehicle was a privilege reserved for a per-

[33] Y.Peah 3.9 17d.
[34] B.Bava Batra. 135b; 152a. see also: M.Gittin 7.3.

son in contemplation of death.[35] This is borne out in the midrashic literature, where the term *diatheke* is used exclusively in conjunction with a person in ill health, or a person in contemplation of death.[36] In like fashion, we find in the *Sifrut Ha-Ma'sim Livnei Eretz Yisrael* that the deed of a *diatheke* is employed exclusively in conjunction with a person in ill health.[37] In light of the restrictions placed on the use of the *diatheke*, it became necessary to construct an alternative instrument through which disposition could be executed by a person in good health as well. This led to the establishment of a new gift, "a gift from today and after death," whose defining characteristics are the execution of an immediate act of acquisition, מעשה קניין מיידי, resulting in an immediate cession of the possession, or, at the very least, of the bare title.[38]

This enactment was designed to circumvent the legal obstacles standing before a person of good health wishing to dispose of his possessions. On the one hand, such a person was unable to dispose of possessions in a manner that would take effect only after death. Yet such a person may not have desired to cede ownership of the property and usufruct in his lifetime. To accommodate this situation, the sages ordained that such a person in good health should employ the formula, "from today and after death," whereby the ownership would be ceded "from today," immediately, while usufruct remained fully in his control until death, when it would be ceded to the donee, "after death." In this vein the Mishnah states, "If a person desires to give his estate in writing to his sons, he must write, 'this estate is assigned from this day and after my death'; these are the words of Rabbi Yehuda. Rabbi Yose said, this is not necessary. If a person assigned his estate in writing to his son to become his son's after his death, the father may not sell it because it is assigned in writing to the son, and the son may not sell it because it is in the possession of the father." This is likewise what Abaye meant in explicating the beraitha as follows: "It is this that was meant: 'Which is the gift of a person in good health that is regarded as the gift of a dying man in that no possession of its fruit is acquired until after

---

[35] R. Yaron, *Gifts in Contemplation of Death in Jewish and Roman Law* (Oxford 1960) 48.
[36] Tanhuma, Mantova, Lech-Lecha, 8a; Tanhuma, Buber, va-Ethanan, 4; Bamidbar Rabba 2.8.
[37] M. Margaliot, *Hilkhot Eretz Yisrael Min ha-Geniza* (Jerusalem 1973) 47–8.
[38] M.Bava Batra 8.7.

death? Any deed in which it is written 'from this day and after my death.'"[39]

In other words, with the adoption of the restrictive principles, "a deed has no validity after death" and "there is no transfer of title after death," the laws of disposition split into two categories of disposition: the disposition of a person in ill health, and the disposition of a person in good health, instruments designed to remedy the legal obstacle that had emerged whereby an act of cession to take effect only upon death was an invalid act. Without this new enactment, the standard gift formulation of "a gift from today and forever" or, "from today my possessions are ceded" would have left it impossible for the donor to retain usufruct during the course of his life. This gift, upon reflection, can be seen as an amalgam of two previously existing legal conventions. The first is the standard gift, whose wording is "a gift from today."[40] The second is the standard formula of disposition for a person in ill health, "a gift after death." The formulation of this new amalgam is a natural reflection of its two components: "a gift from today" reflecting the standard gift in reference to the ownership, "and after death" reflecting the standard process of disposition, here in reference to usufruct.

The dispute between R. Yehuda and R. Yose in the opening of the mishnah, "If a person desires to give his estate in writing to his sons, he must write, 'this estate is assigned from this day and after my death'; these are the words of R. Yehuda. R. Yose said, this is not necessary,"[41] is expanded upon in the Tosefta: "He who writes over his property to his son has to write in the document, 'From this time forth, and after death,' the words of R. Yehuda. R. Yose says, 'He does not have to do so, because the date of the document proves matters in any event.' Said to him R. Yehuda, 'But does not the date of the document give proof only from the time that it was written?'"[42] R. Yehuda was concerned about the possibility of a person in good health attempting to dispose of possessions after death, and, in accordance with the new enactment that had emerged within the Jewish legal system, insisted upon the inclusion of the term, "from today." This is not a mere technicality of formulation, but an issue

[39] B.Bava Metzia 19a; B.Bava Batra 135b.
[40] T.Bava Batra. 8.10.
[41] M.Bava Batra. 8.7.
[42] T.Ketubot 8.5.

which bears on the very binding force of the deed. The date recorded in the deed, he argues before R. Yose, attests only to the date on which the deed was drafted, but does not connote intention to bestow the property now. Therefore the formulation must bear the term "from today," which indicates the immediate cession of the possession. It is unclear why R. Yose felt that this was unnecessary. It may be that the standard deed of disposition bore no date whatever, and that R. Yose was of the opinion that the inclusion of the date in this new deed of disposition would constitute a distinctive characteristic, one that would grant it immediate binding force from the date of composition of the deed. Alternatively, it may be that the dispute here is of a far more fundamental nature. R. Yose may have maintained that it is possible to dispose of possessions "after death"; in other words, R. Yose maintained that no reform whatever had occurred in the institution of the *diatheke*, and that it was permissible for a person to dispose of his possessions after death.[43]

I would like to suggest that the debate here between R. Yehuda and R. Yose, but particularly the stance taken by R. Yose, are best understood if we assume that this new formulation "from today and after death" was enacted during their era, and that the purpose of the new formulation was to draw attention to the distinction of the new form of disposition. Their debate lacks all coherence if we assume that the age-old formula for disposition likewise included the formulation "from today and after death."[44] If the formula for disposition of a person in good health employed this formula for the purpose of cession only following death, how could it also take effect for the immediate cession of possessions as well? There would be no import in the term "from today" in a bestowal whose entire effect was to occur only after death. It is similarly difficult to accept the proposition that historically the bequest of a person in good health was irrevocable, for that proposition implies that the donor cannot retract, and that the cession takes effect immediately. If so, then the injunction "there is no transfer of title after death" would be of little consequence. Why, if these were in fact the circumstances, did the rabbis feel the need to abolish the historic institution of disposition by a healthy person? It therefore would appear that the early

---

[43] Y. Rivlin, *Inheritance and Will in Jewish Law* (Ramat Gan 1999) 135–79.
[44] Gulak (supra note 25) 160; Katzoff (1990) (supra note 11) 5.

diatheke, which served equally a person of either good or ill health, bore a single formula: "אם מתי, נכסיי לפלוני"—"in the event of my death, may my possessions be ceded to so and so." Regardless of the donor's state of health, the gift took effect only upon death, and regardless of the donor's health, the donor retained the right to retract this gift at any time prior to death. This stands in contradistinction to the later innovation in the gift of a healthy person of the formulation "from today and after death," which was irrevocable.

Use of this convention must have been limited, for no person would want to cede control of his possessions while still fully functional, without any possibility of retraction at a later date. This provokes the question of why is there no allowance anywhere in Talmudic literature for a person of good health to make a gift with the later possibility of retraction. *A priori* we might suggest that the Talmudic jurists were unaware of such a convention. Yet, upon inspection it is clear that the rabbis were aware of conventions that allowed a person to make a gift that included a stipulation that would allow for later retraction. A woman who had remarried could make a gift to her child from her first marriage. The gift would take immediate effect, but could carry the stipulation that the mother could retract the gift at a later point.[45] This convention concurs with Yaron's opinion that the sages, had they wanted, could have allowed a person in good health to dispose of his possessions while retaining the option of selling them later for purposes of personal sustenance, as exhibited in P.Yadin 7.[46] This leaves us with the question: why, in fact, did they not adopt this norm when designing the gift of a healthy person as we have it recorded in the Talmud?

I would suggest that because of the evolution in the use of the *diatheke*, the sages desired to make a clear distinction between the gift of a person in good health and the gift of one on his deathbed. The stipulation that the gift of a healthy person could not be retracted erects the clearest distinction between the two gifts. As we have seen, the deed of a *diatheke*—i.e. the disposition of possessions after death—was considered valid, during the initial stage of its adoption into the Jewish legal system, for any person, regardless of health. When the

---

[45] B.Ketubot 79a.
[46] Yaron (supra note 3) 45.

Jewish legal system incorporated the principles that "a deed has no validity after death" and "there is no transfer of title after death," and restricted use of the *diatheke* for a person in ill health, they effectively denied the healthy person the option of disposing of possessions after death such that the binding force would take effect only after death and that the healthy person could retract his gift at any point during his lifetime. The new option made available to the healthy person was disposition "from today and after death," which denied the right of retraction that had been available prior to the new innovation. The sages deliberately wanted to limit the right of retraction in this gift, and therefore made no provision that would allow such retraction to be binding.

What emerges from the norms reflected in the documents, however, is that some form of retraction was possible. In P.Yadin 7, the donor stipulates that he retains the right to sell the property for personal sustenance, in which event, the beneficiary will enjoy only that portion that remains after the sale. Had the sages designed the gift of a healthy person to include the option of retraction, distinctions between the two would have become blurred, possibly leading to the erroneous conclusion that the gift of a healthy person takes effect after death, a concept that the sages sought to uproot. Moreover, the provisions incorporated in P.Yadin 7, whereby the gift can include future acquisitions, and whereby the donor can sell possessions for the sake of sustenance, strengthen the sense that this act of cession remains unfinished, and only really takes effect after death. This clashes with the norm of "there is no transfer of title after death," and thus the sages sought to undermine it. In order to preserve the integrity of this precept, the rabbis insisted on a convention that would grant immediate cession of the property, remain irrevocable, and disallow the inclusion of future acquisitions. This is the answer to Yaron's questions.

10. *Developments in the Jewish Law of Mattenath Bari*

Only in the post-talmudic period, when the gift of a healthy person had become an accepted norm, do we find attempts to ease the restrictions, and allow for extended use of the property itself and flexibility concerning retraction. Thus we find in an 11th century responsum attributed to Rabbi Yitzhak Alfasi:

> Question: If one bestows a parcel of land as a gift "from today and after death" and stipulates that he wishes to retain the right of retraction concerning that parcel of land in case of need, is the stipulation valid and binding?
>
> Response: All stipulations entered into monetary agreements are valid, and the donor here may retract his gift . . .[47]

From the very question, and from the responsum offered, we can infer that such a stipulation was an uncommon practice under the rubric of a gift by a healthy person. R. Alfasi validates it by the principle that "all stipulations entered into monetary agreements are valid." One can also infer from the language of the stipulation that it is to be exercised only in an hour of need. In other words, the donor does not ask for the full license to retract under any circumstances, but only if he is in need of that parcel of land.

While we find no similar stipulations discussed in the other responsa of R. Alfasi, nor, for that matter, in the responsa of any of his contemporaries, we do find such mention in a deed found in the Cairo Genizah. In it, a father bestows a courtyard upon his daughter on the occasion of her marriage: "This gift of a quarter of the courtyard, made as a gift from now and after death, is made on condition that R. Sasson Dana does not need to sell it for the sake of his sustenance. Yet [should] he claim that he needs it for this purpose, he will be believed at his word, as if two witnesses were attesting to this as fact, and without the need to bring any further proof beyond his word itself."[48] Similar stipulations are found in agreements formulated in subsequent generations as well.[49]

11. A "Gift from Today and After Death"

With this, we return to P.Yadin 19. As we have maintained, the innovation of the gift "from today and after death" was designed so that transfer of title would not occur after death. Indeed, when the ownership of a possession is ceded in immediate fashion to the donee, during the lifetime of the donor, the transfer of title after death is averted. (Upon the death of the donor, the usufruct passes auto-

---

[47] R.Yitzhak Alfasi, Responsa 86.
[48] TS 10J7.6a.
[49] Rivlin (supra 43) 170–7.

matically to the owner, the donee; there is no process of cession or transfer that takes place at this time). Yet Katzoff's interpretation[50] leaves us with several difficulties: The first is the problem of ceding the possession after death. His proposal, whereby half of the possessions are ceded now, and half after death, is incongruous with the standard use of the convention "from today and after death," whereby what is ceded "today" is the substance of the possession, and what is ceded "from after death" is usufruct, and runs counter to the precept of "there is no transfer of title after death." Second, the agency of "from today and after death" was intended specifically for a person in good health, while Katzoff here applies it to a person in ill-health. Third, in a gift of a person on his deathbed, there is no need to split the gift into two parcels. Fourth, if we are speaking here of a person contemplating death, in a manner which is publicly known, this process of 'leaving over' some portion of the gift until after death, makes the gift null and void upon his recovery. There would therefore be no purpose served by the donor retaining half of the courtyard. Fifth, the 'leaving over' stated here, is done so with regard to the half that is bestowed in an immediate gift, concerning which there is no issue of "leaving over."

Therefore, if we wish to see in this document a reflection of the practices of the Jewish legal system, we must discern here two gifts: one an immediate gift, and one a disposition after death. This, of course, rests on the question of the health of the donor in this document. If, as Katzoff asserts, the donor is in ill-health, then we could posit here a standard process of disposition after death. As we saw above, the rabbis did not restrict the capacity of a person in ill health to dispose of his possessions after death. And, of course, there is no problem with making an immediate gift, which a person may execute regardless of health. Usually, disposition is executed through the formulation of נתינה, "bestowing," or "giving," but we have it in the name of R. Shimon ben Gamliel that the use of the Greek term *diethemên* is valid, even though it expresses the notion of "bequest," ירושה.[51] This document is composed in Greek; nonetheless the choice of verbs to execute the cession is of interest. The reading of "bequeath" concerning the half of the structure being ceded immediately is not

---

[50] Katzoff (1990) (supra note 11) 7–8.
[51] Y.Bava Batra. 8.9 16c.

a certain one, as Lewis has pointed out. According to this interpretation, no juridical consequence would emerge from leaving over the small courtyard, as I previously explained.

However, there is also the possibility that the donor here, Judah, was actually in good health, which then makes it more difficult to dovetail the norms reflected here with those of Jewish law. Of course, the first act of cession, the immediate gift, poses no problem. Yet concerning the second gift, we would have to make one of several assumptions: first, that this document reflects the earlier practice whereby a person in good health was permitted to dispose of possessions from after death, and second, that the disposition here was executed not through the standard process of disposition, but through the agency of "the inheritance of R. Yohanan ben Beroka," namely that a donor can bequeath his possessions to the donee who, by norm, stands to succeed him anyway.[52] Because Shelamzion is the successor of Judah, he was able to bequeath to her. This, incidentally, would explain the use of the term להוריש, "to bequeath." But, I should add, this would be so only according to one opinion in the Talmud, that maintains that a healthy person could employ this vehicle as well.[53]

12. *Conclusion*

My conclusion therefore is that the documents before us may indeed be seen as reflective of the following mechanisms of gift and disposition found in the halachah of the Tannaitic period: First, the immediate gift which cedes to the donee. The donor may not retract his gift, nor does he retain any usufruct. This mechanism is available to a person regardless of the state of his health. Second, we see here the process of disposition of possessions after death. Disposition of this sort, which had once been executed through the *diatheke*, underwent evolutionary change during the Tannaitic period. Initially even a person in good health could employ this tool, but subsequently it became limited for use by persons in ill health. At all times this was a retractable gift, whereby the donor could retract, retain the property in his own possession, or cede it to another, a transaction which

---

[52] M.Bava Batra 8.5.
[53] B.Bava Batra 131a.

was considered null and void in the event of the recovery of the donor. Third, we see here the gift of a person in good health, "from today and after death," whereby the substance of the possession is ceded immediately to the donee, while the donor retains usufruct for the remainder of his life.

These documents incorporate other stipulations: The gift can include all possessions that the donor stands to acquire in the future on the one hand, while on the other hand, the gift can be retracted should the donor need to sell them for his sustenance. The rabbis were aware of the availability of these conventions, and were even prepared to honor them, and grant them binding force. Yet they did not incorporate them as part of the standard model, which they felt would have been interpreted as a validation of the possibility of the transfer of title after death. We recall, of course, that Rabbi Meir maintained that a person could cede a possession that did not yet exist, and that R. Yose felt that a possession could be ceded to a beneficiary who did not yet exist. The rabbis were prepared to honor such legal acts, provided they were spelled out explicitly. The stipulation of a donor allowing him to sell his possession for the purpose of his own sustenance was valid and binding, as we saw in the post-talmudic literature.

REFLECTIONS ON THE DEEDS OF SALE FROM THE JUDAEAN DESERT IN LIGHT OF RABBINIC LITERATURE

Lawrence H. Schiffman

The publication of a substantial number of deeds of sale and other transfers of real estate in the collection of texts from the Judaean Desert[1] makes possible detailed comparison of these contracts with the rules, regulations and accounts of transactions which are preserved in Talmudic texts. Such comparisons allow us to gain a much better perspective on the manner in which materials preserved in rabbinic sources relate to what one might term "real life" in the tannaitic period and on the extent to which tannaitic law reflects practices which were part of the legal world of Greco-Roman times. We do not intend here to enter into the question of to what extent those who lived around the southern part of the Dead Sea in the first two centuries CE did or did not conform to the standards of Jewish law as understood by the early rabbis. These people lived a complex life of interaction between various ethnic and religious groups and various political entities within the Roman Empire. For this reason, we should not be surprised at what appears to be their eclecticism. That they appeared to live at times according to Hellenistic law, at times according to Roman law, at times according to mishnaic law, and at times according to Nabatean law should not surprise us. But certainly, one legal tradition in which they found themselves very much at home, if we are to judge from the documents at our disposal, was that of Jewish law. We will look here at the way in which that segment of their legal life recorded in the Hebrew and Aramaic documents in this corpus compares with the tannaitic understanding of Jewish law as opposed to that of the non-Jewish world around.

---

[1] J.T. Milik, "Textes hébreux et araméens," in P. Benoit, J.T. Milik, and R. de Vaux, *Les Grottes de Murabbaʿât* (= *DJD* II, Oxford 1960) 118–49; N. Lewis, *The Documents from the Bar Kokhba Period in the Cave of Letters: Greek Papyri* (Jerusalem 1989) 83–87, 88–93; A. Yardeni, "Aramaic and Hebrew Documentary Texts," in H.M. Cotton and A. Yardeni, *Aramaic, Hebrew and Greek Documentary Texts from Naḥal Ḥever and Other Sites* (= *DJD* 27, Oxford 1997) 9–51, 76–94, 106–10, 123–9; H.M. Cotton, "Greek Documentary Texts," *ibid.*, 174–223, A. Yardeni, "Documentary Texts Alleged to be from Qumran Cave 4," *ibid.*, 292–8; K. Beyer, *Die aramäischen Texte vom Toten Meer* II (Göttingen 1994) 167–73, 188–91.

To be sure, tannaitic texts and the documents now in our hands reflect a common legal tradition. We have no doubt that this legal tradition itself represents influences from ancient Near Eastern and Greco-Roman practices upon the development of Jewish law. To the extent that rabbinic texts dealing with Roman Palestine and the documents from the Judaean Desert do indeed reflect common elements, such elements must have been part of the usual legal practice of the Jewish population of the land of Israel. That such "Jewish" practices may not have been the sum total of the legal practice of Jews living under Roman rule in a period of increasing Hellenization in no way detracts from the significance of these parallels.

We may already note one important conclusion of the material to be presented below. It is futile to use rabbinic parallels to conclude that specific practices represent a document's adherence to Jewish law. Such an approach is extremely oversimplified. Rabbinic sources codified the practices in customary use in this domain of life, so that the usages in evidence in our documents generated the rabbinic rulings in question. Parallels, therefore, show that the tannaim and amoraim adapted to and lived with this system which combined elements of Jewish law with the legal formulary of the ancient Near Eastern and Greco-Roman world. Indeed, Jews had behaved this way as far as we know from as early as the Persian period[2] and most probably before that as well. In this respect, these procedures became Jewish and were totally assimilated into the tannaitic legal system. But it is clear that in some cases the tannaim envisaged other procedures, and that the rabbis were discussing common practices and their legal implications, not legislating them. This is characteristic of the legal formulae in ancient and medieval Jewish legal texts. They are never specifically codified in the classical codes, but the codes deal with the ramifications of these contracts in case of disputes.

In undertaking this research we are fortunate to be able to utilize the excellent analysis and outline of the form of these contracts which has been prepared by Ada Yardeni. She has prepared a formal and literary outline of the various features included in these contracts.[3] In her Hebrew edition of the texts from Nahal Hever, she has divided the modern Hebrew translation of the texts so as

---

[2] R. Yaron, *Introduction to the Law of the Aramaic Papyri* (Oxford 1961).
[3] Yardeni (supra note 1) 13–17.

to illustrate these formal characteristics.[4] Making use of her outline and numeration, but including all of the available contracts from the Judaean Desert dating to the first and second centuries CE, we will present below rabbinic traditions which illustrate or contrast with these legal practices. Along the way, we will also mention, where relevant, practices followed in the Greek documents.

The basic elements required in a legal contract were set forth by M.Gittin 3.2 in the context of discussing whether or not documents may be prepared in advance by a scribe. The primary types of documents—divorces, loan contracts, and deeds of sale—are all mentioned. Regarding deeds of sale, the following elements are specified: the buyer, the seller, the price, the field (that is, its measurements), and the date. The debate there regarding whether or not a contract may indeed be prepared in advance will not concern us here. Our interest is in the list of elements that must be included in the contract in the case of a real estate transaction. The very same list of elements is found in T.Bava Batra 11.1 according to the text in the editio princeps which in this case is to be preferred to the manuscripts.[5] This list of required elements is not all-inclusive. The context of the presentation of these lists is the case in which blanks are to be left in a pre-prepared contract to be filled in later. Accordingly, features required in the contract which do not change according to the needs of the particular transaction are not specified in this tannaitic list. The absence of a full text of the document for sale of land, and for that matter of virtually all other transactions in rabbinic literature (the *get* is an exception), is explained by Lieberman as resulting from the fact that this information was well-known.[6] Our documents do indeed attest to the widespread diffusion of these practices, but we see the lack of codified deeds in tannaitic texts as resulting from the customary aspect of this area of legal practice which was not legislated from the top down by the rabbinic elite.

---

[4] A. Yardeni, *'Naḥal Ṣe'elim' Documents* (Beer Sheva and Jerusalem 1995) 17, 33, 45, 53, 98, 103.

[5] S. Lieberman, ed., *Tosefta: Neziqin* (New York 1988) 166; cf. S. Lieberman, *Tosefta Ki-Fshutah: Neziqin*, pt. 10 (New York 1988) (henceforth *TK*) 452.

[6] *TK* 10, 453.

1. *The Date*

To be sure, according to the evidence of contracts in our hands, the first element of any ancient Jewish contract was the date.[7] For example, "On the four[teenth] of Iyyar, year three of the freedom of Israel in the name of Shimon son of Kosibah,[8] the prince of Israel" (P.Hever 7). The dating must be done according to a very particular form as specified in T.Bava Batra 11.2.[9] Here we find the requirement to include in the body of the contract the day, the week (or perhaps Sabbatical cycle or week of a particular priestly course), the month, the year, and a specification of the government according to which the date is being given.[10]

Greek papyri from the Cave of Letters contain elaborate dating schemes.[11] In a document of concession of rights we read: "Year fourteenth of Imperator Traianus Hadrianus Caesar Augustus, in the consulship of Fabius Catullinus and Flavius Aper thirteen days before the kalends of July, according to the compute of the new province of Arabia year twenty-fifth on the thirtieth of Daisios, in Maoza in the district of Zoara . . ." (P.Yadin 20).[12] Even the Aramaic documents preserve such detailed and accurate dating as in this deed of gift: "During the consulate of Lucius Catilius Severus for the second time, and of Marcus Aurelius Antoninus, in the third year of the Imperator Caesar Trajanus Hadrianus Sebastos and according to the era of this province on the 24th of Tammuz in the 15th year. . . ."[13]

M.Gittin 8.5 mentions the requirement of the identification of the government which is being used to date a legal document. While this passage is in the context of discussion of divorce documents, it also treats various other types of transactions, and it is apparent that its restrictions would have been applied by the rabbis to land sale deeds as well. Several disqualifications are mentioned there which in the case of divorce would result in the document's being sufficient

---

[7] Yardeni (supra note 1) 14.
[8] This last phrase can be omitted as in P.Hever 8a.
[9] Lieberman, *Tosefta: Neziqin*, 167.
[10] Lieberman, *TK* 10, 452 nn. 4–5. On p. 453 he prefers the notion that Sabbath here refers to the weeks of the month, which is the view of Maimonides, Gerushin 1.26.
[11] Cf. Lewis (supra note 1) 27–8; Cotton (supra note 1) 146–9.
[12] Lewis (supra note 1) 91.
[13] Beyer (supra note 1) 169. My translation.

to terminate the marriage but requiring as well the writing of an additional writ of divorce. These disqualifications are as follows: if the text was dated according to the era of an inappropriate government, that is one which was not in authority where the document was executed, or to the government of Media, that is, the Persian Empire (since it was defunct), or to what is termed the Greek Empire which must refer to the empire of Alexander the Great,[14] or to the building of the temple or its destruction.[15] T.Gittin 6(8).3[16] indicates several methods for dating a contract which were considered legal. These are dating according to the Roman province, the consul, or one of two simultaneous kings. From the formulation, it is clear that the acceptance of any one of these dating formulas is only post facto and that the correct dating procedure would have been to include all three.[17] Indeed, from the documents at our disposal it appears that date of the province, the consuls, and the emperor or emperors was the norm.

2. *Place*

By place we refer to the location in which the contract was written, which is sometimes, but not always, specified in the Judaean Desert documents,[18] e.g. "at Kefar *Bryw*" (P.Hever 8a).[19] I was unable to find a direct reference requiring indication of the place of execution of a contract for land sale in rabbinic literature. Yet allusion can be found to indication of place in a contract of debt in the Tosefta (Ketubot 12[13].6 = Bava Batra 11.3). Here the text speaks of a contract of Babylonia or a contract of the land of Israel. At issue is what the value of currency would be, presumably in a case in which both currencies had the same name or where the currency was not explicitly stated. One may assume that a Palestinian or Babylonian contract would be one in which a place found in Palestine or Babylonia

---

[14] The Seleucid era, however, continued to be used by Jews into the Middle Ages.
[15] For the specifics of the determination of the regnal year, see M.Rosh Hashana 1.1, and Babylonian and Palestinian Talmudim.
[16] Lieberman, *Tosefta: Nashim* (New York 1973) 270.
[17] Cf. *TK*, 890–1.
[18] Yardeni (supra note 1) 14.
[19] Yardeni (supra note 1) 36.

was entered into the contract as its place of execution. Accordingly, this passage in the Tosefta, dealing according to one reading explicitly with loan documents,[20] reflects the very same practice of those contracts which indicate the place.

This parallel raises a further important issue. The purpose of the contract and its halakhic status must be carefully delineated. Does the execution of the contract affect the transfer of ownership (*kinyan*) or is it simply a means of recording a transaction which does not go into effect unless the payment is subsequently made? If it is the latter, then we would easily understand why so many parallels exist between documents for the sale of land and those for entering into loans. On other hand, if the document serves by its very execution to effect the transfer, some of these parallels would be difficult to understand. Yet in all the Judaean Desert documents at our disposal, the inclusion of a specific clause indicating that payment has been made in toto (see below) indicates that these contracts are, in fact, a means of recording a transaction that has taken effect as a result of the exchange of money which has actually been completed.[21]

3a. *Names of the parties*

It is normal legal practice that contracts specify the names of both the buyer and the seller.[22] Accordingly, these features are mentioned in the list of elements found in the Mishnah and Tosefta. The names of the parties are normally stated according to the personal name, patronymic, and in some cases place of origin or some special appellative, as in "Yehonathan son of Eli from Kefar *Brw* said to Sha'ul son of Harrashah from there: I sold to you today the house . . ." (P.Hever 8).[23]

3b. *Declaration of sale*

The Judaean Desert documents always include a statement of the sale made by the seller.[24] This statement can be in one of two

---

[20] Ms. Erfurt to Ketubot 12(13)16; Lieberman, *Tosefta: Nashim*, 99.
[21] Cf. M.Y. Lipkovitz, *Emek ha-Sha'ar* in Hai Gaon, *Sefer ha-Mekah veha-Mimkar* (Bene Berak 1993/4) chap. 13, p. 168 n.a.
[22] Yardeni (supra note 1) 14–5.
[23] Yardeni (supra note 1) 28.
[24] Yardeni (supra note 1) 14–5.

forms—either by indirect speech, "x said to y," followed by a procla-
mation in the name of the seller, or through direct speech by the
seller, "I x sold to you, you y." For example, "I, Hazaq son of Mattat
have sold to you, you Elazar son of Levi the wine seller, of the sons
of Israel, who dwells in the village of . . ." (P.Hever 7).[25] In origin,
these two forms may reflect the same practice as in M.Bava Batra
where land sales may be made out by the seller either in the presence of the buyer (to whom he might make direct address) or in the
absence of the buyer.[26] Often free will is mentioned in the seller's
declaration. "I, of my own will, sold you today . . ." (P.Hever 8a).[27]

What might have been contained in the declaration of sale according to rabbinic halakhah is found in a baraita in B.Kidushin 26a.[28]
Here we learn that one seeking to sell a field by means of entering
into a contract might state in the document, "my field is sold to
you." In such a case the sale is considered valid. Rabbinic authorities, however, debate the question of whether the contract itself can
effect transfer, and the amoraim conclude that such a contract only
functions where a financial settlement is made. It is very possible
that the original use of contracts was to effect transfer of ownership,
and that at a later stage the contract became effectively a proof
(*reayah*) that the financial consideration had in fact been transferred.
Such seems to be the case in the documents from Judaean Desert.

4. *Identification and dimensions of property*

Specific identification for the property is always included,[29] for example: "The house that I own and the courtyard of the beam(?)-house
in Kefar *Brw* and the/its room that opens to the east inside that
large house and the/its upper storey that opens to the west." (P.Hever
8)[30] or, "The house of mine that opens (to the) north into my courtyard that you might open it into your house" (P.Hever 8a).[31] Often
the specific parts of the property which are associated with the real

---

[25] Yardeni (supra note 1) 21.
[26] Cf. Lieberman, *TK* 10, 457.
[27] Yardeni (supra note 1) 36.
[28] Cf. B.Kidushin 9a.
[29] Yardeni (supra note 1) 15.
[30] Yardeni (supra note 1) 28.
[31] Yardeni (supra note 1) 36.

estate transaction may be specified, for example, "those places—within their boundaries: the stones, the walls, the beams, the ground, the depth and the height, the [. . .] and the gate and the key, the entrance and the exit, as is fitting" (P.Hever 21)[32] or, "That place—within its boundaries and within its borders: fig-trees, and everything which is in it and which is fitting to it, the entrance and the exit, as is fitting" (P.Hever 50 + Mur 26).[33] In the Babatha archives a Greek papyrus deed of gift locates a courtyard ". . . together with entrances and exits, bricks, roofs, doors, windows and existing appurtenances of every kind" (P.Yadin 19).[34]

This item is closely related to 6, the description of the property, and most of its elements will be discussed there. The naming of the type of property does seem to fit the list of property types found in M. and T.Bava Batra, but this fact is simply a result of shared material culture, as are the parallels with the Greek documents.

It is self-evident that any contract must state what the item to be sold is. This is assumed by rabbinic sources, and it was legal practice in the ancient Near East from time immemorial. It is nowhere specifically legislated, although it is possible that the "field" for which a space has to be left blank in a pre-prepared document according to the tannaitic list we have discussed above indicates this requirement.

5. *Boundaries*

The contracts from the Judaean Desert are very careful to describe the boundaries of the property in terms of a list for all four directions of what properties or roads abut the property in question.[35] A straightforward example is: "To the south—Elazar the buyer; (to) the east—Yehonathan and/son of Yeshua; to the north—the courtyard; (to) the west—Hadad the seller" (P.Hever 8a).[36] Sometimes only one of several owners on one side may be specified as in "west—Yehudah the buyer and others" (P.Hever 9).[37] Roads may also be mentioned as in "East—the road and others" (P.Hever 9), that is,

---

[32] Yardeni (supra note 1) 80.
[33] Yardeni (supra note 1) 128.
[34] Lewis (supra note 1) 85.
[35] Yardeni (supra note 1) 15.
[36] Yardeni (supra note 1) 37.
[37] Yardeni (supra note 1) 42.

other land holders. Such formulae are also known from the Elephantine
papyri as well as from various medieval documents. A Greek loan
on hypothec says of a courtyard, "the abutters of said courtyard
being, on the east the camp and Yeshua son of Mandron, west the
camp and the factory of the said Elazar my father, south a market
and Simon son of Matthew, north a street and the camp headquarters . . ." (P.Yadin 11).[38]

It is probable that this feature is referred to as the "field" in the
tannaitic lists to which we have alluded. Tannaitic sources for such
practice are not particularly strong and legal usage appears in this
respect to follow patterns set out in ancient Near Eastern society
and in the Hellenistic world. These customary usages have shaped
the practices in our documents as well as in later rabbinic rulings.
It is interesting that the setting forth of such boundaries, each known
as a *metsar*, is not referred to at all in tannaitic sources nor in the
Palestinian Talmud, but is discussed in some detail by early Babylonian
amoraim (B.Bava Batra 62a–b). Apparently, from the contracts at
our disposal, this was the normal practice in the land of Israel. Its
absence from tannaitic sources supports the notion that it entered
Jewish legal tradition from outside.

6. *Description of the property*

The contracts then describe the property in terms of what is contained in it.[39] Essentially, this is a description of that which is within
the boundaries set forth in the previous section. For example, ". . . the
place of mine that is called the F[iel]d of the Orchard, [the area of
sowing of] three *seah*" (P.Hever 9).[40] Also found in this section is
always a description of the means of ingress and egress. This section usually comes to a close with the expression, "as is fitting." A
Greek deed of gift from Nahal Hever even includes the water rights
that come with the property: "I acknowledge that I have given you
as a gift from this day and for ever . . . a date orchard called the

---

[38] Lewis (supra no. 1) 44; See also P.Yadin 16 (p. 68), which mentions abutters,
a road and the sea, as well as the names of persons who owned land abutting the
property. The complex question of the order of directions has been studied by others and will not detain us here.
[39] Yardeni (supra note 1) 15.
[40] Yardeni (supra note 1) 42.

Garden of Asadaia with the water allowance (of that orchard), once a week on the fourth day, for one half-hour. . . ." (P.Hever 64).[41]

Often the description of the property includes its dimensions, as we have seen. Usually a phrase indicating that the sale is "as is" is added, for example, "Whether it is more or less it is (the responsibility of) the buyer" (P.Mur. 30).[42] The purpose here is to guard against minor imprecisions in the measurements becoming an object of dispute and litigation.

The Babylonian Talmud (B.Bava Batra 69b) alludes to a clause, "acquire for yourself the palms, tall trees, smaller trees, and small palms"[43] which indicates that contracts usually specified transfer of the trees along with the field. If the laws of the tannaim regarding the sale of real estate and its appurtenances (M.Bava Batra 4.8–9) were in practice (on this see below), these clauses would be unnecessary.

The specification of such details seems to fly in the face of the passages in the Mishnah (Bava Batra 4–7) and Tosefta (Bava Batra 3–4) which go out of their way to indicate exactly what is included and what is not included in real estate transactions. Indeed, the Mishnah even mentions the possibility that the seller might stipulate, "it and everything which is in it [the house]" which again indicates that standardization of practice had not yet been achieved. These passages include information regarding the purchase of a house, residential courtyard, olive press, field, vineyard, bath house and even an entire city. It seems difficult to understand why such complicated clauses would have been placed into contracts if the tannaitic regulations were being observed. It seems best, therefore, to follow the view of A. Gulak who would see in these laws the standardization and codification into tannaitic law of that which was normally formulated for inclusion in Hellenistic contracts.[44] What is clear from our contract documents is that Jews were making use of similar detailed formulations in their documents, so that the incorporation of a standardization of such regulations in the Mishnah and Tosefta was appropriate. Therefore, the fact that numerous clauses in our contracts are in agreement with the specifics of tannaitic law says

---

[41] Cotton (supra note 1) 212.
[42] Milik (supra note 1) 146.
[43] Following the reading of the Arukh.
[44] A. Gulak, *Legal Documents in the Talmud in Light of Greek Papyri and Greek and Roman Law*, Edited and supplemented by R. Katzoff (Jerusalem 1994) 118–41 (Hebrew).

little more than that Jews in the Greco-Roman period followed legal norms and procedures of the society in which they lived.

The same is the case with two particular aspects of these contracts. Despite the rabbinic view that the purchaser of real estate was entitled to use of the ground below as well as what we could term air rights,[45] these documents, like their Greco-Roman counterparts,[46] regularly specify such rights. Further, these texts always set forth the right of entrance and exit. Tannaim disputed as to whether there was a need to specify access in the contract or whether it was included automatically.[47] The Babylonian Talmud shows that this was an ongoing dispute in the Talmudic academies.[48] Again, we must understand that the tannaitic codes reflect what was common procedure at that time, but enforcement of such regulations depended on the language of the contract since one could not reasonably expect the tannaim to enforce these rulings under direct Roman rule. This was certainly the case in the region of the Dead Sea where Jews lived in the "boondocks" of the province in Judaea or in Arabia, and after 106 CE in the Roman province of Arabia.

7. Price

The documents before us, from the point of view of Talmudic law, reflect a procedure whereby in exchange for the execution of the contract at its being handed to the new owner, a cash payment must be surrendered to the seller. It is this cash payment which from the point of view of tannaitic halakhah effects the transfer.[49] For this reason, we find that the list of blank spaces to be included in a pre-written contract includes the space for a report of the price. Indeed, the inclusion of the price in the tannaitic requirements indicates that we are no longer dealing with acquisition by means of contract but rather with contracts which recorded land sales which have taken place—deeds in our terminology.

---

[45] M.Bava Batra 4.2; T. Bava Batra 3.1; Lieberman, *TK* 10, 359–60.

[46] Gulak (supra note 44) 120 note 4 and especially the addition by R. Katzoff in square brackets.

[47] M.Bava Batra 4.2.

[48] B.Bava Batra 64a–65a

[49] Cf. M. Kidushin 1.5, which indicates that cash payment was one of three means for acquiring real property. See also Yardeni, DJD 27, 15.

To avoid confusion about the value of the coinage involved, the purchase price is usually given in two currencies expressed as an equivalency.[50] An example is: "That I have sold to you for thirty-six silver *zuzin* which are (equal to) nine *sil'in*" (P.Hever 8).[51] That confusion regarding currency could take place is made clear in M.Bava Batra 10.2 which specifically refers to the practice of writing the price in two denominations and which deals with irregularities that might take place in an incorrectly written document. Additional material is found in T. Bava Batra 11.2,[52] discussing the issue of whether the currency was calculated according to a gold or silver standard and confusions which might result in this regard. That passage also refers specifically to the expression of price in two currencies. This same practice was followed, as noted by Lieberman, in Greek documents from the Judaean Desert. This is also true of the Greek texts, as for example: "I acknowledge that I have received and owe to you in loan sixty denarii of Tyrian silver, which are fifteen staters . . ." (P.Yadin 11).[53]

In this case, we are dealing with a practice which was followed in contracts and which has been codified in the Mishnah and Tosefta only as regards cases of irregularities or partly preserved documents. The legal formulary in question is assumed by rabbinic texts and not legislated by them. At the same time, we should remember that the use of money as a means for effecting ownership of land and the associated "immovable property" was regarded by the rabbis as being a Torah law. This form of acquisition is mentioned alongside of acquisition by contract (to be distinguished from the use of a contract to record acquisition by payment) as well as by tenure (*hazaqah*) (M.Kidushin 1.5). According to some views, land can even be purchased by exchange (*halifin*).[54] Certainly, the evidence of our land contracts indicates that popular practice followed the notion, enshrined as well in the prevailing non-Jewish legal practice, that only transfer of money did effect transfer of land, and it is in order to record such transactions that our documents are written.

---

[50] Yardeni (supra note 1) 15.
[51] Yardeni (supra note 1) 28.
[52] Lieberman, *Tosefta: Neziqin*, 167; *TK* 10, 453–4.
[53] Lewis (supra note 1) 44.
[54] Cf. H. Albeck, *Shishah Sidre Mishnah: Seder Nashim* (Jerusalem 1958) 410–2.

8. *Receipt clause*

The documents exhibit a receipt clause in which the seller indicates that he has received full payment from the buyer.[55] The nature of this clause in these particular documents reflects the expression, "full payment," which appears in Babylonian, neo-Assyrian, Wadi Daliyeh and Nabatean deeds as well.[56] An example is:

"And the silver coins I received, the full price" (P.Hever 8).[57] Effectively, this clause functions as a receipt, as in the subscriptions on some contracts. It is not required by Jewish law, which would allow land tenure along with possession of a contract to validate the ownership of the buyer in a case where there was a subsequent dispute about title to the property.

9. *Ownership clause*

This clause indicates the full rights of the new owner who has taken possession.[58] A well-preserved example is the seller's statement: "Forever entitled is Shaul the buyer[59] regarding those places, to dig and to deepen and to do with them whatever he desires from this day and forever" (P.Hever 8). It specifies that he is the owner in perpetuity and that its possession may pass to his heirs with no limitation, as in: "Forever entitled and empowered are Yehudah the buyer and his inheritors regarding that sale, to buy and to sell, and to do with it whatever you desire, from this day and forever" (P.Hever 9).[60] Further, the new owner has the right to excavate, or build on and use the property in any way he may see fit. It is usual for this clause to end with the words, "from this day forth and forever." A parallel in the Greek texts from the Babatha archives states: ". . . the aforesaid Shelamzious shall have the half of the aforesaid courtyard and rooms from today . . . validly and securely for all time, to build, raise up, raise higher, excavate, deepen, possess, use, sell and manage in whatever manner she may choose, all valid and secure" (P.Yadin 19).[61]

---

[55] Yardeni (supra note 1) 15–6.
[56] Cf. Genesis 23:9.
[57] Yardeni (supra note 1) 28.
[58] Yardeni (supra note 1) 16.
[59] Correcting Yardeni (supra note 1) 28.
[60] Yardeni (supra note 1) 42–3.
[61] Lewis (supra note 1) 85.

These contracts generally explicitly permit the buyer to dig below the surface of the earth or to build above the present height of the structure which he has acquired. M.Bava Batra 4.2 specifically alludes to the rights of "depth and height" which were normally written into such land contracts. However, some other parallel texts included allusion to "from the depth of the earth and to the height of heaven" (B. Bava Batra 63b). Indeed, the Babylonian Talmud sought to distinguish between the technical meaning of these two formulations which must originally have been variations on the same theme.

10. *Responsibility and "cleansing"*

In this clause, the seller, who is effectively the speaker in the contract expresses his responsibility to the buyer to the effect that the real estate being transferred is free and clean of all liens and that he, the seller, will make good on ("cleanse") any claims against the buyer or his heirs. In this clause it is usual for the seller to pledge as surety against this commitment not only property which he owns at the time of the sale, but all future property which he may at any time acquire.[62] A well-preserved example is: "And I, Yehonathan, the seller, and whatever I own and whatever I shall acquire, are responsible and a security to establish and to cleanse those places from any dispute and challenge which will come upon you. . . ." (P.Hever 8).[63]

The responsibility of the seller in real estate transactions is so significant a part of the contractual relationship that real estate is termed "property for which there is responsibility" (e.g. M.Kidushin 1.5). In this respect real property and that which is attached to it differs from immovable property for which there is no responsibility to guarantee that the sale object is free of lien. According to tannaitic law, in a case in which a property is previously mortgaged, the previous debtor may reclaim his debt by taking possession of the property even from later buyers who presumably should have been aware of the lien but were not.[64] The seller of real estate must guarantee the buyer against such claims. In Hellenistic law, such guar-

---

[62] Yardeni (supra note 1) 16.
[63] Yardeni (supra note 1) 28.
[64] Cf. M.Bava Batra 10.8.

antees rendered the person himself surety in loan documents. Defaulting on payment could result in the debtor's being sold into slavery.[65]

Such a specific contract clause which is in some ways parallel to that in our contract texts is found in B.Bava Metzia 15a. Further, direct allusion to this responsibility clause is found in B. Bava Batra 169a in regards to the case of a duplicate contract (on which see below), from which this clause was omitted to prevent the buyer from collecting twice on the same legal obligation.

The fundamental problem posed by this clause for our study is that of why it was necessary, if in fact the responsibility to "cleanse" the obligation and to pay back the buyer was enshrined in Jewish law. From the fact that it was ruled by the tannaim that even if this clause was left out of a real estate transaction it was still considered in force, it is easy to see that it was the norm in contracts in the tannaitic period. But it is also clear that the necessity to include this clause resulted from the fact that otherwise such a guarantee could not be enforced within the prevailing legal system of the Roman empire. Only with the insertion of the clause was this regulation enforceable. Even if from the point of view of tannaitic halakhah this clause was assumed to exist even where it was not written, enforcement was only possible where it was in fact inscribed in the contract.

11. *Guarantee*

In this clause, which survives only in fragmentary state for the most part, the seller guarantees to reimburse the buyer for any costs that he may incur as a result of claims against his ownership of the property.[66] For example, "And the payment will be from my property and from whatever I shall acquire according to that" (P.Hever 8).[67]

In particular, the most important aspect of this clause is probably the allusion to property not yet in possession of the seller at the time of the sale. The seller promises to indemnify the buyer even from property that he has not yet bought. This condition appears in the discussion of a loan contract in T.Ketubot 4.12 and Y.Ketubot 4.8

---

[65] Gulak (supra note 44) 142.
[66] Yardeni (supra note 1) 16.
[67] Yardeni (supra note 1) 28.

29a.[68] It is explicitly discussed as well in B. Bava Batra 44b. Gulak concludes that this procedure was originally alien to Jewish law and that in the amoraic period doubts about its halakhic legality were raised.[69] It appears that we have here a case of the entry into Jewish law of a feature from the non-Jewish legal system, which feature then becomes the subject of halakhic discussion.

12. *Replacement of the deed*

It seems to be an essential element of these contracts, and of other documents from the Judaean Desert collection, that the initiator of the document promises the other party that he will replace the document if it is lost:[70] "And at any time that you say to me, I shall exchange for you this document as is fitting" (P.Hever 8).[71]

Such a procedure no doubt was important in a society where legal documents were not always safely kept. Most important, it presumes the absence of an archive or depository, such as existed in Petra, for example, under the Roman provincial administration. Such a depository had existed in Jerusalem on the eve of the Great Revolt,[72] and Roman archives existed at Sepphoris and Tiberias.[73] Apparently, there was no such depository for Hebrew and Aramaic Jewish documents from this period.

Y.Ketubot 9.10 33c makes allusion to just such a case where the contact might be lost. In such cases it was the practice to draw up a second copy. For this reason, when a man made a second loan from another, he would write in the contract that it was besides the original transaction. Thus, it could never be claimed by the borrower, in an effort to avoid his obligation to repay the loan, that this was simply a duplicate of the other document.[74] Such clauses were inserted also into Greek contracts. But despite this assumed practice, we have no stated legal requirement in tannaitic law to

---

[68] Gulak (supra note 44) 143–5. Contrast T.Ketubot 4:12, where Lieberman, ad loc., p. 250 emends the Tosefta to accord with the Yerushalmi.

[69] Gulak (supra note 44) 145.

[70] Yardeni (supra note 1) 16.

[71] Yardeni (supra note 1) 28.

[72] Josephus, *BJ* 12.427.

[73] Josephus, *Vit.* 38; S. Miller, *Studies in the History and Traditions of Sepphoris* (= SJLA 37, Leiden 1984) 46–55.

[74] Gulak (supra note 44) 147–8.

write a duplicate contract and no express allusion to the practice. Clearly this is a case where common practice is assumed by the law and adjustments are made for it, especially when it appeared to further the aims of a just and lawful society, but the rabbinic tradition did not initiate the practice.

13. *Signatures*

The final element of these contracts, as in all Jewish contracts, is the signatures. These include not only the witnesses but often the parties.[75] In general, most of these documents are double (tied) deeds, with the witnesses signed on the knots of the document, as was also the practice at Elephantine. The first two signatures may be those of the buyer and the seller, but sometimes the seller alone signs. In a text in which the wife had to attest that she agreed to the sale and had no claims, the wife had to sign as well, or a signature could be entered at her instruction.

An example may be cited from P.Hever 8a where in this "simple" (untied) deed, the seller signed, then three witnesses. Above, Hadad's wife attested her agreement and lack of claims against the transfer of ownership.[76] But in this case there is no signature of the buyer, a fact which would not invalidate the document since it is phrased as an assertion that he transferred the property to the buyer. Other documents may lack the buyer's "John Hancock" as well. But in the Greek documents the buyer's signature is clear in some examples (P.Yadin. 21–22).[77] A full tabulation of this data for the Judaean Desert corpus still needs to be made.

One thing is clear, though. Tannaitic sources speak almost exclusively about the signatures of the witnesses (M.Bava Batra 10.1–2; T.Gittin 6(8).9;[78] T.Bava Batra 11.1)[79] and late Jewish legal tradition

---

[75] Yardeni (supra note 1) 17.
[76] Yardeni (supra note 1) 36–7.
[77] Lewis (supra no. 1) 95.
[78] S. Lieberman, *TK: Nashim*, pt. 8 (New York 1973) 899–900. See also L.H. Schiffman, "Witnesses and Signatures in the Hebrew and Aramaic Documents from the Bar Kokhba Caves," *Semitic Papyrology in in Context: A Climate of Creativity: Papers from a New York University Conference Marking the Retirement of Baruch A. Levine* (ed. Lawrence H. Schiffman; Culture and History of the Ancient Near East 14; Leiden: Brill, 2003) 165–86.
[79] But cf. T.Bava Metzia 1.13, Y.Gittin 8.12 49d, Y.Bava Batra 10.1 17c

often assumes the signatures to be of the members of the court before whom transactions may be formalized. This entire procedure by which the witnesses' signatures are accompanied by those of the parties to the contract results from Greco-Roman legal practice. When we add the fact that the tied deeds are tied in the style of the Hellenistic documents it is clear that the Jewish requirement of witnesses with specific qualifications has been grafted onto non-Jewish legal procedures.

Conclusion

This investigation shows that the relationship of these contracts to tannaitic law is exceedingly complex. Certainly, many of the procedures outlined here are the same as those required by the early rabbis. In these cases we may be dealing with the effects of Jewish law on the contracts, but just as often with the reverse—the effect of the contractual formulations of antiquity on the tannaim who often are codifying or reacting to processes known from the wider society. In some cases, it is difficult to square the procedures of the contracts in our possession with the specific requirements or assumptions of the tannaitic halakhic system. For the most part, the procedures in these documents, even when reflecting non-Jewish approaches, did not in any way run counter to Jewish sentiment. Further, many of those practices go far back in time in both non-Jewish and Jewish use.

The bottom line, however, is that to the extent that these contracts are in accord with tannaitic law, it is because the legal system of the tannaim absorbed elements of legal practice and formulation from the very same sources which nourished the Hellenistic legal practice of the Near East. These processes and requirements were only partly codified in tannaitic sources or set forth in the amoraic discussions in Palestine or Babylonia. But side by side with these official legal codes, the Jewish legal process continued to develop, as always, in perpetual dialogue with the practices of the Jewish people's non-Jewish neighbors. When contracts were eventually codified in collections in the middle ages, starting with the collection of Hai

---

regarding a subscription consisting of a first person declaration by a party to the contract followed by his signature.

Gaon,[80] this aspect of the law remained outside of the major codes—the Mishneh Torah of Maimonides, the Tur of Jacob ben Asher, and the Shulhan Arukh of Yosef Karo. Rather, there seems to have been an implicit recognition of the need to allow contract texts to develop in tandem with the legal structures within which Jews were living, as they had in the Mishnaic period as evidenced in the contracts from the Judaean Desert.

---

[80] S. Assaf, ed., *Sefer ha-Shetarot le-Rav Hai Ga'on, Tarbiz* 1.3 Suppl. (Jerusalem 1929/30); cf. also Judah ben Barzilai of Barcelona, *Sefer ha-Shetarot,* ed. S.J. Halberstam (Berlin 1898, repr. Jerusalem 1966/7).

HALAKHIC OBSERVANCE IN THE JUDAEAN DESERT DOCUMENTS

Ze'ev Safrai

The Problem

The Judaean Desert documents are being published in ever-increasing numbers. The general picture in all its diversity is beginning to emerge. Almost all the Judaean Desert documents were written by Jews, as can be seen by the names of the individuals mentioned in the texts: Eleazar, Simeon, Johanan, etc. The question of the degree to which observance of the commandments and the behavioral norms demanded by the rabbinic sources is reflected in the documents is central to the scholarly research of these writings. This question is of interest and importance for several reasons, and from a number of aspects. The publishers of the documents, especially the impressive series of publications by Hannah Cotton, seek possible comparisons between the documents and any plausible source. It is only natural that they fruitfully compare the documents with the papyri in Egypt, but also with rabbinic sources. This question is of interest also to scholars investigating rabbinic literature.

One of the principal questions in the study of the period of the Mishnah and the Talmud is the extent to which Jewish society is reflected in rabbinic literature. If this society was religiously observant, then the rabbis were its leaders, and their literature guided the society. Consequently, the Jewish sources are likely to depict many aspects of the life of this society, just as the Roman law constitutes an important (but not the sole) source for our understanding of Roman society. If, however, it transpires that the society of the authors of the Judaean Desert documents was not religiously observant, this would indicate that the halakhah did not determine the way of life in the Jewish society, and therefore rabbinic literature is to be regarded as a source that was detached from reality and that was reflective of an esoteric group, a subsociety removed from the general public. Furthermore, rabbinic literature portrays an at least generally observant society (reservations to this assertion will be raised below). The question is whether this picture is accurate or utopian, and obviously, whether rabbinic literature is a realistic literature of law and thought, or rather is a tendentious genre that relates to a utopian society—as it should be, and not to the society as it was. If troubling discoveries were concealed, repressed, or reported in an untrue manner, it would be difficult to use rabbinic literature as a reliable source for the social history of the period. If the Judaean Desert documents are reflective of a society that was not religiously observant, then rabbinic literature would presumably seem to be utopian and tendentious, and, accordingly, of marginal value as a historical source. If so, then the needs of the Mishnaic-Talmudic dialectic, on the one hand, and those of the construction of the aggadic narrative, on the other, transformed the literary testimonies into a nonrealistic source. If so, then the rabbinic sources become a fascinating literary document, but not a historical source, or perhaps a nonhistorical one.[1]

The questions are important and far-reaching, but we will restrict ourselves to a single limited aspect: the comparison of rabbinic literature with the Judaean Desert documents.

The Geographic Scope of the Society of the Judaean Desert Documents

For the purposes of our discussion, we should determine the area represented by the extant documents. Even the most precise answer that we can provide, however, will still be insufficiently clear. The documents came to us from the Judaean Desert caves to which refugees had fled. Almost all the place names in the documents are from the eastern Judaean hill country, in the desert or in the desert fringe. Nonetheless, this picture may be brought into somewhat greater focus. There are three groups of documents. The first, from Murabba'at, was published mainly in *DJD*, vol. 2. These documents, that originated with the refugees from 'En-Gedi, mention inhabitants of the Judaean hill country. The second group was discovered in the Cave of Letters and published by Lewis.[2] Most of the refugees most

---

[1] For the most extensive list of scholars who participated in the discussion, see, e.g.: J. Neusner, *The Talmud as History* (Westmount, Quebec 1979); Z. Safrai, *The Economy of Roman Palestine* (London 1994) 3–15; and many more sources.

[2] N. Lewis, *The Documents from the Bar Kokhba Period in the Cave of Letters* (Jerusalem 1989).

likely came from settlements along the Dead Sea basin, mainly from the southern part of the basin. All the papyri published by Lewis are from Zoar and its environs. We learn that inhabitants from the nearby villages streamed to the area: Eleazar b. Catushion and his family (and, obviously, including Babatha), who came from 'En-Gedi, and Judah b. Cimber.[3] The third group, discovered in the Nahal Hever cave, was published by Cotton and Yardeni in *DJD*, vol. 27.[4] This assemblage consists of two parts: one from the archives of Salome daughter of Comais,[5] and an additional group of documents of people from different villages in the southern Hebron hill country, although some of the identifications are less clear-cut. One of them mentions an estate in Zoar,[6] but the payer, from whose archives this document came, may possibly have lived in another village. An additional group of papyri found by H. Eshel in Katef Jericho apparently originated in settlements in the Jericho region; however, these have not been published in their entirety.

As we shall see, as regards questions relevant to the current discussion, the various groupings differ significantly. A detailed examination of the geographical background of the different groupings would exceed the scope of the present discussion, and the general definition presented here will suffice for our purposes.

Religious Observance in the Dead Sea Basin According to the Rabbinic Sources

For the purposes of this paper, we will assume that the extant documents reflect the basin around the Dead Sea. Above, we accepted the simple assumption that rabbinic literature portrays an observant society. We must now limit and clarify this premise. The Mishna in Tractate Gittin establishes that one who brings a writ of divorce from abroad must attest to its nature, and how it was written and sealed, because those living abroad did not possess legal expertise.[7] The formulation of this explanation in the PT is "that *haverim* [i.e.,

---

[3] *Ibid.* no. 18.
[4] See also: A. Yardeni, *'Nahal Se'elim' Documents* (Jerusalem 1995) (Hebrew).
[5] P.Hever 62, 63, and more.
[6] *P.Hever* 60 pages 169–70.
[7] M.Gittin 1.1.

scholars] were not to be found abroad," or "they were not expert in the details of writs of divorce."[8] The halakhah relates specifically to the Dead Sea basin, stating "Rabban Gamliel says, Even if he brings from Rekem or from Heger."[9] Rabban Gamliel lived in the Yavneh generation, during which most of the Judaean Desert documents were written. Rabbi Judah, who lived about a generation after him, adds "From Rekem eastwards, and Rekem is like the East,"[10] i.e., Rekem itself is regarded as if it were outside the Land of Israel.

Accordingly, the "Rekem" area is like "abroad," like a place where people are not expert in the laws. Rekem is also mentioned in the *Baraita de-Tehumim*[11] as the southeast boundary of the Land of Israel. Rekem is, as is well-known, Petra,[12] but the Jewish settlement plainly did not extend to the latter. Mazar correctly maintains that Rekem and Heger are the fortified fringe area, on the southern Dead Sea-Rafiah line, which became the Roman "Limes"[13] in the fourth century. In the first century there patently was not the organized line of fortifications that there was in the fourth century, but apparently something already existed.[14] Many important scholars have exam-

---

[8] Y.Gittin 1.1 43b; and in B.Gittin 2b: "because they are not expert regarding [the rule that it must be written] for her sake."

[9] M.Gittin 1.1.

[10] *Ibid.*, 1.2.

[11] Y. Sussmann, "The 'Boundaries of Eretz-Israel'," *Tarbiz* 45 (1976) 213–57 (Hebrew) and English summary in II–III; Z. Safrai, "Israel's Borders as Regards Halachic Issues," in S. Israeli, et al., eds., *Jubilee Volume In Honor of Moreinu Hagaon Rabbi Joseph B. Soloveitchik* (Jerusalem 1984) 1097–119 (Hebrew).

[12] Sussman (supra note 11) 239.

[13] B. Mazar, "The Rekem and the Hagar," *Tarbiz* 20 (1950) 316–9 (Hebrew); G.I. Davies, "Hagar, el-Heğra and the location of Mt Sinai," *Vetus Testamentum* 22 (1972) 152–63.

[14] Many works have been devoted to a description of the "Limes"; see: A. Alt, "Limes Palaestinae," *PJB* 26 (1930) 43–82; M. Avi-Yonah, "The Date of the 'Limes Palestinae'," *ErIsr* 5 (1958) 135–7; idem, *Historical Geography of Palestine from the End of the Babylonian Exile up to the Arab Conquest* (Jerusalem 1963) 168–78 (Hebrew); idem, *The Holy Land. From the Persian to the Arab Conquests (536 BC to AD 640). A Historical Geography* (Grand Rapids, Michigan 1966) 119–21, 162–4. S. Applebaum, "The Initial Date of the Limes Palestinae," *Zion* 27 (1962) 1–10 (Hebrew); M. Gichon devoted a series of essays to the subject, beginning with the unpublished dissertation, *The Limes in the Negev from Its Foundation Down to Diocletian's Times* (Jerusalem 1967) (Hebrew); idem, "The Site of the *Limes* in the Negev," *ErIsr* 12 (1975) 149–66 (Hebrew). For a more complete list of his articles, see: I. Shatzman, "Security Problems in Southern Judaea following the First Revolt," *Cathedra* 30 (1984) 3–32; Y. Tsafrir, "Why Were the Negev, Southern Transjordan and Sinai Transferred from Provincia Arabia to Provincia Palaestina at the End of the Third Century AD?" *Cathedra* 30 (1984) 35–56. For a clarification of the military aspects and the

ined the question of whether the "Limes" already existed in the first and second centuries. Alt, Applebaum, and Avi-Yonah assumed that this was the case, but they did not deal with this issue in detailed fashion. According to Gichon, the line of fortifications was established by Herod. Afterwards, in the time of the Flavian emperors (70–98 CE), an orderly line of fortifications was constructed, which continued during the time of the Severian emperors, as in Germany.[15] Gichon also agrees that the Limes dates mainly from the reign of Diocletian, when it assumed its final form. Only the fortress in Beersheva seems to be earlier, from the first century, but this dating has not been proven. Shatzman goes so far as to argue that there was no need to build a line of fortifications in the south of the Land of Israel until the fourth century, because security problems were not serious. Gichon based his response on the Talmudic sources, including the Mishnah in Gittin cited above,[16] and on two fortresses excavated in the Yattir region.[17] This line of reasoning requires further clarification, since these may not have been Roman fortresses at all, but rather fortified farmsteads. At any rate, an additional fortress, Kasr Hamrawi, to the south of Susya,[18] dates from the first century. This structure belongs to the line of fortresses of identical architectural nature passing between the settled area and the desert in the eastern fringe of the Hebron hill country, and this entire line of fortifications is to be dated approximately to the first century.[19]

Roman security concept, see E. Luttwak, *The Grand Strategy of the Roman Empire from the First Century AD to the Third* (Baltimore 1976), and for an opposing view B. Isaac, *The Limits of Empire* (Oxford 1990) 372–418.

[15] M. Gichon, "Edom, Idumea, and the Herodian Limes," *Doron le-Prof. Benzion Katz* (Festschrift in Honor of Prof. Benzion Katz) (Tel Aviv 1967) 205–18.

[16] M. Gichon, "When and Why Did the Romans Commence the Defense of Southern Palestine?" in: V.A. Maxfield and M.J. Dobson, eds., *Roman Frontier Studies 1989* (Exeter 1991) 318–25.

[17] D. Alon, "Nahal Yatir Site," in A. Kloner and Y. Tepper, eds., *The Hiding Complexes in the Judean Shephelah* (Tel Aviv 1987) 154–9 (Hebrew); idem, "Horvat Salit (Khirbet Salantah)," *Excavations and Surveys in Israel 1986* (vol. 5) 94–6; idem, "The Underground Caves in the Judean Plain," in E. Schiller ed., *Zev Vilnay's Jubilee Volume*, II (Jerusalem 1987) 107–14 (Hebrew). In the opinion of the excavator, these are part of a series of fortresses.

[18] Y. Barouch, "The Roman Castles in the Hills of Hebron," in Z.H. Erlich and Y. Eshel, eds., *Judea and Samaria Research Studies: Proceedings of the 4th Annual Meeting— 1994* (Kedumim 1995) 137–43 (Hebrew), English summary in XV–XVI.

[19] Y. Hirschfeld, "A Line of Byzantine Forts Along the Eastern Highway of the Hebron Hills," *Qadmoniot* 12 (1979) 78–84 (Hebrew); A. Kloner and Y. Hirschfeld, "Khirbet el-Qasr—A Byzantine Fort with an Olive Press in the Judean Desert," *ErIsr* 19 (1987) 132–41 (Hebrew).

The exact location of Rekem cannot be easily determined. The
Baraita de-Tehumim provides a concise description of the boundary of
the Jewish settlement: מלח רזיזא רקם דניאה ונייה דאשקלון "Melah
Rezizah [i.e., of Ziza], Rekem of Gyia, and Ginea of Ashkelon."[20]
"Ziza" is apparently Ziza, to the east of the Dead Sea, mentioned in
Notitia Dignitatum,[21] and in the *Geography* of Ptolemy (second century).[22]
Therefore, the boundary line described in the *Baraita de-Tehumim* was
supposed to pass south of the Dead Sea to Ashkelon, apparently
along the southern border of the province of Judaea, approximately
paralleling the "Limes" as it was later formed.

A line of fortifications, at least a part of which dates from the first
century, was discovered in the settlement fringe in the eastern Hebron
hill country.[23] This line also was included in the Rekem mentioned
above.

Zoar is located within the province of Arabia, and apparently was
included within this same "Rekem." One of the documents mentions inhabitants from Ziph and Aristobolea, which are 10 km. to
the north of this "Rekem," a few kilometers from Kefar Aziz, where
R. Ishmael lived, but the inhabitants of these two settlements were
already active in the Zoar region.[24] This papyrus belongs to the third
group of documents, and not the second, which comes from Zoar.
The sources relating to Rekem are from the time of R. Gamaliel,
that is, the period in which the Judaean Desert documents were
written. R. Judah, from the following generation, provides detail and
expands upon R. Ishmael's teachings.*

Testimony regarding the nature of the settlement in "Rekem" is
also provided by another source: "All stains coming from Rekem are
pure. R. Judah declares them impure, because they are converts and
err."[25] According to the Sages, the majority of the inhabitants were
Gentiles, for whom menstruation does not impart impurity; while
R. Judah maintains that most of the inhabitants were Jews, and only

---

* See Additional note, p. 236.

---

[20] Sussman (supra note 11) 238–9.
[21] Avi-Yonah, *Historical Geography* (supra note 14) 175.
[22] Ptolemaeus 5.16.4.
[23] Hirschfeld, "Khirbet el-Qasr" (supra note 19).
[24] P.Hever 69.
[25] M.Niddah 7.3.

a portion were converts who err, i.e., they were not knowledgeable in the halakhah; or possibly, this is to be interpreted as meaning that some of the Jews were converts, and another part erred. In his *Commentary on the Mishnah*, Maimonides writes: "This was a place of non-Jews, among whom Israelites live, and they followed most of the former's ways." This then was a mixed settlement, in which the Jews were not particular in their observance of the commandments. The disagreement ensues from the fact of the Jewish population being mixed among the Gentile population, and following the practices of the non-Jews.

The Talmudim learned from this mishnah that converts from Palmyra are to be accepted, and they apparently understood that these converts came from the local Palmyran tribes.[26] The law that Palmyran converts are to be accepted may possibly date from the Yavneh generation.[27] The connection to Rekem is solely Talmudic, and Palmyran military units most likely were encamped there only in the time of the Amoraim. This testimony is of importance for our understanding of the creation and development of the third-century line of fortifications, but is not relevant to the subject at hand.[28] Consequently, according to the rabbinic sources, the inhabitants of Rekem are not expert in the laws of writs of divorce, do not count *haverim* among their numbers, and are regarded as erring.

Some Methodological Problems

Our examination must be preceded by a methodological discussion. Scholars generally compare the Judaean Desert documents with the Talmudic material and with the laws and practices in Egypt, as reflected in the papyri. This research effort is intended to reveal which elements are derived from Roman law, and which may be connected to the rabbinic sources. A number of important studies

---

[26] Y.Kiddushin 4.1 65c; Yevamot 1.6 3b; B.Yevamot 16a; Bava Kamma 38b; Niddah 56b.

[27] In the Talmud Yerushalmi it is transmitted to the Rabbis in Yavneh in the name of the prophet Haggai, as part of the well-known discussion of the daughter's co-wife (M.Yevamot 1.4; T.Yevamot 1.10–12), though the incident and the mention of the Palmyrean converts appears only in the Talmudim.

[28] The *Notitia Dignitatum* represents the fourth century, and it enumerates the military units in the region. If the proposed interpretation is correct, then the arrival of the Roman army in the region may be advanced to the mid-third century.

have been written in this realm, albeit employing somewhat different approaches. Three matters, however, pose difficulties for the scholar:

(a) The lack of clarity, fragmentary nature, and ambiguous language of some of the documents do not facilitate scholarly research and historical reconstruction.

(b) Jewish law on many civil topics was close to Roman practice. Thus, e.g., the entire method of a "folded" writ of divorce, in the language of the rabbis, or "a 'bald' writ of divorce that has more folds than witnesses."[29] Does the discovery of folded writs of divorce in the Dead Sea caves attest to Jewish influence? We cannot give a definite answer to this question, because such a practice was common in Egypt as well, and most probably also in the Land of Israel in the First Temple period.[30] And again: the practice of not leaving more than a single blank line between the text and the signatures of the witnesses is a halakhic requirement,[31] but this was also an accepted practice, with a logic of its own. Generally speaking, in many areas the Jewish practice was drawn from, or was close to, the general custom, and it is frequently difficult to determine the origin of a certain procedure appearing in the papyri. This methodological question has occupied a central position in the scholarly discussion of this topic to the present.[32]

(c) Accepted scholarly practice calls for a comparison of the finds from the papyri with that indicated by the papyri from Roman Egypt. Such a comparison, however, is like searching for a lost article near a streetlight rather than where it was lost. The local Roman-Egyptian custom, which was not identical with the imperial laws, held sway in Egypt. In the Syrian sphere, Syrian-Roman practice is known to us from lawbooks beginning in the fourth century.[33] This, however, is a lawbook, and not testimony regarding the accepted legal practice in effect. Furthermore, the collection was formulated not before the fifth century, three centuries after the writing of the Judaean Desert documents. Thus, e.g., the right of guardianship of a woman, which we shall discuss below, will exemplify the incor-

---

[29] M.Gittin 8.10; Bava Batra 10.1, and many others.
[30] Jer. 32:11, 14.
[31] T.Gittin 7.11.
[32] See the discussion of P.Yadin 18, below.
[33] K.G. Bruns and E. Sachau, eds., *Syrisch-Römisches Rechtbuch* (Leipzig 1880); A. Vööbus, *The Syro-Roman Lawbook* (Stockholm 1982–3); idem, *An Unknown Recension*

poration of the Syrian-Roman element in our discussion. The Yadin papyrus mentions a Julia Crispina who was appointed to be a guardian.[34] Ilan argued that such an action was in opposition both to Roman law and the Jewish halakhah.[35] Cotton correctly showed that the halakhah permits the appointment of a woman as guardian, providing that this was in accordance with her late husband's wishes.[36] Consequently, the appointment of a female guardian is to be regarded as exhibiting Jewish influence. The Syrian-Roman law also entitles a woman to demand such an appointment, in the absence of a clear directive from her husband, and if he had no brothers.[37] Consequently, we must also take into account the Syrian-Roman law in all its versions during our discussion, comparisons, and analysis. The lack of substantive knowledge of the first-century law and legal practice in Arabia and Syria hinders any study of the sources of the law practiced in the Judaean Desert region in the period under discussion.

(d) The law is not reflective of reality in all its diversity. The law and legal practice were part of reality and influenced the latter, but are not identical to it. This has been known for some time to scholars investigating the Roman Empire,[38] and should also be understood by those examining Talmudic law. An outstanding example of this is the question of the property of a married woman, which we shall discuss below, along with a concise discussion of writs of marriage.

There is much relevant material, and to facilitate our discussion, the main findings have been summarized, with a division of the documents by language; bilingual documents were classified in accordance with the body of the text (these are generally documents in Greek with only the summary, the unfolded part in plain view, in Aramaic).

---

of the *Syro-Roman Lawbook* (Stockholm 1977). The lack of a scientific edition and a parallel examination of papyri from the Syrian East does not make the scholar's task easier.

[34] P.Yadin 20 and more.

[35] T. Ilan, "Julia Crispina, Daughter of Berenicianus, a Herodian Princess in the Babatha Archive: A Case Study in Historical Identification," *JQR* 82 (1992) 361–81.

[36] H. Cotton, "The Guardianship of Jesus Son of Babatha: Roman and Local Law in the Province of Arabia," *JRS* 83 (1993) 94–108.

[37] Vööbus, *Lawbook* (supra note 33) section 4, p. 4.

[38] R. MacMullen, *Changes in the Roman Empire* (Princeton 1990) 56–66.

Documents Written in Greek

Most of these documents have been the subject of intensive discussion. We cannot cite all the details in this paper, and will merely state that, as a general rule, they do not correspond to the Tannaic halakhah familiar to us. Many of their details contradict this halakhah, while many elements appearing in the halakhah are absent from these documents.[39] Thus, for example, the writs of divorce and marriage contracts do not contain the main clauses that we would expect to find, interest-bearing loans are mentioned, etc.

All of these writs are addressed to the courts of the civil authorities, which will be discussed below, along with other elements that are inconsistent with what is indicated by rabbinic literature. One example will suffice for the current discussion. P.Yadin 18, which aroused lively scholarly interest, contains the marriage contract of Shelamzion daughter of Judah b. Eleazer Khthusion.[40] Katzoff indicated six elements that he regarded as Jewish.[41] Wasserstein, in contrast, argued that all of these elements may be interpreted within the context of practices in Roman Egypt.[42] In the most recent discussion, Katzoff retracted some of his arguments. He also agrees now that the papyrus is not generally "Jewish," and is not the Greek version of an Aramaic contract of a Jewish nature; at most, elements that come from a Jewish background may be identified in it.[43] As was noted above, the Jewish writs were similar in nature to those in use in the East, which poses a difficulty for the isolation of the Jewish component, which must remain in the realm of conjecture. Thus, for example, mention is made of an addition to the marriage writ; this sentence is likely to be a Greek translation of the term known only from Amoraic sources, "*tosefet ketubah*,"[44] but may also be an ordinary non-Jewish term. The fact that the term is exclusively Amoraic does not constitute decisive proof that it did not

---

[39] H. Cotton, "A Cancelled Marriage Contract from the Judaean Desert," *JRS* 84 (1994) 64–86 at 81–2; idem, "Loan with Hypothec: Another Papyrus from the Cave of Letters," *ZPE* 101 (1994) 53–60 at 53–7; *P.Yadin 15* pages 58–64.

[40] *P.Yadin* pages 77–9.

[41] N. Lewis, R. Katzoff, and J.C. Greenfield, "Papyrus Yadin 18," *IEJ* 37 (1987) 229–50.

[42] A. Wasserstein, "A Marriage Contract from the Province of Arabia Nova: Notes on Papyrus Yadin 18," *JQR* 80 (1989) 93–130.

[43] R. Katzoff, "Papyrus Yadin 18 Again: A Rejoinder," *JQR* 82 (1991) 171–6.

[44] Y.Ketubot 12.1 34d.

already come into existence in the first century, but, on the other hand, it does not facilitate such an early dating either. One of Katzoff's more persuasive arguments is that the writ guarantees the maintenance of the children. Although this element appears in writs from Egypt, it is extremely rare. It is explicitly discussed, in contrast, in Jewish sources, and was formulated as an obligatory regulation in the Usha generation. At any rate, the writers of the contract acted to great degree in accordance with the demands of the halakhah and did not deviate from it, although it would be difficult to prove if they did so out of an awareness of the halakhah or because this was the accepted practice in their society.

There is a low level of *correspondence* between Jewish law and the Greek documents. Even so in my assessment, the *deviation* from the practice indicated by the rabbinic literature is much smaller than is usually assumed. This distinction is based, inter alia, on my allusion to the differences between the authoritative halakhah and the common practice. Within the context of this article, which presents the broad picture, without excessive focus upon details, one additional illustration will suffice. The halakhah distinguishes between betrothal (אירוסין) and "instruments of women's betrothal [*shtarei erusin* שטרי אירוסין]"[45] which detail the financial arrangements of the marriage. A similar distinction apparently existed regarding writs of divorce. The seeming writs of divorce in Greek may therefore not be writs of divorce at all, but rather monetary contracts which do not require the inclusion of halakhic formulas. They do not fit the halakha, but they do not contradict it either.

The differences between the groups of documents are clear. The assemblage in the Cave of Letters, representing the archives of Babatha of Zoar, is extremely distant from the halakhah. There are few differences between the papyri in the archives of Salome daughter of Comais and what is indicated by rabbinic literature, and the documents in the group from the Hever cave hardly raise any problems of practices opposed to the halakhah. The group from Murabba'at corresponds to what is indicated by the rabbinic sources.

---

[45] M.Moed Katan 3.3. The Mishnah mentions the writing of writs of "betrothal, and writs of divorce," but it was forbidden to wed during *chol ha-mo'ed* (the intermediary days of the Festival). It would therefore seem that these were not instruments of marriage, but rather prior agreements including all the details of the financial arrangements.

Documents Written in Aramaic

These have been the subject of less scholarly attention, but they generally correspond to the halakhic system to a greater degree. A number of examples will suffice:

(a) P.Mur. 18: a promissory note—from the 20th year of Nero (55–56 CE),[46] and therefore beyond the scope of our discussion. At any rate, the document apparently does not allude to interest payments.[47] The writ mentions the Sabbatical year, during which the borrower may have been exempt from paying; or, to the contrary, he paid, despite the fact that this was the Sabbatical year and despite his consequent difficult financial situation. In either event, the document expressed the special nature of the year, and probably alluded to a certain observance of its laws. According to the halakhah, the seventh year cancels debts; Hillel, however, instituted the *prozbol* [for circumventing the remission of debts], and this text does not present any halakhic difficulty. The document also mentions the mortgaging of property to the creditor, also in accordance with the halakhah, although this formulation is also common in other judicial systems.

(b) a future bill of sale, P.Jericho 3. A future sale is halakhically permitted only at the produce price to be determined in the future; consequently, this sale was conducted in accordance with the halakhah.[48]

(c) a writ from the time of Bar Kokhba, P.Hever 8,[49] mentioning the mortgaging of property of the owner to guarantee the sale. The sale includes all the listed parts of the house, as the halakhah demands, and as is reflected in rabbinic literature.[50] Once again, this detailing does not necessarily attest to an essential link to the halakhah; rather, this was a practice common in the East that entered the halakhah

---

[46] *P.Mur.* p. 101.

[47] In contrast with the reconstruction of J.A. Fitzmyer et al., *A Manual of Palestinian Aramaic Texts* (Rome 1976) 247–64; E. and H. Eshel, "Fragments of Two Aramaic Documents which were Brought to Abi'or Cave during the Bar-Kokhba Revolt," *ErIsr* 23 (1992) 276–85 at 278 (Hebrew).

[48] B.-Z. Eliash, "Ideological Roots of the Halakhah: A Chapter in the Laws of Interest," *Shenaton ha-Mishpat ha-Ivri, Annual of the Institute for Research in Jewish Law* 5 (1978) 7–72 at 18–9, 64–7 (Hebrew).

[49] First published: Y. Yadin et al., "A Deed of Land Sale in *Kefar Baru* from the Period of Bar Kokhba," *Cathedra* 40 (1986) 201–13 (Hebrew).

[50] M.Bava Batra 4.1–2; see above, the discussion of P.Mur. 18.

as well. The mortgaging of property is mentioned in many Aramaic papyri, and not only in papyri from the Land of Israel.[51]

(d) P.Mur. 19:[52] a writ of divorce written in the sixth year of Masada (73 CE?). The writ contains the formula: די את רשיא בנפשכי למהך ולמהוי אנת לכל נבר יהודאי די תצבין וכדין להוי לכי ספר תרכין ונט שבקין "You yourself are permitted to be the wife of any Jewish man that you wish; a book of divorce and writ of divorce properly [given]"; the formulation of R. Judah in the Mishnah reads: ודין דיהוי ליכי מנאי ספר תרכין ואגרת שבקין ונט פטורין ולמהך ולהתנסבא לכל נבר די תצבין.[53] "And this shall be to you from me a writ of divorce and a letter of release and a bill of dismissal, wherewith you may go and marry any man that you please." These, of course, are later limitations. The restriction that the woman is free to marry only a Jew is comprehensible in the area with a mixed population in which this document was written, and certainly was acceptable to the rabbis. The Mishnah also contains a lengthy discussion regarding the validity of such restrictive additions, and states expressly that a writ prohibiting marriage to a Gentile is valid.[54] This was so, even though they usually opposed conditional writs.

(e) P.Mur. 20: a marriage contract,[55] containing the formula: "be to me a wife in accordance with the law of M[oses]. . . ." The contract further distinguishes between the rights of sons and daughters, apparently in the spirit of the Mishnaic rule: "The sons inherit, and the daughters receive maintenance."[56] The contract also contains the formula that all the property is "surety and pledged," which also appears in the Mishnah.[57] In line 6 is the beginning of the conditional clause: אם תש . . . "if you will be c . . .," which is the beginning of the Mishnaic formula: אם תשתבאי אפרקינך "If you will be taken captive, I will redeem you." This formula will be discussed below, incidental to P.Yadin 10, and is clearly, and uniquely, Jewish.

---

[51] P.Hever 15, 24, and others; Fitzmyer (supra note 47) 156–8.

[52] P.Mur. 19, pages 105–6.

[53] M.Gittin 9.3. The Talmudim emphasize additional restrictions, such as the necessity to write "ודין" and not "ודין" (Y.Gittin 9.3 50b; B.Gittin 85b); see *ad loc.* for additional restrictions not in this document.

[54] M.Gittin 9.3 and 9.2.

[55] *P.Mur.* p. 110.

[56] M.Ketubot 4.6.

[57] Ibid., 4.7.

(f) P.Mur. 21, a marriage contract,[58] stipulates that the sons will inherit the sum of the contract, in accordance with the rules stated in the Mishnah.[59] Although the papyrus is fragmentary, this document also seems to resemble the Mishnah stylistically. The document also established the right of the woman to live in her husband's house after his death. The halakhah offers two possibilities: either the wife lives in her husband's house and is maintained from his property, or she takes the amount of her marriage contract and leaves his house. The Jerusalemites and Galileans gave the woman the right to choose, while the Judaeans afforded this privilege to the heirs. This marriage contract follows the Jerusalemite formulation, and corresponds to the view of the rabbis. The Tosefta states that all lands followed the Jerusalem practice.[60]

(g) P.Mur. 26: a bill of sale.[61] The wife most likely confirmed the sale, which may possibly be a Jewish practice. The husband's property was mortgaged to the wife's marriage contract, and her approval was therefore required.[62] All the property of the seller is אחריא וערבה "surety and pledged" for the sale, a formulation to which the sources allude. In the Mishnah, the formulation is אחראין and in the Talmud אחראין וערבאין.[63]

(h) P.Mur. 42: confirmation of a sale.[64] Those confirming are the leaders of the community.[65] Once again, the leadership of the town acts as a court, as was the accepted practice in the Jewish community. There is no extant parallel information regarding the leadership of the non-Jewish village, but it plainly cannot be proved that this was a uniquely Jewish practice. An analysis of the structure and power of the community in the Gentile village in the Land of Israel still lies before us, and the paucity of sources does not enable us to draw unequivocal conclusions.

---

[58] *P.Mur.* p. 114.
[59] M.Ketubot 4.10.
[60] M.Ketubot 4.12; T.Ketubot 4.6; the Talmudim *ad loc.*
[61] *P.Mur.* p. 137.
[62] See below.
[63] M.Ketubot 4.7; B.Gittin 37a.
[64] *P.Mur.* p. 156.
[65] Z. Safrai, *The Jewish Community in the Talmudic Period* (Jerusalem 1995) 79 (Hebrew).

(i) P.Yadin 10: a marriage contract.[66] This is the marriage contract of Babatha. In contrast to the Greek marriage contracts, and especially with the marriage contract this same individual, Judah b. Eleazar Khthousion, wrote for his daughter,[67] it contains numerous Jewish elements, not all of which were discussed in the detailed publication of the contract. These elements are: the formula: כדין משה ויה[ו]דאי" "in accordance with the law of Moses and the Jews" (line 5); the commitment to maintain and provide clothing for his wife (line 5); the commitment to redeem the wife, which is formulated almost identically with the language of the Mishnah: אפרקנך מן ביתי ומן נכסי [ואת]בנך לי לאנתה ואם תשבתאי "And if you are taken captive, I will redeem you from my house and from my property, and I will return you to marital relations" (line 10) and in the Mishnah: אם תשתבאי אפרקנך ואתיבנך לי לאנתו "If you will be taken captive, I will redeem you and I will return you to marital relations." *Intu* means "marital relations," and not "for a wife," as the translation of the editors. The halakhic rationale they gave also is erroneous. The husband is permitted and obligated to take her into his house and return her to marital relations,[68] not because she is believed that she was not violated, as stated by the first editors, but because a violated woman is permitted to her Israelite husband; she is believed that she did not consent, but rather was raped. The question of the woman's return to full marital relations is explicitly discussed in the rabbinic sources.[69]

In lines 13–14 the husband makes a commitment that the daughters will be maintained מן בתי ומן נכסי "from my house and from my property" until they wed; here as well, the formulation is almost exactly as it appears in the Mishnah.[70] As in other marriage contracts, the widow is guaranteed the right to receive maintenance, and she has the choice of receiving maintenance in the house of the

---

[66] First published: Y. Yadin et al., "Babatha's *Ketubba*," *IEJ* 44 (1994) 75–101.

[67] P.Yadin 18.

[68] M.Ketubot 4.8; T.Ketubot 4.5; the Talmudim *ad loc.*

[69] *Sifrei*, Num., *Naso* 7, p. 12. Cf. Y. Yadin, J.C. Greenfield, and A. Yardeni, "Babatha's *Ketubba*," *IEJ* 44 (1944) 75–101 at 93. Contra: S. Safrai, "Two Observations on Babatha's Ketuba," *Tarbiz* 65 (1996) 717–9 (Hebrew) at 719, and M.A. Friedman, "Babatha's *Ketubba*: Some Preliminary Remarks," *IEJ* 46 (1996) 55–76 at 71.

[70] M.Ketubot 4.11.

husband (and the heirs), or of receiving the amount of her marriage contract, as we have seen above.[71]

On the other hand, the sum stipulated in the marriage contract, 400 *zuz*, which are 100 Tyrean *sela*, does not exactly correspond with the halakhah. According to Jewish law, the marriage contract sum of a widow is 100 *kesef* (silver), or a *maneh*, but the intent is to 100 *zuz*, and not to 100 Tyrean *sela*. This is not in opposition to the halakhah, but it does not necessarily conform to it. Four hundred *zuz* is mentioned in the Syrian-Roman law as the sum given to the woman upon her divorce,[72] and was also the practice of the Jewish priests, "and the rabbis did not protest this."[73] In other words, this was the practice of the elite in the East, to which the rabbis acquiesced.[74]

(j) the Bar Kokhba letters: mention is made of the arrangements for the supply of the Four Species and their tithing.[75]

Additional examples are to be found throughout the documents, some of which are also examined in the article by Lawrence Schiffman in this collection.[76]

Documents Written in Hebrew

(a) P.Mur. 24:[77] a single text containing ten government leases from the time of the second revolt (i.e., that of Bar Kokhba), which mention the Sabbatical year and the setting aside of tithes.

---

[71] M.Ketubot 4.12.

[72] A. Vööbus, *Syriac and Arabic Documents Regarding Legislation Relative to Syrian Asceticism* (Stockholm 1960) 192, no. 19.

[73] M.Ketubot 1.5. The Khthousion family most likely was not of priestly lineage; there is no allusion to such stock, and the halakhah prohibits the return of a priestly woman captive.

[74] Fitzmyer (supra note 47) 156–8.

[75] P.Yadin 57.

[76] P.Hever 13 is not against any halakhic rule. See A. Schremer, "Papyrus Se'elim 13 and the Question of Divorce Initiated by Women in Ancient Jewish Halakha," *Zion* 63 (1998) 377–90 (Hebrew); H.M. Cotton and E. Qimron, "P. XHev\Se ar 13 of 134 or 135 CE: A Wife's Renunciation of Claims," *JJS* 49 (1998) 108–18. Contra: B.J. Brooten, "Konnten Frauen im alten Judentum die Scheidung betreiben? Ueberlegung zu Mk. 10, 11–12 und Kor. 7, 10–11," *Evangelische Theologie* 42 (1982) 65–80; T. Ilan "Notes and Observations On a Newly Published Divorce Bill from Judaean Desert," *HThR* 89 (1996) 195–202.

[77] P.Mur. pages 124–33.

(b) P.Mur. 29:[78] a bill of sale from the second year of the revolt. The bill of sale is signed by the wife, which is in accordance with halakhic practice.[79]

(c) P.Mur. 30:[80] a bill of sale from the end of Tishrei, the fourth year of the revolt. The writ may possibly be from the time of the earlier revolt against the Romans, but such a question is of secondary importance to the current discussion. The wife declares: "I have no claims whatsoever regarding this sale, forever."[81] The version in the Mishnah is: "I have no claim whatsoever against you."[82] According to the document, the property of the seller is "surety and pledged to conclude [or, to finish] before you this sale," a formulation which also appears in halakhic texts.

(d) the Bar Kokhba letters,[83] which mention a number of halakhot, such as *tikkun*[84] [the setting aside] of tithes, Shabbat,[85] care for the poor, and the burial of the dead.[86]

(e) a bill from the second year of the revolt, P.Hever 49,[87] mentioning the obligation to repay "from my house and from my property." This formulation also is to be found in the halakhah, but not necessarily exclusively so.

Discussion and Conclusions

The classification by language yields extremely clear distinctions. Writs and letters in Hebrew were characteristic particularly of the second revolt. Close to half of the correspondence by Bar Kokhba (or more accurately, the correspondence written in his headquarters)

---

[78] P.Mur. pages 141–2. [For the date see the contribution of Eshel, Broshi and Jull in this volume.]

[79] See below.

[80] P.Mur. pages 145–6.

[81] Lines 6, 27–8.

[82] M.Ketubot 10.6 and parallels.

[83] P.Mur. 42–52.

[84] P.Mur. 44.4. In Rabbinic terminology, "*le-taken*" means to set aside tithes.

[85] P.Mur. 44.6.

[86] P.Mur. 46.5.

[87] First published: M. Broshi and E. Qimron, "I.O.U. Note from the Time of the Bar Kochba Revolt," *ErIsr* 20 (1989) 256–61 (Hebrew); English version: "A Hebrew I.O.U. Note from the Second Year of the Bar Kokhba Revolt," *JJS* 45 (1994) 286–94.

and official documents by his officials were similarly written exclusively in Hebrew. Some of the Hebrew documents most probably date from the first revolt; the use of Hebrew is characteristic of both national uprisings. The observance of the commandments is clearly expressed in these letters. Scholars have already discussed such observance in the "court" of Bar Kokhba, and this is indicated by his letters, and the Four Species of the Sukkot holiday, in accordance with halakhic rules, appear on his coins.[88] Bar Kokhba refrained from referring to himself as king, and called himself only *Nasi*, probably to avoid openly proclaiming himself king. This corresponded with the Talmudic conception that the "king" is the Messiah, the anointed king. According to rabbinic traditions, the rabbis supported the revolt, thus attesting that Bar Kokhba was perceived by himself and by the rabbis as a leader who went in the proper path. The rabbis also tell of many individuals who were circumcised in the time of Bar Kokhba, or who had stretched their foreskins and underwent a second circumcision, i.e., assimilated Jews who returned to the Jewish society.[89]

Accordingly, the time of the revolt is portrayed as a period of national-religious revolution, with the return to Hebrew constituting part of this process. Although a detailed discussion of the "language war" at the time would exceed the scope of this paper, the rabbis manifestly thought of Hebrew as the sacred tongue, which was to be preferred to other languages.[90] Nonetheless, they did not wage an intense battle on its behalf. A majority of the writs in rabbinic literature are written in Aramaic.[91] Writs and letters in Hebrew from this period are oppositionist, challenge societal norms, and reveal a religious-national orientation.

The Aramaic writs are generally reflective of the halakhot of the rabbis, and are close to the Jewish practice and context. This affinity is expressed in the subjects included in the documents, and in the wording they employ. This is quite pronounced in a writ of divorce

---

[88] A. Oppenheimer, "Bar-Kokhva and the Practice of Jewish Law," in: A. Oppenheimer and U. Rappaport, eds., *The Bar-Kokhva Revolt: A New Approach* (Jerusalem 1984) 140–6 (Hebrew).

[89] T.Shabbat 15(16).9.

[90] An exhaustive discussion of this question would exceed the purview of the current work.

[91] E.g., M.Ketubot, chapter 4; T.Bava Metzia 9.13; M.Gittin 9.3, and more.

from Masada (P.Mur. 19) and the marriage contract of Babatha (Yadin 10), and in less striking fashion in the other Aramaic documents. The Greek documents, in contrast, reflect a society following Roman norms, and it is difficult to find and identify Jewish elements and characteristics. Some scholars have found allusions to Jewish practices, and a number of details may be explained within a Jewish perspective, but the documents themselves are not from the world of the rabbis, and at most contain allusions to some Jewish background. This is also the general conclusion reached by H. Cotton,[92] who is undoubtedly correct in her analysis. Nonetheless, the significance of the testimony must be reconsidered, which we shall do presently.

The problem does not consist of the use per se of a foreign language. A writ of divorce written in Greek is halakhically valid, as is even a bilingual writ.[93] Rather, the language is a cultural indicator and a means for social-religious analysis. The Jews of Rekem generally, and especially of Zoar, were not Hellenizers, but they were highly assimilated in the society of their Nabatean-Aramean neighbors.

The Greek, Aramaic, and Hebrew writs are reflective of the same society. The same people wrote these documents in the various languages. Judah b. Eleazar Khthousion wrote for his wife a halakhic marriage contract in Aramaic (P.Yadin 10), and a marriage contract for his daughter in Greek (P.Yadin 18). The refugees who brought these Greek documents with them also came with *mezuzot* and phylacteries. This is not a question of majority or minority, in which language most of the documents were written. Not only are the extant finds random, the same society transmitted a multitude of messages, some of them possibly even contradictory.

The differences in the degree of correspondence to the rabbinic halakhah are not dependent solely upon the language of the document, but also upon the place where it was written. The documents from Zoar are patently the farthest from what is indicated by the rabbinic tradition, those from Nahal Hever represent an interim position, and the disparities between the rabbinic halakhot and the papyri from Murabba'at are the smallest. Nor are there contrasts between the small amount of material known, at this stage, from Jericho and the rabbinic halakhot. This situation corresponds to the rabbinic

---

[92] Cotton, "Marriage Document" (supra note 39).
[93] M.Gittin 9.8 and parallels; but see Y.Gittin 9.9 50d.

characterization of Rekem as a place whee "they are converts and err," that is, a society with a higher degree of assimilation than that of other rural communities in the Judaean hill country.

As we established in our introduction, the central question, in terms of the current discussion, is not whether the populace heeded the instructions of the rabbis, or whether the halakhah dictated its way of life, but whether rabbinic literature is reflective of the social reality. We must now examine how and in what manner the Greek documents deviate from the reality depicted in rabbinic literature. An examination of all the pertinent questions would exceed the purview of the current work, which will concentrate on a number of major realms.

The Courts of Gentiles

The primary deviation is seemingly the very application to a Gentile court. The rabbis obviously preferred that the public turn to their courts. The very writing of marriage contracts and even promissory notes in accordance with the Nabatean-Roman practice caused them displeasure.[94] Elsewhere I have shown that rabbinic literature itself implies that the public at large did not honor the prohibition of applying to the "courts of Gentiles." In practice, the Jews required the services of this institution. The Tosefta already rules: "All the documents that come to the courts of Gentiles, even though they are signed by Gentiles: R. Akiva validates them all, but the rabbis invalidate, except for writs of divorce and slaves' writs of emancipation."[95] And in the Mishnah: "All the documents that come to the courts of Gentiles, even though they are signed by Gentiles are valid, except for writs of divorce and slaves' writs of emancipation. R. Shimon says, Even these are valid; they were mentioned only when they were drawn up by a layman."[96] The details of the discussion and

---

[94] *Midrash Tannaim*, Deut. 16:18, p. 96; *Mekhilta de-Rabbi Ishmael. Mekhilta de-Nezikin* 1, p. 246; B.Gittin 88b; see also *Midrash Yalkut Ha-Sacili* 145, p. 124; *Midrash Aggadah* on *Mishpatim* 21:1, p. 154 (ed. Buber 654), and more; M.Gittin 9.8; Y.Gittin 9.9 50a; Y.Yevamot 9.4 10b; Ex. Rabbah 30.18; B.Shabbat 116b; *Midrash ha-Gadol*, Deut. 16.18, 368; *Pitron Torah* on Deut., 264, and more; T.Bava Metzia 11.23; *Tanhuma*, ed. Buber, *Shoftim* 1.1, p. 28; *Tanhuma, Shoftim* 1.1; J. Mann, *The Bible as Read and Preached in the Old Synagogue* (New York 1971) 144, and more.

[95] T.Gittin 1.9(4).

[96] M.Gittin 1.5.

the differences between the Mishnah and the Tosefta are significant,[97] but two conclusions are of importance for the matter at hand:

(1) In practice, people without doubt required the writing of legal documents in Gentile courts; otherwise this entire question would not have arisen.

(2) The dispute, and the permission granted, are already from the Yavneh generation (R. Akiva). As we have seen, the non-Jewish court was already needed in order to enforce a writ of divorce. The rabbis generally opposed this, but some validated a writ of divorce granted with the aid of the non-Jewish court. Special laws apply to a writ of divorce, including the requirement that it be granted willingly. All other legal documents may be confirmed by a non-Jewish court with greater halakhic approval. Indeed, the rabbis themselves permitted application to such a court in instances in which this would advance their goals.[98] According to the rabbinic testimony, there was no Jewish court in the Rekem-Zoar region, and it is doubtful if one existed in 'En-Gedi, which was an imperial estate. Since there was no nearby Jewish court, how could the rabbis complain if the residents of Zoar were compelled to turn to non-Jewish courts? Even within the bounds of the Jewish settlement the rabbis permitted such activity, and it is therefore not surprising that they consented to such legal activity by the inhabitants of Zoar, and possibly also by the inhabitants of additional nearby settlements.

Accordingly, application to a court of Gentiles was a normal and accepted "deviation." If a Jew wanted a document between him and his fellow to have legal validity, he was forced to write the document in Greek, and in a manner that would meet the requirements of the court in Petra or in Rabbah. One who wrote his document in Aramaic thereby decided that he would not need the official courts. He did so either out of naivete and good will, or because he relied upon another, unofficial, court, probably a Jewish one. The Shelamzion who received an Aramaic marriage contract knew that she would not have any legal recourse to the Roman court and apparently relied upon another court, or possibly upon a second marriage contract written in Greek. Application to the Gentile courts

---

[97] See: S. Lieberman, *Tosefta ki-Fshutah*, Nashim (New York 1973) 786–91.

[98] Z. Safrai, "The Sages in the Juristic Systems," in A. Sagi et al., eds., *Judaism: A Dialogue Between Cultures* (Jerusalem 1999) 219–34.

is therefore consistent with what is known from rabbinic literature. In the absence of a Jewish court in Zoar, the Jews had no choice but to apply to a Gentile court. It has not been determined who appointed the guardians in 'En-Gedi (P.Yadin 20, 25, and elsewhere). This as well may have been the decision of the council in Petra, because the deceased was an inhabitant of Zoar. The appointment of a Gentile guardian is not surprising, nor was it prohibited. Such an appointment is explicitly mentioned in the Tosefta and in the Palestinian Talmud.[99] The appointment might not have won the enthusiastic blessing of the rabbis, but this was nevertheless an accepted deviation to which the rabbis acquiesced, traces of which appear in their literature.

Women's Property

A well-known halakhah mandates that a married woman possesses no personal property, and everything that she acquires belongs to her husband. Monies that she brought with her from her father's house are given over to her husband, who uses them and "consumes the fruits," that is, derives benefit from the current income. Women mentioned in the Judaean Desert documents, such as Babatha, Shelamzion, and Salome daughter of Comais, undoubtedly had much personal property. The property of women is less prominent in the other documents from Nahal Hever, and even less so in the documents from Murabba'at. The very possession of property by a woman is seemingly in opposition to the halakhah and, more importantly, contrary to what is implicit in rabbinic literature regarding the status of the Jewish woman in this period.

---

[99] T.Bava Metzia 5.8(20); Y.Bava Metzia 5.5 10c. Opposition is even voiced in the Talmud Bavli to the appointment of an *am ha'aretz* (an uneducated person); see B.Pesahim 49b; *Derekh Eretz Zuta* 10.4; *Kallah Rabbati* 2.14. This was not, however, a halakhic ruling, but rather a polemical statement against *amei ha-aretz*. The anti-*am ha-aretz* polemic is characteristic solely of the Talmud Bavli. The dicta deprecating them and the expressions of enmity attest to a fierce struggle against *amei ha-aretz* and to internal social tension. All of these dicta and others in the same vein, however, appear only in the Talmud Bavli, albeit at times in the name of the Tannaim and Amoraim of the Land of Israel; they are absent from Land of Israel sources. It would therefore seem that the testimonies of tension with *amei ha-aretz* reflect only Babylonian teachings. This major argument is worthy of a detailed discussion, which would exceed the purview of the current work. For our purposes, the traditions that *amei ha-aretz* are invalid to serve as guardians also are exclusively Babylonian.

Notwithstanding the halakhic stance in principle, in practice women did own private property. A number of halakhot are expressly based on such ownership. Thus, for example, a woman sets aside for the Nazirite sacrifice a beast from her possessions,[100] a writ of divorce may be given to a woman in her courtyard,[101] and a stubborn and rebellious son is not punished unless he steals from his father and from his mother.[102] A woman gives charity,[103] and the praises afforded such generous women attest that the charity funds were given from the woman's property. The BT (exclusively) contains a discussion of the laws relating to a husband who sells a field to his wife,[104] and alludes to money belonging to the wife that was not given over to the husband.[105] The mishnayot also discuss the prohibition of going forth on the Sabbath with a ring; this explicitly refers to a woman going forth while wearing a ring with a seal. Such a piece of jewelry attests to a businesswoman who required a seal. Another mishnah, on the other hand, discusses the law of a ring without a seal that is used for purely decorative purposes, and which has a different legal status.[106]

The two Talmudim struggle with the question of how a woman could have "private" property. They search for a legal answer, and propose a special case in which the woman received a gift on condition that her husband had no part in it.[107] The PT offers two additional solutions: the first, "by controlling his property,"[108] that is, the woman received permission to control her husband's courtyard in

---

[100] M.Nazir 4.4.

[101] M.Gittin 8.1.

[102] M.Sanhedrin 8.3.

[103] E.g., Y.Horayot 2.7 48a; Y.Taanit 2.4 64b–c; B.Taanit 23b; Esther Rabbah 4.3 and more.

[104] B.Bava Batra 51a.

[105] See also the discussion regarding the setting aside of *ma'aser sheni* (second tithes): T.Maaser Sheni 4.4 and many parallels; see S. Lieberman, *Tosefta ki-Fshutah* (New York 1955), *Zera'im* 769.

[106] M.Shabbat 6.1–3; see also B. Shabbat 62a. In the course of the discussion, the Talmud assumes that the ring with the seal belongs to the husband, who gave it to the woman to bring from one place to another. A parallel explanation also is offered, that she is a "*gizbarit* [charity overseer]," but an ordinary woman would not have a ring with a seal, since the woman, unlike the man, has no intention of using the seal. This entire discussion, however, is merely dialectic, and can hardly be regarded as reflecting the actual social reality.

[107] B.Sanhedrin 71a; Gittin 77a; Nazir 24b; Kiddushin 23b; Y.Nazir 4.4 53b; Sanhedrin 8.4 26b.

[108] Y.Gittin 8.1 49b.

practice, and this de facto permission suffices for the courtyard to
be considered her property for the purpose of receiving a writ of
divorce. The economic importance of such an arrangement is likely
to be marginal. The second, and more important, solution is meant
to explain how a son could steal from the property of his mother:
"that she would receive paying guests, and make [= serve] meals,
and he [the son] would steal from them."[109] This apparently refers
to a woman who rents out rooms in her house and gives the ten-
ants "*shiro*," that is, a meal—activity that, as is indicated by this discussion, is independent.

The Talmudic discussions are an attempt to find a legal context
for a social situation, and in actuality, any such legal quest is
superfluous. These mishnayot and laws are naturally to be interpreted within the perspective of a social reality in which property
belonged de jure to the husband, while de facto the wife managed
these possessions and had effective control of them. The scope of
this phenomenon was most likely not inconsiderable, but its legal
status was problematic. It is not inconceivable that the rabbis did
not wish to grant excessive validity to this "loophole" in which the
wife, in practical terms, was independent, in light of the tendencies
of the Talmudic legislation regarding the woman's "rightful" place
and her "desired" status—that is, closeted in the home. This aspect
of the rabbinic legislation is well-known.

In the course of the discussions in the Talmudim regarding the
property of women, the Mishnah (Ketubot 9.1) mentions: "If a husband gives to his wife a written commitment, 'I have no claims
against your property. . . .'" This is the text of a document meant
to circumvent the halakhah that a wife's property, or at least the
deriving of benefit from it, is transferred to the household economy,
that is, to the husband. The Tannaim already sought to limit the
scope of this arrangement, and some even rejected its validity, because
it contained a condition contradictory to the "law of the Torah."
This orientation is explicit in the Talmud of the Land of Israel, and
only in it. According to the PT, this law applies only to the period
of betrothal.[110] Its plain meaning, however, is that this is a popular
stipulation that circumvented the halakhah. The rabbis wrestled with

---

[109] Y.Sanhedrin 8.4 26b.
[110] Y.Ketubot 9.1 32d.

the question of its extent and validity, but the popular condition was stronger than these authorities, as can be seen from the testimonies cited above and below.

PT Shevuot[111] tells of R. Marinus who was a surety for his daughter-in-law. In this instance, the daughter-in-law managed some business, and apparently borrowed money. This, therefore, is a woman from rabbinic circles who engages in commercial activity and is supported by her father-in-law, one of the rabbis. The sources contain similar testimonies concerning women who were active in the economic sphere. Thus, for example, the midrashim are concerned with the return of stolen property to women,[112] and *Midrash Tehillim* tells of David who, in his madness, wrote that the wife of Achish owed him a considerable sum of money.[113] This narrative is patently completely aggadic, albeit within the bounds of reason, and it is possible for a woman to be a debtor in this legendary narrative.

The Talmud Bavli in Tractate Bava Kama tells of a woman who showed a dinar to R. Hiyya, so that he would examine its quality.[114] R. Hiyya lived and was active in the Land of Israel. While the narrative has no Land of Israel parallel, there is no reason to assume that it is not authentic.[115] Additional testimonies in a similar spirit can be collected, leading us to conclude that in practice women controlled and derived benefit from property. The property of Babatha, like that of Salome, is neither exceptional nor surprising. The Tosefta expressly states: "A man may borrow with interest from his wife and from his children, but he thereby educates them to engage in usury."[116] Consequently, it is permissible to borrow with interest from the members of one's family, but the rabbis are cognizant of the educational harm caused by such an action. The very act of borrowing from the wife is therefore a reasonable and normal possibility, despite the halakhic principle that what the wife acquired is acquired by her husband. The loan by Babatha to her husband does not exceed accepted bounds. Moreover, P.Yadin 17 should possibly be interpreted on the basis of this halakhah: this document includes a clause

---

[111] Y.Shevuot 6.2 37a.

[112] *Sifrei Zuta* 5.8; *Sifrei, Naso* 4; Num. Rabbah 8.5.

[113] *Midrash Tehillim* 34.1, p. 24.

[114] B.Bava Kamma 99b.

[115] It may be assumed that the narrative was brought to Babylonia by Rav, who also was a participant in this incident.

[116] T.Bava Metzia 5.15.

stating explicitly that Babatha is loaning money to her husband without interest. It is seemingly strange that the loan was extended without interest, in light of the taking of interest in other documents, especially, the interest that Babatha herself suggests, and the halakhic permission granted for the taking of interest in such cases. This document may have been intended to impart Roman legal validity to the Jewish practice. Upon marrying, the woman's property becomes a deposit managed by the husband, who is entitled to "consume the fruits," while the principal remains for the woman. This halakhah was expressed within the context of the non-Jewish law in the following manner: the wife loaned this sum of money to her husband, with the date of repayment determined by the wife and her heirs.

Another possible explanation of this document is the halakhah that "A marriage contract is drawn up as a loan," that is, it was customary to write the sum of the marriage contract as if it were a loan, probably without interest, from the wife to the husband.[117] The rabbis agreed to this practice, to which this document may allude. The practice is also well-known in the Egyptian-Roman law, and appears in papyri.[118]

The question of wives' property is therefore a fine example of a number of scholarly research principles: to what degree rabbinic literature is variegated, on the one hand, and to what extent the law and the judicial system only partially express the social reality. P.Yadin 17, for its part, exemplifies the wealth of possible explanations of the legal background of the marriage agreement between a husband and his wife.

The Text of the Marriage Contract

At first glance, the Judaean Desert marriage contracts in Greek reflect a Jewish society that is not submissive to the halakhah. Tractate Ketubot contains a list of directives for the marriage contract text.[119] On occasion, identical legal principles can be discerned, but not a single marriage contract from the Judaean Desert corresponds exactly with the version in the Mishnah.[120] The Aramaic marriage contracts

---

[117] T.Ketubot 4.13; Y.Yevamot 15.3 14d; Ketubot 4.8 29a.
[118] A. Gulak, *Legal Documents in the Talmud*. Edited and supplemented by R. Katzoff (Jerusalem 1994) 89 (Hebrew).
[119] M.Ketubot 4.7–12.
[120] Cotton, "Marriage Contract," (supra note 39) 85.

correspond to what is indicated by the Mishnah. They are generally close to the halakhah: they do not exactly preserve the mishnaic text, but are proximate to it, especially the marriage contract
in P.Yadin 10 and the writ of divorce, P.Mur. 18. The Greek marriage contracts, in contrast, reflect a completely different set of conventions. The subjects discussed in the Tannaitic marriage contract
are not mentioned in the Greek marriage contracts from the Judaean
Desert, and especially not the uniquely Jewish topic: what would
happen if the wife were to fall into captivity.[121] The Jewish marriage
contract was a significant religious document, and the disregard for
the directives of the Mishnah would seem to attest to a high degree
of assimilation within the Jewish settlement in the Dead Sea region.

The mishnayot in chapter 4 of M. Ketubot strongly suggest that
marriage contracts not in accordance with the halakhah were at
times written throughout the Land of Israel as well. Recurrent in
these mishnayot is the formula: "If one did not do such and such,
he is liable, for this is a condition imposed by the court"—"If [a
husband] did not write a marriage contract for her . . . because this
is a condition imposed by the court"—a total of six times! Accordingly,
this was a demand issued by the rabbis, but many did not write the
marriage contract as required. Furthermore, what is defined in the
Mishnah as an absolute obligation is the subject of a disagreement
in the Tosefta, and various limitations are imposed.[122]

The practice that a wife brings property with her is mentioned in
or is implied by the majority of the Greek marriage contracts.
Although not an integral part of the marriage contract text in the
Mishnah, it is discussed extensively in the Tannaitic sources, and
clearly was accepted. The rabbis neither supported nor opposed this,
and it therefore is not mentioned as a part of the marriage contract,
but their teachings contain recognition of it as an existing social custom. The Mishnah (Ketubot 6.6) even hints that it was accepted to
write this in some document, possibly in that of the marriage contract itself: "An orphan . . . and they wrote for her one hundred, or
fifty *zuz*, when she attains her majority, she may recover it from
them." The obligatory practice that a bride brings with her a dowry
penetrated into the halakhah as an obligation to aid the daughter

---

[121] See the following note.
[122] Cf. M.Ketubot 4.9 with T.Ketubot 4.5 and the Talmudim *ad loc.*

of poor parents in amassing the money. This obligation, known as
"*hakhnasat kallah*" [literally, bringing in the bride], appears frequently
in the sources.[123] The bringing of a dowry is patently not an exclusively Jewish custom, nor it is necessarily a Gentile practice.

This is also the case regarding the clause termed by the halakhah
"the inheritance of male children," that is, the stipulation that the
sons of the wife will inherit the sum of her marriage contract, or
even the dowry, in addition to their share of the inheritance. This
clause appears in the Mishnah,[124] and there are allusions to it in
Greek documents from the Dead Sea basin; once again, however,
this is not an exclusively Jewish clause, and it also appears in Egyptian
papyri.

All this teaches that the Greek marriage contracts do not run
counter to the halakhah, and in actuality the practice reflected in
these documents does not differ from that in the Mishnah, but the
marriage contracts are different and lack the uniquely Jewish characteristics. It would not be out of place to conjecture that the Jews
of the region had two marriage contracts, one practical, that ordered
the conditions of the marriage, and the other ritual, close to the version of the Mishnah. Such a reality is known from the different dias-
poras in our times. This hypothesis cannot, however, be proved until
we are fortunate enough to find two parallel marriage contracts of
the same woman. Up to now, all that has been found are two marriage contracts in different languages for the same male, to be precise, an Aramaic document that the husband wrote to his wife and
a Greek document that the same man wrote for his daughter. As
we have seen, the marriage contracts in Greek may possibly not be
ketubot in the halakhic sense of the term, but rather writs that order
the financial terms of the marriage. The same may be said for writs
of marriage, as we suggested above.

Another question is the degree to which the writing of the marriage contract was widespread. Did every wife have a marriage contract? The answer is not clear, neither in our documents nor in those
from Egypt. There patently were many marriage contracts in this
land, but their quantity is insufficient to estimate for how many
women they were written, and to which social strata such women

---

[123] M.Ketubot 6.5–6; Y.Ketubot 6.6 30d; T.Ketubot 6.8, and additional sources.
[124] M.Ketubot 4.10 and parallels.

belonged. The Syro-Roman lawbook clearly indicates that the marriage contract was quite rare until the fourth century, when it was established as an obligatory practice.[125] In the Jewish halakhah the marriage contract is obligatory, and a man may not marry a woman without such a document. Furthermore, already in the Tannaitic period the marriage contract had become a partially ritual document. The differential between the amount of money that the husband was required to guarantee and the sum of money that he actually promised already attests to a ritual component of the *ketubah*. The Mishnah even proposed a somewhat legal method of circumventing the *ketubah* and in practice give less than the necessary minimum.[126] This clause devoids the *ketubah* of all content, and attests to the adaptation of a document whose text is obligatory (and archaic) to the context of actually existing social procedures.

Interest

The last issue to be examined within this context is that of interest. A loan without interest is a special act of kindness, namely, the waiving of the creditor's rights with no tangible recompense. It is difficult to believe that a major creditor would waive the interest, unless this was a case of neighborly relations or of Jews complying with the halakhah. The prohibition of interest applies only when the creditor and debtor are both Jews. There is no stricture, however, against taking interest from a non-Jew, and certainly not of paying interest to a Gentile. It may be argued that documents in which the terms of interest are not mentioned were written by Jews, or the interest was concealed within the principal, such as, possibly, the loan document from an officer in the Roman army in 'En-Gedi.[127] We must now examine the significance of the documents in which interest is mentioned. It is not clear who is the creditor and who the debtor

---

[125] The scholarly literature on the Syrian-Roman lawbook contains many discussions of the shortcomings of the *"phernita"* (marriage contract) and explicit statements about "peoples" that are not accustomed to write a *"phernita."* See, e.g., Vööbus, *Lawbook* (supra note 33) II page 17 § 46, page 21 §50, page 23 §51; idem, *The Synodicon in the West Syrian Tradition* (Louvain 1976) 176.

[126] M.Ketubot 5.1. According to the Mishnah, the husband is permitted to demand that his wife write him a receipt according to which she already received part of the sum written in her marriage contract. The tremendous sums in the Judaean Desert marriage contracts may therefore possibly be fictitious amounts.

[127] *P.Yadin* 11.

in P.Mur. 114. In P.Hever 66[128] the creditor is most likely a Gentile, and interest to Gentiles was permitted. The guardians of Jeshua b. Jeshua also loaned money at 6 percent interest per annum, and Babatha offered them annual interest of 9 percent.[129] It has not been determined to whom the guardians, one of whom was a Gentile, loaned the money, but Babatha patently had no halakhic sanction to offer and pay any interest, even if the guardian were a Gentile. This is an explicit and unchallenged halakhah.[130] What, however, was to be expected from a mother who sees how the property of her son does not yield the desired profits? Moreover, according to the testimony of the rabbis, there were many breaches of the prohibition of lending with interest. The rabbinic halakhot are concerned with loans and documents containing an agreement regarding interest. The question is not whether interest is forbidden or permitted, but rather how to relate to a transgression that had already been committed, such as: "The person who happens to find a writ on interest should tear it up. If it should come to a court, they tear it up. R. Simeon b. Gamaliel says, All *is in accordance with the accepted practice for the region* (מדינה)."[131] This, then, is not a private transgression, but the accepted practice for the region. Similarly, "If one lends to his fellow with interest and comes before the court, he is fined,"[132] "If one lends to his fellow with interest . . .,"[133] "If one lends to his fellow with interest and repents . . .,"[134] and additional sources. Consequently, not only did Babatha have good reasons to pay interest to the guardians, this was not regarded as exceptional in the Jewish society. Moreover, the permission granted to a father to pay interest to his son[135] also applies to a case such as this, in which the mother pays interest to her son. It cannot be assumed that Babatha studied the writings of the Tannaim before making such an offer to the guardians, nor, on the other hand, was her proposal irregular, neither in the Jewish society nor in the view of the rabbis.

---

[128] Cotton "Loan with Hypothec," (supra note 39).
[129] *P.Yadin* 15.
[130] T.Bava Metzia 5.20.
[131] T.Bava Metzia 5.23.
[132] *Ibid.* 5.22; Y.Bava Metzia 5.1 10a; Pesahim 2.2 29a; Gittin 4.4 46a; B.Bava Metzia 72a.
[133] T.Bava Metzia 5.23.
[134] *Ibid.* 5.25.
[135] T.Bava Metzia 5.15.

Summary

The Judaean Desert documents present a complex picture of a mixed multinational and multireligious society. The extant documents are in Hebrew, Aramaic, and Greek, and they were all written by the same population.

(1) The observance of the halakhah is stressed in the Hebrew documents, all of which were written at the time of the Bar Kokhba rebellion. The use of Hebrew is to be connected with the religious-national awakening characteristic of the uprising. This is also of significance for an understanding of the rebellion, which exceeds the scope of our discussion.

(2) The documents in Aramaic roughly correspond to the demands of the halakhah. Like the halakhah itself they contain external influences, but this is not surprising.

(3) The Greek documents reflect a legal practice different from that manifest in the Jewish sources. The Greek documents contain virtually no violations of the rabbinic halakhah, but the writs were not produced in the study hall, even though they contain traces of halakhic influence. A large number of the halakhic irregularities have parallel testimonies in the Talmudic literature, which indicate that these were irregularities, albeit reasonable ones.

The picture that emerges also is indicated by rabbinic literature itself. The Zoar region was outside the bounds of "the Land of Israel," and apparently was the "Rekem" whose inhabitants are defined as "erring converts or as "converts *and* those who err." According to the testimony of the rabbis, there were no courts in the region (as in Egypt even before the diaspora revolt), and the Jews of the region had no recourse other than to apply to the local Roman courts. Rabbinic literature contains testimonies of the need for Gentile courts, and of the displeasure of the rabbis at this situation. An identical picture emerges from a study of rabbinic literature itself, which does not reflect a tendentious viewpoint, but accurately describes the reality. A social revolution in which the rabbis became the dominant elite in the Jewish people occurred during the Yavneh generation. This was the founding generation of the revolution, which was obviously completed only later, in the third century CE. The Yavneh generation constituted the founding period of the Jewish society led by the rabbis, and as is only to be expected in a first generation, the social processes were not concluded, and the rule of the halakhah was not yet total. Rabbinic literature mainly portrays the Jewish society from the viewpoint of the rabbis. Nonetheless, the image of the society as a whole also is indicated by the rabbinic sources. The testimonies from the Judaean Desert documents correspond well with the socioreligious world as it is reflected in the Tannaitic literature. This was a world that respected the teachings of the rabbis, but did not always heed them. The world reflected in rabbinic literature is reflected faithfully, although rabbinic literature cannot be relied upon as a historical mirror without precise and selective study.

Additional note

In the description of the deeds of the monk Barsauma, as yet only partly published by F. Nao, "Histoire de Barsauma de Nisibe," *ROC* 9 (1913) 272–282, 10 (1914) 278–289, a place called Rekem Gea in the northwestern Negev is mentioned. The reference is to Halutza, or perhaps to Kadesh Barnea (Nitzana), which is rendered in the Aramaic translations as Rekem Gea. In that case, Rekem in the eastern Negev and Rekem Gea in the west, and the line of fortified settlement in the northern Negev, are the Rekem in general.

INDEX OF PASSAGES

I. Jewish Literature

II. Greek and Roman Literature

III. Papyri and Inscriptions

INDEX OF NAMES